ISBN 1-57999-017-7

1 2 3 4 5 6 7 8 9 10 11 12 13 14 15 16 17 18 19 20

Our Growing Years
a hymnal

GIA Publications, Inc.
Chicago

PREFACE

Introduction. Hymns can be lifelong companions. In early childhood we learn "Jesus loves me." In our older years we sing, "The Lord has promised good to me, His word my hope secures; He will my shield and portion be as long as life endures," from the hymn "Amazing grace, how sweet the sound."

This hymnal was designed by a committee of residents at Westminster-Canterbury, a continuing-care retirement community in Richmond, Virginia. This committee realized that the purpose of hymns is to enable as many persons as possible to enjoy the faith which was expressed by hymn writers and composers. Thus by singing and reading hymns, we can share spiritual insights and can experience the assuring reality of God's love.

An eminent American hymnologist, Louis FitzGerald Benson (1855–1930), expressed this same idea in a lecture at Princeton Theological Seminary: "So inspiring and uplifting can the spiritual ministry of poetry and music to human lives be made that I venture to propose this task and opportunity of getting the hymnal back into the homes and hands and hearts of Christian people as one of the most rewarding that can engage us."

Since the residents of most retirement communities belong to a variety of denominations, the committee decided that the contents of this hymnal should be ecumenical in scope. Almost half of the hymns are drawn from the list of hymns selected by the Consultation on Ecumenical Hymnody.

Early in its deliberations the committee determined that the book should be light enough to be comfortably held. In addition, the texts should be clearly legible.

The liturgical resources at the beginning of the hymnal were selected to provide for ecumenical worship as well as for private devotions. Furthermore, the publisher has provided additional denominational worship materials for this hymnal, which can be placed in the pocket inside the back cover. These include Roman Catholic, Lutheran, Episcopal, and mainline Protestant supplements for the celebration of Eucharist, or Holy Communion.

The Liturgy

General Worship. The hymnbook begins with a liturgical section designed to be laity-friendly so that almost anyone will feel comfortable leading worship. Each component of the liturgy is included except for the scripture readings and the devotion or homily. There are four options for each section of the liturgy. A community may choose to use all of the (A) options for the first week of the month, (B) options for the second week, and so on, or options may be chosen at will. This allows for variation in weekly worship.

Morning and Evening Prayer. A similar structure has been designed for both the morning and evening prayer services. It is our hope that this format will encourage people to feel more comfortable in leading worship or prayer services.

Prayers. The prayers in this section represent various cultures throughout the ages of Christian faith. They were chosen for their relevance in our prayer life today.

The Psalms and Canticles

Psalms and biblical canticles are the songs found in sacred Scripture. Twenty-eight songs immediately precede the hymn section. Some are printed with full melody, but most follow the form of a refrain and verses. Several methods of performance may be employed.

The refrain, which usually summarizes the psalm, is set to an easily singable melody, often a phrase from a familiar hymn. This refrain almost always belongs to the entire congregation, and may be sung first by a soloist (cantor) to be repeated by all, or sung immediately by all after an instrumental introduction. The verses may then be recited by a worship leader, with the recurring refrain sung by the congregation, or the verses may be chanted according to one of the five tones provided on the pull-out card bound into the back of the accompaniment edition. Each of these tones is given in several keys, so that any one tone may be used with various psalms in this section.

Chanting is a form of singing in which the normal speech flow of the text governs the musical rhythm. These tones each consist of two musical phrases, which correspond to two verse lines of text. The first line of text is sung on the single pitch of the first chanting tone, followed by the mediant cadence (three notes), which begins at the dot. The second line is then chanted on the reciting note after the bar line, with the final cadence sung where the second dot occurs. The tone is repeated for each two lines of text. Often, the final pitch of either cadence will have more than one syllable. This final note is always somewhat stressed (as is the case of the downbeat of a measure in metered music). When the last word of the phrase ends on one or two weak syllables—e.g., "mountain," "heavens," "satisfied," etc.—the final pitch is sung on the accented syllable and repeated for each of the weak syllables.

The following two examples show how selected psalm verses would look if interlined with the tone, and how they would look if written as sung:

As written:

As sung:

One must always be careful to avoid placing a stress on a syllable that is not stressed in normal speech. The tendency to do this occurs when a weak syllable falls on the first cadence note, as is found above on both cadences of the excerpt from Psalm 23. Both "in" and "the" should not be stressed, even though they begin the cadences. Rather, the natural accents will fall on the syllable before each cadence. In performance, then, the singer would place the stresses as follows:

The Hymns

Hymns have two principal uses. They can be sung and they can be read. Both purposes are equally important. Three versions of this hymnal provide formats which serve these two functions.

Full music edition. For the accompanist, this edition has the complete music score with the text interlined between the staves. Also, the many persons who enjoy singing hymns in harmony will use this edition.

Melody-only edition. This edition displays only the melody interlined with the first stanza, with the remaining stanzas given below in poetic form. This arrangement enables a person, while singing in corporate worship, to read the tune more easily and, in private, to ponder the meaning of the hymn at leisure.

Large-print edition. The preceding edition has been enlarged for the benefit of the visually impaired.

A leading hymnologist, Erik Routley (1917–1982), wrote, "When I remember how in my own youth, say thirty years back, men and women in so many branches of the church in England, my home country, would read their hymnals as eagerly and regularly as they read their Bibles, and would, if whipped off to the hospital, reach for the hymn book as well as the Bible, I simply grieve to think this particular pleasure and religious nourishment is withheld from so many or ignored by so many in these later days."

Residents are therefore urged to purchase their own copies so that the hymnal can be on their bedside tables or beside their reading chairs for private devotions and memorization. Then the books can be brought to chapel for corporate worship.

In order to find a hymn for a specific need, several means are furnished. The Table of Contents indicates the thirty broad categories of hymns. And since many hymns have several emphases, the extensive Topical Index gives further help in finding a desired hymn.

Exchanging texts and tunes. If the leader of worship wants to use a particular hymn text but knows that the tune is unfamiliar and there is not enough time or skill to teach the new tune, the Metrical Index is the means for discovering an appropriate substitute melody.

Each tune has a name, which is located just below the hymn title. Alongside the tune name are code numbers or abbreviations like 7.6.7.6.D, CMD, or SM. These symbols indicate the metrical framework of the text. In other words, these numbers and alphabetical abbreviations indicate the exact number of syllables per line or phrase.

To illustrate, consider the familiar Bishop Ken Doxology, "Praise God from whom all blessings flow." This stanza has eight syllables in each of the four lines. This formula is called Long Meter (LM) or 8.8.8.8. Here are two tunes with which the Doxology words could be sung—DUKE STREET (Jesus shall reign) or GERMANY (Where cross the crowded ways), although its traditional melody is the OLD HUNDREDTH.

Two other popular meters are the Common Meter (CM) and the Short Meter (SM). The meter of "O God, our help in ages past" is Common with 8.6.8.6 syllables in the four lines. "Blest be the tie that binds" is in Short Meter with the formula 6.6.8.6.

These three metrical pattern symbols are occasionally followed by "D" which means Doubled. For instance, a meter of 6.6.8.6.6.6.8.6 is shown as SMD or Short Meter Doubled. The text "This is my Father's world" with the tune TERRA BEATA is an example of SMD meter.

The metrical identities of the remainder of the tunes are shown by numerals. These meters are shown in rising serial order from 4 to 14. One popular meter is 8.7.8.7.D. Beethoven's HYMN TO JOY with "Joyful, joyful, we adore thee" is a well-known melody and text in this meter.

To assist you in introducing this hymnal, GIA Publications has published a manual entitled *Introducing a New Hymnal* by James R. Sydnor. Other guides written by Sydnor are *Hymns and Their Uses*, and *Hymns: A Congregational Study* (Agape).

Acknowledgments

This project was conceived by W. Ray Inscoe, Director of Pastoral Care at Westminster-Canterbury Richmond, in consultation with James R. Sydnor. Its publication was arranged by Robert J. Batastini of GIA Publications, Inc., with support from W. Thomas Cunningham, Jr., President of Westminster-Canterbury Richmond. W. Ray Inscoe chaired the editorial committee comprised of Mary Mohr, Edward Peple, Elizabeth Reynolds, Johnni Johnson Scofield, Dorothy and Mann Valentine. These committee members gave enthusiastic and knowledgeable aid to the editorial task. J. Frederick Holper, Professor at Union Theological Seminary in Virginia, was a liturgical consultant. James L. Mays, Professor Emeritus at Union Theological Seminary in Virginia, was the psalmody consultant.

Jeffry Mickus coordinated the project for GIA Publications, Inc. Engraving and typesetting was prepared by staff engravers Marc Southard and Philip Roberts. Proofreading was done by Victoria Krstansky and Clarence Reiels. The topical indexes were prepared by Robert H. Oldershaw.

The committee offers this hymnal to all persons, retirees and young people alike, so that they can have a life enriched by this treasure of hymns. This desire is expressed in a hymn of gratitude by David Mowbray for which a new tune (#65) was composed for this hymnal by Richard Proulx.

Lord of our growing years. . .
Your grace surrounds us all our days;
For all your gifts we bring our praise.

Robert J. Batastini
James Rawlings Sydnor
Editors

CONTENTS

THE LITURGY
WORSHIP
An Outline for Worship (2-17)

Gathering
Prayer before Worship
Call to Worship
Prayer of the Day or Opening Prayer
Hymn of Praise, Psalm, or Spiritual
Confession and Pardon
The Peace
Canticle, Psalm, Hymn, or Spiritual
The Word
Prayer for Illumination
First Reading
Psalm (45-64)
Second Reading
Anthem, Hymn, Psalm, Canticle, or Spiritual
Gospel Reading
Sermon
Affirmation of Faith
Concluding Prayers
Prayers of the People
Lord's Prayer
Hymn, Spiritual, Canticle, or Psalm
Charge and Benediction

Gathering

Prayers for Use Before Worship

The following prayers may be used by worshipers as they prepare for the service.

A. Eternal God,
you have called us to be members of one body.
Join us with those
who in all times and places have praised your name,
that, with one heart and mind,
we may show the unity of your church,
and bring honor to our Lord and Savior,
Jesus Christ. **Amen.**

B. Everlasting God,
in whom we live and move and have our being:
You have made us for yourself,
so that our hearts are restless
until they rest in you.
Give us purity of heart and strength of purpose,
that no selfish passion may hinder us from knowing your will,
no weakness keep us from doing it;
that in your light we may see light clearly,
and in your service find perfect freedom;
through Jesus Christ our Lord,
who lives and reigns with you and the Holy Spirit,
one God, now and for ever. **Amen.**

C. Almighty God,
you pour out the spirit of grace and supplication
on all who desire it.
Deliver us from cold hearts and wandering thoughts,
that with steady minds and burning zeal
we may worship you
in spirit and in truth;
through Jesus Christ our Lord. **Amen.**

BCP

D. God of grace,
you have given us minds to know you,
hearts to love you,
and voices to sing your praise.
Fill us with your Spirit,
that we may celebrate your glory
and worship you in spirit and in truth;
through Jesus Christ our Lord. **Amen.**

In preparation for worship, the people may wish to meditate on the law or the summary of the law.

The Ten Commandments

God spoke all these words, saying,
I am the Lord your God, you shall have no other gods before me.
You shall not make for yourself an idol, whether in the form of anything that is in heaven above or that is on the earth beneath, or that is in the water under the earth.
You shall not bow down to them or worship them.
You shall not make wrongful use of the name of the Lord your God.
Remember the Sabbath day, and keep it holy.
Honor your father and your mother.
You shall not murder.
You shall not commit adultery.
You shall not steal.
You shall not bear false witness against your neighbor.
You shall not covet your neighbor's house;
you shall not covet your neighbor's wife, or anything that belongs to your neighbor.

Ex. 20:1-17

Summary of the Law

Our Lord Jesus said:
You shall love the Lord your God with all your heart,
and with all your soul, and with all your mind.
This is the greatest and first commandment.
And a second is like it: You shall love your neighbor as yourself.
On these two commandments hang all the law and the prophets.

Matt. 22:37-4

Call to Worship

A. Our help is in the name of the Lord,
who made heaven and earth.

Ps. 124:8

B. This is the day that the Lord has made;
let us rejoice and be glad in it.

Ps. 118:24

C. O come, let us sing to the Lord
and shout with joy to the rock of our salvation!
Let us come into God's presence with thanksgiving,
singing joyful songs of praise.

Ps. 95:1, 2

D. Cry out with joy to the Lord, all the earth.
Worship the Lord with gladness.
Come into God's presence with singing!
For the Lord is a gracious God,
whose mercy is everlasting;
and whose faithfulness endures to all generations.

Ps. 100:1, 2, 5

Opening Prayer

A. Almighty God,
to whom all hearts are open, all desires known,
and from whom no secrets are hid:
Cleanse the thoughts of our hearts
by the inspiration of your Holy Spirit,
that we may perfectly love you
and worthily magnify your holy name;
through Christ our Lord.   **Amen.**

BCP

B. God of all glory,
on this first day you began creation,
bringing light out of darkness.
On this first day you began your new creation,
raising Jesus Christ out of the darkness of death.
On this Lord's Day grant that we,
the people you create by water and the Spirit,
may be joined with all your works
in praising you for your great glory.
Through Jesus Christ,
in union with the Holy Spirit,
we praise you now and for ever.   **Amen.**

C. O God, light of the hearts that see you,
life of the souls that love you,
strength of the thoughts that seek you:
to turn from you is to fall,
to turn to you is to rise,
to abide in you is to stand fast for ever.
Although we are unworthy to approach you,
or to ask anything at all of you,
grant us your grace and blessing
for the sake of Jesus Christ our Redeemer.   **Amen.**

D. O God, you are infinite,
eternal and unchangeable,
glorious in holiness,
full of love and compassion,
abundant in grace and truth.
Your works everywhere praise you,
and your glory is revealed
in Jesus Christ our Savior.
Therefore we praise you, blessed and holy Trinity,
one God, for ever and ever.   **Amen.**

Hymn of Praise

Confession

Call to Confession

A. If we say we have no sin,
we deceive ourselves,
and the truth is not in us.
But if we confess our sins,
God who is faithful and just
will forgive us our sins
and cleanse us from all unrighteousness.
In humility and faith
let us confess our sin to God.

1 John 1:8, 9

B. The proof of God's amazing love is this:
While we were sinners
Christ died for us.
Because we have faith in him,
we dare to approach God with confidence.
In faith and penitence,
let us confess our sin before God and one another.

Rom. 5:8; Heb. 4:16

C. Remember that our Lord Jesus can sympathize with us in our weaknesses,
since in every respect he was tempted as we are,
yet without sin.
Let us then with boldness approach the throne of grace,
that we may receive mercy
and find grace to help in time of need.
Let us confess our sins
against God and our neighbor.

See Heb. 4:14-16

D. This is the covenant
which I will make with the house of Israel,
says the Lord:
I will put my law within them,
and I will write it upon their hearts;
and I will be their God,
and they shall be my people.
I will forgive their evil deeds,
and I will remember their sin no more.
In penitence and faith,
let us confess our sins to almighty God.

Jer. 31:33, 34

Confession of Sin

A. Merciful God,
we confess that we have sinned against you in thought, word, and deed,
by what we have done, and by what we have left undone.
We have not loved you with our whole heart and mind and strength.
We have not loved our neighbors as ourselves.
In your mercy forgive what we have been,
help us amend what we are, and direct what we shall be,
so that we may delight in your will and walk in your ways,
to the glory of your holy name.   **Amen.**

B. Holy and merciful God,
in your presence we confess our sinfulness, our shortcomings,
and our offenses against you.
You alone know how often we have sinned in wandering from your ways,
in wasting your gifts, in forgetting your love.
Have mercy on us, O Lord,
for we are ashamed and sorry for all we have done to displease you.
Forgive our sins, and help us to live in your light,
and walk in your ways, for the sake of Jesus Christ our Savior.   **Amen.**

C. Eternal God, our judge and redeemer,
we confess that we have tried to hide from you,
for we have done wrong.
We have lived for ourselves, and apart from you.
We have turned from our neighbors and refused to bear the burdens of others.
We have ignored the pain of the world
and passed by the hungry, the poor and the oppressed.
In your great mercy forgive our sins and free us from selfishness,
that we may choose your will and obey your commandments;
through Jesus Christ our Savior.   **Amen.**

D. Merciful God,
you pardon all who truly repent and turn to you.
We humbly confess our sins and ask your mercy.
We have not loved you with a pure heart,
nor have we loved our neighbor as ourselves.
We have not done justice, loved kindness,
or walked humbly with you, our God.
Have mercy on us, O God, in your loving-kindness.
In your great compassion, cleanse us from our sin.
Create in us a clean heart, O God, and renew a right spirit within us.
Do not cast us from your presence, or take your Holy Spirit from us.
Restore to us the joy of your salvation and sustain us with your bountiful Spirit.   **Amen.**

Declaration of Forgiveness

A. The mercy of the Lord
is from everlasting to everlasting.
I declare to you, in the name of Jesus Christ,
we are forgiven.
May the God of mercy,
who forgives you all your sins,
strengthen you in all goodness,
and by the power of the Holy Spirit
keep you in eternal life. **Amen.**

B. Hear the good news!
The saying is sure and worthy of full acceptance,
that Christ Jesus came into the world to save sinners.
He himself bore our sins
in his body on the cross,
that we might be dead to sin,
and alive to all that is good.
I declare to you in the name of Jesus Christ,
you are forgiven. **Amen.**

1 Tim. 1:15; 1 Peter 2:24

C. Hear the good news!
Who is in a position to condemn?
Only Christ,
and Christ died for us,
Christ rose for us,
Christ reigns in power for us,
Christ prays for us.
Anyone who is in Christ
is a new creation.
The old life has gone;
a new life has begun.
Know that you are forgiven
and be at peace. **Amen.**

Rom. 8:34; 2 Cor. 5:17

D. Hear the good news!
In baptism you were buried with Christ.
In baptism also you were raised to life with him,
through faith in the power of God
who raised Christ from the dead.
Anyone who is in Christ is a new creation.
The old life has gone;
a new life has begun.
I declare to you in the name of Jesus Christ,
you are forgiven. **Amen.**

Col. 2:12; 2 Cor. 5:17

The Peace

Since God has forgiven us in Christ,
let us forgive one another.

The peace of our Lord Jesus Christ be with you all.
And also with you.

John 20:19, 21, 26

People may turn and briefly greet their neighbor.

Hymn

The Word

Prayer for Illumination

Let us pray.

A. Lord, open our hearts and minds
by the power of your Holy Spirit,
that as the scriptures are read
and your Word is proclaimed,
we may hear with joy what you say to us today. **Amen.**

SWT

B. Prepare our hearts, O God,
to accept your Word.
Silence in us any voice but your own,
that, hearing, we may also obey your will;
through Jesus Christ our Lord. **Amen.**

C. O God,
by your Spirit tell us what we need to hear,
and show us what we ought to do,
to obey Jesus Christ our Savior. **Amen.**

D. O Lord our God,
your Word is a lamp to our feet
and a light to our path.
Give us grace to receive your truth in faith and love,
that we may be obedient to your will
and live always for your glory;
through Jesus Christ our Savior. **Amen.**

First Reading

Psalm

Second Reading

Hymn of Meditation

Gospel Reading

Sermon or Devotion

Affirmation of Faith

Let us confess the faith of our baptism, as we say:

Apostles' Creed
I believe in God the Father Almighty, Maker of heaven and earth;
And in Jesus Christ His only Son our Lord;
who was conceived by the Holy Ghost, born of the Virgin Mary,
suffered under Pontius Pilate, was crucified, dead, and buried;
He descended into hell; the third day He rose again from the dead;
He ascended into heaven,
and sitteth on the right hand of God the Father Almighty;
from thence He shall come to judge the quick and the dead.
I believe in the Holy Ghost; the holy catholic Church;
the communion of saints; the forgiveness of sins;
the resurrection of the body; and the life everlasting. **Amen.**

Nicene Creed
I believe in one God, the Father Almighty,
Maker of heaven and earth, and of all things visible and invisible;
And in one Lord Jesus Christ, the only-begotten Son of God,
begotten of His Father before all worlds;
God of God; Light of Light; Very God of Very God;
Begotten, not made; Being of one substance with the Father,
by whom all things were made;
Who for us men, and for our salvation, came down from heaven;
And was incarnate by the Holy Ghost of the Virgin Mary, and was made man;
And was crucified also for us under Pontius Pilate.
He suffered and was buried;
And the third day He rose again according to the Scriptures;
And ascended into heaven; And sitteth on the right hand of the Father,
And He shall come again with glory to judge both the quick and the dead;
Whose kingdom shall have no end.
And I believe in the Holy Ghost; The Lord and Giver of Life;
Who proceedeth from the Father and the Son;
Who with the Father and the Son together is worshipped and glorified;
Who spake by the prophets. And I believe one holy Catholic and Apostolic Church.
I acknowledge one Baptism for the remission of sins.
And I look for the Resurrection of the dead; And the Life of the world to come. **Amen.**

Concluding Prayers

Prayers of the People

A. Almighty God,
in Jesus Christ you taught us to pray,
and to offer our petitions to you in his name.
Guide us by your Holy Spirit,
that our prayers for others may serve your will
and show your steadfast love;
through the same Jesus Christ our Lord.   **Amen.**

Let us pray for the **world.**
Silent prayer.
God our creator,
you made all things in your wisdom,
and in your love you save us.
We pray for the whole creation.
Overthrow evil powers, right what is wrong,
feed and satisfy those who thirst for justice,
so that all your children may freely enjoy the earth you have made,
and joyfully sing your praises;
through Jesus Christ our Lord.   **Amen.**

Let us pray for the **church.**
Silent prayer.
Gracious God,
you have called us to be the church of Jesus Christ.
Keep us one in faith and service,
breaking bread together,
and proclaiming the good news to the world,
that all may believe you are love,
turn to your ways,
and live in the light of your truth;
through Jesus Christ our Lord.   **Amen.**

Let us pray for **peace.**
Silent prayer.
Eternal God,
you sent us a Savior, Christ Jesus,
to break down the walls of hostility that divide us.
Send peace on earth,
and put down greed, pride, and anger,
which turn nation against nation and race against race.
Speed the day when wars will end
and the whole world accepts your rule;
through Jesus Christ our Lord.   **Amen.**

Let us pray for **enemies.**
Silent prayer.
O God, whom we cannot love unless we love our neighbors,
remove hate and prejudice from us and from all people,
so that your children may be reconciled
with those we fear, resent, or threaten;
and live together in your peace;
through Jesus Christ our Lord.   **Amen.**

Let us pray for those who **govern** us.
Silent prayer.
Mighty God, sovereign over the nations,
direct those who make, administer, and judge our laws;
the President of the United States
and others in authority among us (especially N., N.);
that, guided by your wisdom,
they may lead us in the way of righteousness;
through Jesus Christ our Lord.   **Amen.**

Let us pray for **world leaders.**
Silent prayer.
Eternal Ruler, hope of all the earth,
give vision to those who serve the United Nations,
and to those who govern all countries;
that, with goodwill and justice,
they may take down barriers,
and draw together one new world in peace;
through Jesus Christ our Lord.   **Amen.**

Let us pray for the **sick.**
Silent prayer.
Merciful God, you bear the pain of the world.
Look with compassion on those who are sick (especially on N., N.);
cheer them by your word,
and bring healing as a sign of your grace;
through Jesus Christ our Lord.   **Amen.**

Let us pray for those who **sorrow.**
Silent prayer.
God of comfort, stand with those who sorrow (especially N., N.);
that they may be sure that neither death nor life,
nor things present nor things to come,
shall separate them from your love;
through Jesus Christ our Lord.   **Amen.**

Let us pray for **friends** and **families.**
Silent prayer.
God of compassion,
bless us and those we love,
our friends and families;
that, drawing close to you,
we may be drawn closer to each other;
through Jesus Christ our Lord. **Amen.**

B. Gracious God,
because we are not strong enough to pray as we should,
you provide Christ Jesus and the Holy Spirit to intercede for us in power.
In this confidence we ask you to accept our prayers.
God of mercy,
hear our prayer.

Let us pray for the **church.**
Silent prayer.
Faithful God, you formed your church from the despised of the earth
and showed them mercy,
that they might proclaim your salvation to all.
Strengthen those whom you choose today,
that they may faithfully endure all trials
by which you conform your church to the cross of Christ.
God of mercy,
hear our prayer.

Let us pray for **creation.**
Silent prayer.
Creator of all, you entrusted the earth to the human race,
yet we disrupt its peace with violence
and corrupt its purity with our greed.
Prevent your people from ravaging creation,
that coming generations may inherit lands brimming with life.
God of mercy,
hear our prayer.

Let us pray for the **world.**
Silent prayer.
Sovereign God, you hold both the history of nations
and the humble life of villages in your care.
Preserve the people of every nation from tyrants,
heal them of disease,
and protect them in time of upheaval and disaster,
that all may enter the kingdom that cannot be shaken.
God of mercy,
hear our prayer.

Let us pray for **peace.**
Silent prayer.
Judge of the nations,
you created humanity for salvation, not destruction,
and sent your Son to guide us into the way of peace.
Enable people of every race and nation
to accept each other as sisters and brothers,
your children, on whom you lavish honor and favor.
God of mercy,
hear our prayer.

Let us pray for those who **govern** us.
Silent prayer.
God Most High,
in Jesus of Nazareth you show us the authority that pleases you:
for he rules not by power or might, but serves in obedience to your will.
We pray for all in authority over us:
for our President, N., for Congress,
for our Governor, N., and our state legislature, (and N., N.).
Deliver them from vain ambitions
that they may govern in wisdom and justice.
God of mercy,
hear our prayer.

Let us pray for this **community.**
Silent prayer.
Merciful God, since Jesus longed to protect Jerusalem
as a hen gathers her young under her wings,
we ask you to guard and strengthen all who live and work here.
Deliver your people from jealousy and contempt
that they may show mercy to all their neighbors.
God of mercy,
hear our prayer.

Let us pray for all **families**
and those who **live alone.**
Silent prayer.
Holy God, from whom every family on earth takes its name:
Strengthen parents to be responsible and loving
that their children may know security and joy.
Lead children to honor parents by compassion and forgiveness.
May all people discover your parental care
by the respect and love given them by others.
God of mercy,
hear our prayer.

Let us pray for all who suffer any **sorrow** or **trial.**
Silent prayer.
Compassionate God,
your Son gives rest to those weary with heavy burdens.
Heal the sick in body, mind, and spirit.
Lift up the depressed.
Befriend those who grieve.
Comfort the anxious.
Stand with all victims of abuse and other crime.
Awaken those who damage themselves and others
through the use of any drug.
Fill all people with your Holy Spirit
that they may bear each other's burdens
and so fulfill the law of Christ.
God of mercy,
hear our prayer.

Let us give thanks for the lives of the **departed**
who now have rest in God.
Silent prayer.
Eternal God,
your love is stronger than death,
and your passion more fierce than the grave.
We rejoice in the lives of those
whom you have drawn into your eternal embrace.
Keep us in joyful communion with them
until we join the saints of every people and nation,
gathered before your throne in ceaseless praise.
God of glory,
you see how all creation groans in labor as it awaits redemption.
As we work for and await your new creation,
we trust that you will answer our prayers with grace,
and fulfill your promise
that all things work together for good for those who love you;
through Jesus Christ our Lord.   **Amen.**

C. As God's people, called to love one another,
let us pray for the needs of the church,
the whole human family,
and all the world, saying: Hear our prayer.
That churches of all traditions
may discover their unity in Christ
and exercise their gifts in service of all,
we pray to you, O God:
hear our prayer.

That the earth may be freed
from war, famine and disease,
and the air, soil and waters cleansed of poison,
we pray to you, O God:
hear our prayer.

That those who govern and maintain peace in every land
may exercise their powers in obedience to your commands,
we pray to you, O God:
hear our prayer.

That you will strengthen this nation to pursue just priorities
so that the races may be reconciled;
the young, educated; the old, cared for;
the hungry, filled; the homeless, housed;
and the sick, comforted and healed,
we pray to you, O God:
hear our prayer.

That you will preserve all who live and work
in this city (town, village, community)
in peace and safety,
we pray to you, O God:
hear our prayer.

That you will comfort and empower
those who face any difficulty or trial:
the sick (especially N., N.),
the disabled, the poor, the oppressed,
those who grieve and those in prison,
we pray to you, O God:
hear our prayer.

That you will accept our thanksgiving
for all faithful servants of Christ now at rest,
who, with us, await a new heaven and a new earth,
your everlasting kingdom,
we pray to you, O God:
hear our prayer.

Merciful God, as a potter fashions a vessel from humble clay,
you form us into a new creation.
Shape us, day by day,
through the cross of Christ your Son,
until we pray as continually as we breathe
and all our acts are prayer;
through Jesus Christ
and in the mystery of the Holy Spirit, we pray.   **Amen.**

The Lord's Prayer

As our Savior Christ has taught us, we are bold to pray:

Our Father, who art in heaven,
hallowed be thy name,
thy kingdom come,
thy will be done,
on earth as it is in heaven.
Give us this day our daily bread;
and forgive us our debts,
as we forgive our debtors;
and lead us not into temptation,
but deliver us from evil.
For thine is the kingdom,
and the power, and the glory,
for ever.   Amen.

Hymn

Charge

A. Go out into the world in peace.
Love the Lord your God with all your heart,
with all your soul, with all your mind;
and love your neighbor as yourself.

Matt. 22:37-40

B. Whatever you do, in word or deed,
do everything in the name of the Lord Jesus, giving thanks to God through him.

Col. 3:17

C. Be watchful, stand firm in your faith,
be courageous and strong.
Let all that you do be done in love.

1 Cor. 16:13, 14

D. God has shown you what is good.
What does the Lord require of you but to do justice,
and to love kindness, and to walk humbly with your God?

Micah 6:8

Blessing

A. The grace of the Lord Jesus Christ,
the love of God,
and the communion of the Holy Spirit
be with you all.
Alleluia! **Amen.**

2 Cor. 13:13

B. The Lord bless you and keep you.
The Lord be kind and gracious to you.
The Lord look upon you with favor
and give you peace.
Alleluia! **Amen.**

See Num. 6:24-26

C. The peace of God,
which passes all understanding,
keep your hearts and minds
in the knowledge and love of God,
and of God's Son, Jesus Christ our Lord;
and the blessing of God almighty,
the Father, the Son, and the Holy Spirit,
remain with you always. **Amen.**

See Phil. 4:7

D. May the God of hope
fill you with all joy and peace in believing,
so that you may abound in hope
by the power of the Holy Spirit.
Alleluia! **Amen.**

Rom. 15:13

DAILY PRAYER

MORNING PRAYER

An Outline of Morning Prayer (18-25)

Opening Sentences
Morning Psalm or Morning Hymn
Psalm(s)
Psalm (45-64)
Silent Prayer
[Psalm Prayer]
Scripture Reading
Silent Reflection
[A Brief Interpretation of the Reading, or a Nonbiblical Reading]
Canticle
Canticle of Zechariah or Other Canticle   (37-44)
Prayers of Thanksgiving and Intercession
Thanksgivings and Intercessions
Concluding Prayer
Lord's Prayer
[Hymn or Spiritual]
Dismissal
[Sign of Peace]

When a person is worshipping alone, or in a family group, or when circumstances call for an abbreviated order, the following is suggested:
Psalm (45-64)
Scripture Reading
Silent Reflection
Prayers of Thanksgiving and Intercession

Opening Sentences

All may stand.

O Lord, open my lips.
And my mouth shall proclaim your praise.

And one of the following:
Sunday
The Lord's unfailing love and mercy never cease,
fresh as the morning and sure as the sunrise.

Lam. 3:22-23

Monday
You created the day and the night, O God;
you set the sun and the moon in their places;
you set the limits of the earth;
you made summer and winter.

Ps. 74:16, 17

Tuesday
I pray to you, O Lord;
you hear my voice in the morning;
at sunrise I offer my prayer
and wait for your answer.

Ps. 5:2b-3

Wednesday
O depth of wealth, wisdom, and knowledge of God!
How unsearchable are God's judgments,
how untraceable are God's ways!
The source, guide, and goal of all that is,
to God be glory for ever!   **Amen.**

Rom. 11:33, 36

Thursday
Alleluia!
For the Lord our God the Almighty reigns.
Let us rejoice and exult and give God the glory.

Rev. 19:6, 7

Friday
Through Jesus let us continually offer up a sacrifice of praise to God,
the fruit of lips that acknowledge God's name.

Heb. 13:15

Saturday
You are worthy, our Lord and God,
to receive glory and honor and power
for you created all things,
and by your will they existed
and were created.

Rev. 4:11

Morning Psalm or Morning Hymn

One of the morning psalms (95:1-7; 100; 63:1-8; 51:1-12) or a morning hymn may be sung or spoken.

Psalms

Scripture Reading

At the conclusion of the reading of scripture, the reader may say:

The Word of the Lord.
Thanks be to God.

Silence may follow for reflection on the meaning of the scripture.
The scripture may be briefly interpreted, or a devotion may be read.

Canticle

The Canticle of Zechariah or another canticle may be sung or spoken. (37-44)
All may stand.

Prayers of Thanksgiving and Intercession

Satisfy us with your love in the morning,
and we will live this day in joy and praise.

One of the following, or other prayers of thanksgiving and intercession, may be spoken:

Sunday

Mighty God of mercy, we thank you for the resurrection dawn bringing the glory of our risen Lord who makes every day new. Especially we thank you for

the beauty of your creation . . .
the new creation in Christ and all gifts of healing and forgiveness . . .
the sustaining love of family and friends . . .
the fellowship of faith in your church. . . .

Merciful God of might, renew this weary world, heal the hurts of all your children, and bring about your peace for all in Christ Jesus, the living Lord. Especially we pray for

those who govern nations of the world . . .
the people in countries ravaged by strife or warfare . . .
all who work for peace and international harmony . . .
all who strive to save the earth from destruction . . .
the church of Jesus Christ in every land. . . .

Monday

We praise you, God our creator, for your handiwork in shaping and sustaining your wondrous creation. Especially we thank you for

the miracle of life and the wonder of living . . .
particular blessings coming to us in this day . . .
the resources of the earth . . .

gifts of creative vision and skillful craft . . .

the treasure stored in every human life. . . .

We dare to pray for others, God our Savior, claiming your love in Jesus Christ for the whole world, committing ourselves to care for those around us in his name. Especially we pray for

those who work for the benefit of others . . .

those who cannot work today . . .

those who teach and those who learn . . .

people who are poor . . .

the church in Europe. . . .

Tuesday

Eternal God, we rejoice this morning in the gift of life, which we have received by your grace, and the new life you give in Jesus Christ. Especially we thank you for

the love of our families . . .

the affection of our friends . . .

strength and abilities to serve your purpose today . . .

this community in which we live . . .

opportunities to give as we have received. . . .

God of grace, we offer our prayers for the needs of others and commit ourselves to serve them even as we have been served in Jesus Christ. Especially we pray for

those closest to us, families, friends, neighbors . . .

refugees and homeless men, women and children . . .

the outcast and persecuted . . .

those from whom we are estranged . . .

the church in Africa. . . .

Wednesday

God of all mercies, we praise you that you have brought us to this new day, brightening our lives with the dawn of promise and hope in Jesus Christ. Especially we thank you for

the warmth of sunlight, the wetness of rain and snow, and all that nourishes the earth . . .

the presence and power of your Spirit . . .

the support and encouragement we receive from others . . .

those who provide for public safety and well-being . . .

the mission of the church around the world. . . .

. . . l God, strengthen us in prayer that we may lift up the brokenness of this world for healing, and share in the saving love of Jesus Christ. Especially we pray for

those in positions of authority over others . . .

the lonely and forgotten . . .

children without families or homes . . .

agents of caring and relief . . .

the church in Asia and the Middle East. . . .

Thursday

Loving God, as the rising sun chases away the night, so you have scattered the power of death in the rising of Jesus Christ, and you bring us all blessings in him. Especially we thank you for

>   the community of faith in our church . . .
>
>   those with whom we work or share common concerns . . .
>
>   the diversity of your children . . .
>
>   indications of your love at work in the world . . .
>
>   those who work for reconciliation. . . .

Mighty God, with the dawn of your love you reveal your victory over all that would destroy or harm, and you brighten the lives of all who need you. Especially we pray for

>   families suffering separation . . .
>
>   people different from ourselves . . .
>
>   those isolated by sickness or sorrow . . .
>
>   the victims of violence or warfare . . .
>
>   the church in the Pacific region. . . .

Friday

Eternal God, we praise you for your mighty love given in Christ's sacrifice on the cross, and the new life we have received by his resurrection. Especially we thank you for

>   the presence of Christ in our weakness and suffering . . .
>
>   the ministry of Word and Sacrament . . .
>
>   all who work to help and heal . . .
>
>   sacrifices made for our benefit . . .
>
>   opportunities for our generous giving. . . .

God of grace, let our concern for others reflect Christ's self-giving love, not only in our prayers, but also in our practice. Especially we pray for

>   those subjected to tyranny and oppression . . .
>
>   wounded and injured people . . .
>
>   those who face death . . .
>
>   those who may be our enemies . . .
>
>   the church in Latin America. . . .

Saturday

Great and wonderful God, we praise and thank you for the gift of renewal in Jesus Christ. Especially we thank you for

>   opportunities for rest and recreation . . .
>
>   the regenerating gifts of the Holy Spirit . . .
>
>   activities shared by young and old . . .
>
>   fun and laughter . . .
>
>   every service that proclaims your love. . . .

You make all things new, O God, and we offer our prayers for the renewal of the world and the healing of its wounds. Especially we pray for

>   those who have no leisure . . .
>
>   people enslaved by addictions . . .

those who entertain and enlighten . . .
those confronted with temptation . . .
the church in North America. . . .

*Individual prayers of thanksgiving and intercession may be offered.
There may be silent prayer.*

The leader then says one of the following prayers, or a similar prayer.
Sunday
Eternal God,
our beginning and our end,
be our starting point and our haven,
and accompany us in this day's journey.
Use our hands
to do the work of your creation,
and use our lives
to bring others the new life you give this world
in Jesus Christ, Redeemer of all.   **Amen.**

Monday
As you cause the sun to rise, O God,
bring the light of Christ to dawn in our souls
and dispel all darkness.
Give us grace to reflect Christ's glory;
and let his love show in our deeds,
his peace shine in our words,
and his healing in our touch,
that all may give him praise, now and for ever.   **Amen.**

Tuesday
Eternal God,
your touch makes this world holy.
Open our eyes to see your hand at work
in the splendor of creation,
and in the beauty of human life.
Help us to cherish the gifts that surround us,
to share your blessings with our sisters and brothers,
and to experience the joy of life in your presence.
We ask this through Christ our Lord.   **Amen.**

Wednesday
Eternal God,
you never fail to give us each day all that we ever need,
and even more.
Give us such joy in living
and such peace in serving Christ,
that we may gratefully make use of all your blessings,
and joyfully seek our risen Lord
in everyone we meet.
In Jesus Christ we pray.   **Amen.**

Thursday
O God,
you are the well-spring of life.
Pour into our hearts the living water of your grace,
that we may be refreshed to live this day in joy,
confident of your presence
and empowered by your peace,
in Jesus Christ our Lord.   **Amen.**

NZPB, alt.

Friday
Eternal God,
you call us to ventures
of which we cannot see the ending,
by paths as yet untrodden,
through perils unknown.
Give us faith to go out with courage,
not knowing where we go,
but only that your hand is leading us
and your love supporting us;
through Jesus Christ our Lord.   **Amen.**

DP, alt.

Saturday
God our creator,
yours is the morning and yours is the evening.
Let Christ the sun of righteousness
shine for ever in our hearts
and draw us to that light
where you live in radiant glory.
We ask this for the sake of Jesus Christ our Redeemer.   **Amen.**

NZPB, alt.

The Lord's Prayer

Now let us pray the prayer Jesus taught his disciples to pray saying:

Our Father, who art in heaven,
hallowed be thy name,
thy kingdom come,
thy will be done,
on earth as it is in heaven.
Give us this day our daily bread;
and forgive us our debts,
as we forgive our debtors;
and lead us not into temptation,
but deliver us from evil.
For thine is the kingdom,
and the power, and the glory,
for ever. Amen.

[Hymn or Spiritual]

Dismissal

The leader dismisses the people using one of the following:

A. The grace of God be with us all, now and always.
Amen.
Bless the Lord.
The Lord's name be praised.

1 Tim. 6:21

B. May the God of hope fill us with all joy and peace
through the power of the Holy Spirit.
Amen.
Bless the Lord.
The Lord's name be praised.

Rom. 15:13

C. To God be honor and glory for ever and ever.
Amen.
Bless the Lord.
The Lord's name be praised.

1 Tim. 1:17

D. May we continue to grow in the grace and knowledge
of Jesus Christ, our Lord and Savior.
Amen.
Bless the Lord.
The Lord's name be praised.

2 Peter 3:18

A sign of peace may be exchanged by all.

EVENING PRAYER

An Outline of Evening Prayer (26-32)

Opening Sentences
Evening Hymn
Psalm(s)
Psalm (45-64)
Silent Prayer
[Psalm Prayer]
Scripture Reading
Silent Reflection
[A Brief Interpretation of the Reading, or a Nonbiblical Reading]
Canticle
Canticle of Mary or Other Canticle (37-44)
Prayers of Thanksgiving and Intercession
Concluding Prayer
Lord's Prayer
[Hymn or Spiritual]
Dismissal
[Sign of Peace]

When a person is worshipping alone, or in a family group, or when circumstances call for an abbreviated order, the following is suggested:
Psalm (45-64)
Scripture Reading
Silent Reflection
Prayers of Thanksgiving and Intercession

Opening Sentences

All may stand.

A. Our help is in the name of the Lord,
who made heaven and earth.

Ps. 24:34

B. O God, come to our assistance.
O Lord, hasten to help us.

See Ps. 70:1

C. Light and peace in Jesus Christ our Lord.
Thanks be to God.

And one of the following prayers is spoken:

Sunday

God reveals deep and mysterious things, and knows what is hidden in darkness.
God is surrounded by light. To you, O God, we give thanks and praise.

Dan. 2:22-23

Monday

I could ask the darkness to hide me or the light around me to become night,
but even darkness is not dark for you, and the night is as bright as the day;
for darkness is as light with you.

Ps. 139:11-12

Tuesday

The city of God has no need of sun or moon, for the glory of God is its light,
and its lamp is the Lamb.
By its light shall the nations walk, and the rulers of earth shall bring their treasures into it.

Rev. 21:23-24

Wednesday

In the city of God, night shall be no more; they need no light of lamp or sun,
for the Lord God will be their light, and they will reign for ever and ever.

Rev. 22:5

Thursday

God will come, and there shall be continuous day, for at evening time there shall be light.
God is light; in God there is no darkness at all.

Zech. 14:5c, 7, and 1 John 1:5

Friday

God who said, "Out of darkness the light shall shine!" is the same God who made light
shine in our hearts to bring us the knowledge of God's glory shining in the face of Christ.

2 Cor. 4:6

Saturday

You are my lamp, O Lord. My God lightens my darkness.
This God is my strong refuge and has made my way safe.

2 Sam. 22:29, 33

Evening Hymn

An evening hymn is sung or read.

All may be seated.

Psalm(s)

One or more psalms are sung or spoken. (45-64)
Silence for reflection follows each psalm.
A psalm prayer may follow the silence.

Scripture Reading

At the conclusion of the reading of scripture the reader may say:

The Word of the Lord.
Thanks be to God.

Silence follows for reflection on the meaning of the scripture.
The scripture may be briefly interpreted, or a nonbiblical reading may be read.

Canticle

The Canticle of Mary (Magnificat) or Phos Hilaron or another canticle may be sung or
spoken. (37-44)
All may stand.

Prayers of Thanksgiving and Intercession

The following prayers may be used:

Let my prayer rise before you as incense,
the lifting of my hands as an evening sacrifice.

Ps. 141:2

Or

To you, O Lord, I lift my soul.
O God, in you I trust.

Ps. 25:1-2

One of the following, or other prayers of thanksgiving and intercession, are spoken:

Sunday
We lift our voices in prayers of praise, holy God, for you have lifted us to new life in Jesus
Christ, and your blessings come in generous measure. Especially we thank you for
  the privilege of worship and service in this congregation . . .
  the good news of the gospel of Jesus Christ for us . . .
  food and drink to share in the Lord's name . . .
  our calling to discipleship. . . .
We hold up before you human needs, God of compassion, for you have come to us in
Jesus Christ and shared our life so we may share his resurrection. Especially we pray for
  the healing of those who are sick . . .
  the comfort of the dying . . .
  the renewal of those who despair . . .
  the Spirit's power in the church. . . .

Monday

We rejoice in your generous goodness, O God, and celebrate your lavish gifts to us this day, for you have shown your love in giving Jesus Christ for the salvation of the world. Especially we give thanks for

the labors of those who have served us today . . .

friends with whom we have shared . . .

those whom we love and have loved us . . .

opportunities for our work to help others . . .

all beauty that delights us. . . .

Gracious God, we know you are close to all in need, and by our prayers for others we come closer to you. We are bold to claim for others your promises of new life in Jesus Christ, as we claim them for ourselves. Especially we pray for

those in dangerous occupations . . .

physicians and nurses . . .

those who are ill or confined to nursing homes . . .

those who mourn . . .

the Roman Catholic Church. . . .

Tuesday

Eternal God, we thank you for being with us today, and for every sign of your truth and love in Jesus Christ. Especially we thank you for

the gift of peace in Christ . . .

reconciliation in our relationships . . .

each new insight into your love . . .

energy and courage to share your love . . .

the ministries of the church. . . .

Gracious God, we remember in our own hearts the needs of others, that we may reach up to claim your love for them, and reach out to give your love in the name of Christ. Especially we pray for

racial harmony and justice . . .

those imprisoned . . .

strangers we have met today . . .

friends who are bereaved . . .

Orthodox and Coptic churches. . . .

Wednesday

Give us your peace, O God, that we may rejoice in your goodness to us and to all your children, and be thankful for your love revealed in Jesus Christ. Especially we thank you for

> people who reveal your truth and righteousness . . .
>
> courage to be bold disciples . . .
>
> those who show hospitality . . .
>
> surprises that have blessed us . . .
>
> the unity of the church of Jesus Christ. . . .

Give us your peace, O God, that we may be confident of your care for us and all your children, as we remember the needs of others. Especially we pray for

> friends and relatives who are far away . . .
>
> neighbors in special need . . .
>
> those who suffer hunger and thirst . . .
>
> those who work at night while others sleep . . .
>
> Episcopal and Methodist churches. . . .

Thursday

We give you our praise and thanks, O God, for all gifts of love we have received from you, and for your persistent mercy in Jesus Christ. Especially we thank you for

> work we have accomplished pleasing to you . . .
>
> the faithful witness of Christian people . . .
>
> the example of righteousness we see in parents and teachers . . .
>
> the innocence and openness we see in children . . .
>
> all works of Christian compassion. . . .

We give you our cares and concerns, O God, because we know you are kind and care for your children in every circumstance. Especially we pray for

> those who struggle with doubt and despair . . .
>
> people afflicted with disease . . .
>
> those called to special ministries . . .
>
> people neglected or abused . . .
>
> Baptist, Disciples of Christ, and other free churches. . . .

Friday

Merciful God, we praise you that you give strength for every weakness, forgiveness for our failures, and new beginnings in Jesus Christ. Especially we thank you for

> the guidance of your spirit through this day . . .
>
> signs of new life and hope . . .
>
> people who have helped us . . .
>
> those who struggle for justice . . .
>
> expressions of love unexpected or undeserved. . . .

Almighty God, you know all needs before we speak our prayers, yet you welcome our concerns for others in Jesus Christ. Especially we pray for

> those who keep watch over the sick and dying . . .
>
> those who weep with the grieving . . .
>
> those who are without faith and cannot accept your love . . .
>
> the aged who are lonely, distressed or weak . . .
>
> Reformed, Presbyterian, and Lutheran churches. . . .

Saturday

God of glory, we praise you for your presence in our lives, and for all goodness that you shower upon your children in Jesus Christ. Especially we thank you for

> promises kept and hope for tomorrow . . .
> the enjoyment of friends . . .
> the wonders of your creation . . .
> love from our parents, our sisters and brothers, our spouses and children . . .
> pleasures of living. . . .

God of grace, we are one with all your children, for we are sisters and brothers of Jesus Christ, and we offer our prayers for all whom we love. Especially we pray for

> those we too often forget . . .
> people who have lost hope . . .
> victims of tragedy and disaster . . .
> those who suffer mental anguish . . .
> ecumenical councils and church agencies. . . .

Individual prayers of thanksgiving and intercession may be offered.
There may be silent prayer.

The leader then says one of the following prayers, or a similar prayer.

Sunday

As you have made this day, O God, you also make the night.
Give light for our comfort.
Come upon us with quietness and still our souls, that we may listen for the whisper of your Spirit and be attentive to your nearness in our dreams.
Empower us to rise again in new life to proclaim your praise,
and show Christ to the world, for he reigns for ever and ever.   **Amen.**

Monday

Great God, you are one God,
and you bring together what is scattered and mend what is broken.
Unite us with the scattered peoples of the earth that we may be one family of your children.
Bind up all our wounds, and heal us in spirit,
that we may be renewed as disciples of Jesus Christ, our Master and Savior.   **Amen.**

Tuesday

God of all who fear you, make us one with all your saints and with any who are in need.
Teach us to befriend the weak, and welcome the outcast,
that we may serve the Lord Jesus Christ and live to offer him glory.
In his holy name we pray.   **Amen.**

Wednesday

God our shepherd, you have brought us through this day to a time of reflection and rest.
Calm our souls, and refresh us with your peace.
Keep us close to Christ and draw us closer to one another in the bonds of his wondrous love.
We pray through Christ our Lord.   **Amen.**

Thursday

To you, O God we give up the burdens of this day, trusting your love and mercy.
To you, O God, we surrender ourselves, trusting our risen Lord to lead us always
in the way of peace, today, tomorrow, and for ever.   **Amen.**

Friday

Protect your people, O God, and keep us safe
until the coming of your new dawn and the establishment of your righteous rule.
By your Holy Spirit, stir up within us a longing for the light of your new day,
and guide us by the radiance of Jesus Christ your Son, our risen Lord.   **Amen.**

NZPB, alt.

Saturday

Abide with us, O Lord, for evening comes and the day is almost over.
Abide with us, for the days are hastening on and we hasten with them.
Abide with us and with all your faithful people,
until the daystar rises and the morning light appears,
and we shall abide with you for ever.   **Amen.**

The Lord's Prayer

Now let us pray the prayer Jesus taught his disciples to pray saying:

Our Father, who art in heaven,
hallowed be thy name,
thy kingdom come,
thy will be done,
on earth as it is in heaven.
Give us this day our daily bread;
and forgive us our debts,
as we forgive our debtors;
and lead us not into temptation,
but deliver us from evil.
For thine is the kingdom,
and the power, and the glory,
for ever.   Amen.

[Hymn or Spiritual]

Dismissal

The leader dismisses the people using one of the following:

A. May the grace of the Lord Jesus Christ be with us all.
Amen.
Bless the Lord.
The Lord's name be praised.

Phil. 4:23

B. May the Lord, who is our peace,
give us peace at all times and in every way.
Amen.
Bless the Lord.
The Lord's name be praised.

2 Thess. 3:16

C. May the peace of God, which surpasses all understanding,
guard our hearts and minds in Christ Jesus.
Amen.
Bless the Lord.
The Lord's name be praised.

Phil. 4:7

A sign of peace may be exchanged by all.

SPECIAL PRAYERS

Lord, Open Our Eyes

Lord, open our eyes, that we may see you in our brothers and sisters.
Lord, open our ears, that we may hear the cries of the hungry, the cold,
the frightened, the oppressed.
Lord, open our hearts, that we may love each other as you love us.
Renew in us your spirit, Lord, free us and make us one.

Mother Teresa, 1910-1997

Teach Us to Pray

Lord, teach us to pray. Some of us are not skilled in the art of prayer. As we draw near to thee in thought, our spirits long for thy Spirit, and reach out for thee, longing to feel thee near. We know not how to express the deepest emotions that lie hidden in our hearts.

In these moments, we have no polished phrases with which to impress one another, no finely molded, delicately turned clauses to present to thee. Nor would we be confined to conventional petitions and repeat our prayers like the unwinding of a much-exposed film. We know, Father, that we are praying most when we are saying least. We know that we are closest to thee when we have left behind the things that have held us captive so long.

We would not be ignorant in prayer and, like children, make want lists for thee. Rather, we pray that thou wilt give unto us only what we really need. We would not make our prayers the importuning of thee, an omnipotent God, to do what we want thee to do. Rather, give us the vision, the courage, that shall enlarge our horizons and stretch our faith to the adventure of seeking thy loving will for our lives.

We thank thee that thou art hearing us even now. We thank thee for the grace of prayer. We thank thee for thyself.

Peter Marshall, 1902-1944

Unity of Faiths

O God, we are one with you. You have made us one with you. You have taught us that if we are open to one another, you dwell in us. Help us to preserve this openness and to fight for it with all our hearts. Help us to realize that there can be no understanding where there is mutual rejection. O God, in accepting one another wholeheartedly, fully, completely, we accept you, and we thank you, and we adore you, and we love you with our whole being, because our being is in your being, our spirit is rooted in your spirit. Fill us then with love, and let us be bound together with love as we go our diverse ways, united in this one spirit which makes you present in the world, and which makes you witness to the ultimate reality that is love. Love has overcome. Love is victorious.

Thomas Merton, 1915-1968

Comfort Prayer

O Lord God, great is the misery that has come upon me.
My cares overwhelm me: I am at a loss. O God, comfort and help me.
Give me strength to bear what you send, and do not let fear rule over me.
As a loving Father, take care of my loved ones, my wife and my children.
O merciful God, forgive all the sins I have committed
Against you and against my fellow men.
I put my trust in your grace, and commit my life wholly into your hands.
Do with me as is best for you, for that will be best for me too.
Whether I live or die, I am with you, and you are with me.
Lord, I wait for your salvation and for your kingdom.

Dietrich Bonhoeffer, 1906-1945

In Personal Crisis

God of life, there are days when the burdens we carry are heavy on our shoulders and weigh us down, when the road seems dreary and endless, the skies gray and threatening, when our lives have no music in them, and our hearts are lonely, and our souls have lost their courage. Flood the path with light, turn our eyes to where the skies are full of promise; tune our hearts to brave music; give us the sense of comradeship with heroes and saints of every age; and so quicken our spirits that we may be able to encourage the souls of all who journey with us on the road of life, to your honor and glory.   Amen.

Attr. to Augustine of Hippo, 354-430

The Serenity Prayer

God, give us grace to accept with serenity the things that cannot be changed, courage to change the things that should be changed, and the wisdom to distinguish the one from the other.   Amen.

Reinhold Niebuhr, 1892-1971

Give Me Strength

Lord God, you know all things. You know how much I long to be chaste, that I may give my whole self, body and soul, to you. And you know how I struggle to abstain from meat and strong drink, that my mind may be pure for you. I desire never to go against your will; so whenever I fail to keep your commands, I am overcome with sorrow. Now, blessed Jesus, make your will known to me at all times, and give me the strength to obey it.

Margey Kempe, 1373-1432

Seed of Love

What a good friend you are, Lord! You are so patient, willing to wait as long as necessary for me to turn to you. You rejoice at the times when I love you, but you do not hold against me the times when I ignore you. Your patience is beyond my understanding. Even when I pray, my mind fills with worldly concerns and vain daydreams. Yet you are happy if I give only a single second of honest prayer, turning that second into a seed of love. O Lord, I enjoy your friendship so much, why is it not possible for me to think of you constantly?

Teresa of Ávila, 1515-1582

For Personal Devotion

Lord, make me an instrument of your peace. Where there is hatred, let me sow love: where there is injury, pardon: where there is doubt, faith: where there is despair, hope: where there is darkness, light: where there is sadness, joy.

O Divine Master, grant that I may not seek so much to be consoled as to console, to be understood as to understand, to be loved as to love. For it is in giving that we receive, it is in pardoning that we are pardoned, and it is in dying that we are born to eternal life. Amen.

Attr. to Francis of Assisi, 1181-1226

For the Bereaved

O merciful God, you teach us in your Holy Word that you do not willingly afflict or grieve your children. Look with pity on the sorrows of (N., N.) your servant, for whom we pray. Remember him/her, O Lord, in mercy. Strength him/her in patience, comfort him/her with the memory of your goodness, let your presence shine on him/her, and give him/her peace. Through Jesus Christ our Lord. Amen.

BCP

For the Lonely

God of comfort, companion of the lonely, be with those who by neglect or willful separation are left alone. Fill empty places with present love, and long times of solitude with lively thoughts of you. Encourage us to visit lonely men and women, so they may be cheered by the Spirit of Jesus Christ, who walked among us as a friend, and is our Lord for ever. Amen.

For Families

Eternal God, our creator, you set us to live in families. We commend to your care all the homes where your people live. Keep them, we pray, free from bitterness, from the thirst for personal victory, and from pride in self. Fill them with faith, virtue, knowledge, moderation, patience and godliness. Knit together in enduring affection those who have become one in marriage. Let children and parents have full respect for one another: and light the fire of kindliness among us all, that we may show affection for each other; through Jesus Christ our Lord. Amen.

BCP

For Children

Great God, guard the laughter of children. Bring them safely through injury and illness, so they may live the promises you give. Do not let us be so preoccupied with our purposes that we fail to hear their voices, or pay attention to their special vision of the truth; but keep us with them, ready to listen and to love, even as in Jesus Christ you have loved us, your grown-up wayward children. Amen.

For the Aged

O Lord God, look with mercy on all whose increasing years bring them isolation, distress or weakness. Provide for them homes of dignity and peace; give them understanding helpers and the willingness to accept help; and, as their strength diminishes, increase their faith and their assurance of your love. We pray in the name of Jesus Christ our Lord.   Amen.

BCP

For the Sick

O God, the strength of the weak and the comfort of sufferers, mercifully hear our prayers and grant to your servant N. the help of your power, that his/her sickness may be turned into health and our sorrow into joy; through Jesus Christ.   Amen.

BCP

During an Illness

You are medicine for me when I am sick.
You are my strength when I need help.
You are life itself when I fear death.
You are the way when I long for heaven.
You are the light when all is dark.
You are my food when I need nourishment!   Amen.

Ambrose of Milan, 340-397

For Healing

Mighty and merciful God, you sent Jesus Christ to heal broken lives. We praise you that today you send healing in doctors and nurses, and bless us with technology in medicine. We claim your promises of wholeness as we pray for those who are ill in body or mind, who long for your healing touch.

Make the weak strong, the sick healthy, the broken whole, and confirm those who serve them as agents of your love. Then all shall be renewed in vigor to point to the risen Christ who conquered death that we might live eternally.   Amen.

For Social Justice

Yes, Jesus, I want to be on your right side or your left side, not for any selfish reason. I want to be on your right or your best side, not in terms of some political kingdom or ambition, but I just want to be there in love and in justice and in truth and in commitments to others, so we can make of this old world a new world.   Amen.

Martin Luther King, Jr., 1929-1968

For Faithfulness

Give me, O Lord, a steadfast heart, which no unworthy affection may drag downward; give me an unconquered heart, which no tribulation can wear out; give me an upright heart, which no unworthy purpose may tempt aside.

Bestow on me also, O Lord my God, understanding to know you, diligence to seek you, wisdom to find you, and a faithfulness that may finally embrace you; through Jesus Christ our Lord.   Amen.

Thomas Aquinas, c.1225-1274

37   Canticle of Praise to God

Psalm 95:1-7; 96:9, 13   William Boyce

1. O come, let us sing   unto   the   Lord;
3. For the Lord is a   great   God,
5. The sea is his   and   he   made it;
7. For he is the   Lord   our   God;
10. Glory be to the Father and   to   the   Son,

let us heartily rejoice in the   strength of   our sal - vation.
and a great   King   a - bove all   gods.
and his hands pre   -   pared the   dry   land.
and we are the people of his pasture and the   sheep   of   his   hand.
and   to   the   Ho - ly   Ghost;

2. Let us come before his presence with   thanks   -   giving;
4. In his hand are all the corners   of   the   earth;
6. O come let us worship and   fall   down,
8. O worship the Lord in the   beauty of   holiness;
9. For he cometh, for he cometh to   judge the   earth;
   As it was in the beginning, is now and   ev - er   shall be,

and show ourselves   glad   in   him with   psalms.
and the strength of the   hills   is   his   also.
and kneel be   -   fore   the   Lord our   Maker.
let the whole earth   stand in   awe   of   him. *To verse 9*
and with righteousness to
judge the world, and the   peo- ples   with   his   truth. *To verse 10 (opt.)*
world without   end.   A   -   men.

Canticle of God's Glory

38

Luke 2:14; John 1:29; ICET, rev. ELLC

Alexander Peloquin (1972)

Luke 2:14; John 1:29; ICET, rev. ELLC — Alexander Peloquin (1972)

Response

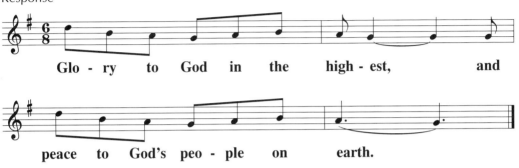

Glo - ry to God in the high - est, and

peace to God's peo - ple on earth.

R

Glory to God in the highest,
    and peace to God's people on earth.
    Lord God, heavenly King,
    almighty God and Father,
    we worship you, we give you thanks,
    we praise you for your glory. **R**

Lord Jesus Christ, only Son of the Father,
    Lord God, Lamb of God,
    you take away the sin of the world:
    have mercy on us;
    you are seated at the right hand of the Father:
    receive our prayer. **R**

For you alone are the Holy One,
    you alone are the Lord,
    you alone are the Most High,
    Jesus Christ,
    with the Holy Spirit,
    in the glory of God the Father. Amen. **R**

39   Canticle of Thanksgiving

Psalm 100; Response, Edward H. Plumptre   Arthur H. Messiter

Response

Re - joice!   Re - joice!   Re - joice,   give thanks and   sing.

R

Make a joyful noise unto the Lord, all ye lands.
Serve the Lord with gladness;
    come before his presence with singing.
Know ye that the Lord, he is God;
it is he that hath made us, and not we ourselves;
    we are his people, and the sheep of his pasture.
Enter into his gates with thanksgiving,
    and into his courts with praise;
be thankful unto him, and bless his name.
For the Lord is good;
his mercy is everlasting;
    and his truth endureth to all generations. R

Canticle of Eventide

40

Phos Hilaron, Greek, c. 200
Tr. by William G. Storey, c. 1970

Plainsong, Mode IV
Harm. by C. Winfred Douglas, 1943, alt.

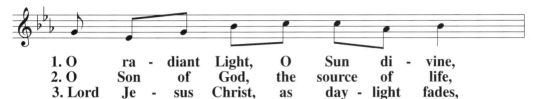

1. O   ra - diant Light,   O   Sun   di - vine,
2. O   Son   of   God,   the   source   of   life,
3. Lord Je - sus Christ,   as   day - light fades,

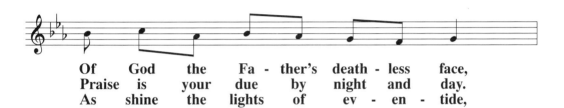

Of   God   the   Fa - ther's death - less   face,
Praise is   your   due   by   night   and   day.
As   shine   the   lights   of   ev - en - tide,

O   im - age   of   the   Light   sub - lime,
Our   hap - py   lips   must   raise   the   strain
We   praise   the   Fa - ther   with   the   Son,

That   fills   the   heav - n'ly dwell - ing place.
Of   your   es - teemed and   splen - did   name.
The   Spir - it   blest   and   with them one.   A - men.

41   **Canticle of Mary**

Luke 1:46b-55, ICET, rev. ELLC
Response, Joachim Neander

LOBE DEN HERREN (99)

Response

Praise to the Lord, the Al - might-y, who rules all cre - a - tion!

R

My soul proclaims the greatness of the Lord,
my spirit rejoices in God my Savior,
    who has looked with favor on me, a lowly servant.
From this day all generations shall call me blessed:
the Almighty has done great things for me
    and holy is the name of the Lord,
    whose mercy is on those who fear God
    from generation to generation.
The arm of the Lord is strong.
    and has scattered the proud in their conceit.
God has cast down the mighty from their thrones
    and lifted up the lowly.
God has filled the hungry with good things
    and sent the rich empty away.
God has come to the aid of Israel, the chosen servant,
    remembering the promise of mercy,
    the promise made to our forebears,
    to Abraham and his children for ever. R

Canticle of Simeon

Luke 2:29-32, ICET, rev. ELLC

LASST UNS ERFREUEN (83)

Response

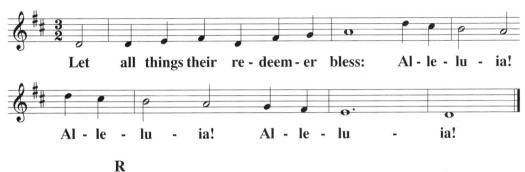

Let all things their re-deem-er bless: Al-le-lu-ia!
Al-le-lu-ia! Al-le-lu-ia!

R

Lord, now let your servant go in peace;
  your word has been fulfilled:
  my own eyes have seen the salvation
  which you have prepared in the presence
of all people,
  a light to reveal you to the nations
  and the glory of your people Israel. R

43   **Canticle of Zechariah**

Luke 1:68-79; ICET, rev. ELLC
Response, James Montgomery (1821)

ELLACOMBE (117)

Response

Hail to the Lord's A - noint - ed, great Da - vid's great-er Son.

R

Blessed be the Lord, the God of Israel,
    who has come to set the chosen people free.
The Lord has raised up for us
    a mighty Savior from the house of David.
Through the holy prophets, God promised of old
    to save us from our enemies,
    from the hands of all who hate us;
to show mercy to our forebears
    and to remember the holy covenant.
This was the oath God swore to our father Abraham:
to set us free from the hands of our enemies,
    free to worship without fear,
    holy and righteous in the Lord's sight,
    all the days of our life. R

And you, child, shall be called the prophet of the Most High,
    for you will go before the Lord to prepare the way,
to give God's people knowledge of salvation
    by the forgiveness of their sins.
In the tender compassion of our God
    the dawn from on high shall break upon us,
to shine on those who dwell in darkness and the shadow of death,
    and to guide our feet into the way of peace. R

Canticle of Light and Darkness

44

Isaiah 9:2; 59:9-10; Psalm 139:11-12;
Daniel 2:20, 22; 1 John 1:5, adapt. by Alan Luff

ADESTE FIDELES (133)

Response

O come, let us a - dore him, Christ, the Lord!

R

We look for light but find darkness,
 for brightness, but walk in gloom.
 We grope like those who have no eyes;
 we stumble at noon as in the twilight. **R**

If I say, "Let only darkness cover me,
 and the light about me be night,"
 even the darkness is not dark to you,
 the night is bright as the day,
 for darkness is as light with you. **R**

Blessed be your name, O God, for ever.
 You reveal deep and mysterious things;
 you are light and in you is no darkness.
 Our darkness is passing away
 and already the true light is shining. **R**

45   Psalm 8

Response   MIT FREUDEN ZART (110)

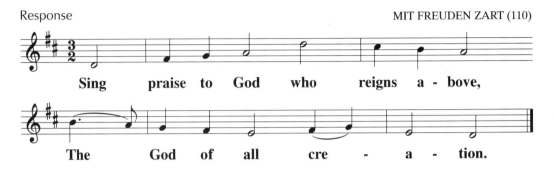

Sing praise to God who reigns a - bove,

The God of all cre - a - tion.

R

1   O Lord, our Lord,
         how majestic is your name in all the earth!
2   Your glory is chanted above the heavens
         by the mouth of babes and infants:
     you have set up a defense against your foes,
         to still the enemy and the avenger.   R

3   When I look at your heavens, the work of your fingers,
         the moon and the stars which you have established;
4   what are human beings that you are mindful of them,
         and mortals that you care for them?
5   Yet you have made them little less than God,
         and crowned them with glory and honor.   R

6   You have given them dominion over the works of your hands;
         you have put all things under their feet,
7   all sheep and oxen,
         and also the beasts of the field,
8   the birds of the air, and the fish of the sea,
         whatever passes along the paths of the seas.
9   O Lord, our Lord,
         how majestic is your name in all the earth!   R

Psalm 16:5-11

46

Response   HYMN TO JOY (92)

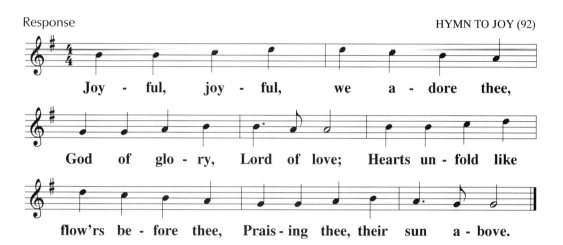

Joy - ful, joy - ful, we a - dore thee, God of glo - ry, Lord of love; Hearts un - fold like flow'rs be - fore thee, Prais - ing thee, their sun a - bove.

R

⁵ The Lord is my chosen portion and my cup;
    you hold my lot.
⁶ **The lines have fallen for me in pleasant places;**
    I have a glorious heritage.
⁷ I bless the Lord who gives me counsel;
    even at night my heart instructs me.
⁸ **I have set the Lord always before me;**
    the Lord is at my right hand;
    I shall not be moved.   R

⁹ Therefore my heart is glad, and my soul rejoices;
    my body also dwells secure.
¹⁰ **For you do not give me up to Sheol,**
    or let your godly one see the pit.
¹¹ You show me the path of life;
    in your presence there is fullness of joy,
    in your right hand are pleasures for evermore.   R

47   **Psalm 19**

Response   LEONI (96)

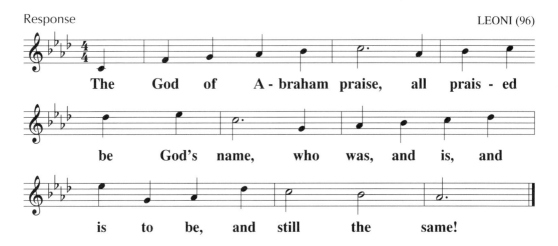

The God of A - braham praise, all prais - ed
be God's name, who was, and is, and
is to be, and still the same!

R

¹ The heavens are telling the glory of God;
       and the firmament proclaims God's handiwork.
² **Day to day pours forth speech,**
       and night to night declares knowledge.
³ There is no speech, nor are there words;
       their voice is not heard;
⁴ **yet their voice goes out through all the earth,**
       and their words to the end of the world.
   In them God has set a tent for the sun,
⁵   which comes forth like a bridegroom leaving his chamber,
       and runs its course with joy like a strong man.
⁶ **Its rising is from the end of the heavens,**
       and its circuit to the end of them;
       and there is nothing hid from its heat.   R

⁷ The law of the Lord is perfect,
       reviving the soul;
   the testimony of the Lord is sure,
       making wise the simple;
⁸ the precepts of the Lord are right,
       rejoicing the heart;
   the commandment of the Lord is pure,
       enlightening the eyes;

9   the fear of the Lord is clean,
        enduring for ever;
    the ordinances of the Lord are true,
        and righteous altogether.
10 More to be desired are they than gold,
        even much fine gold;
    sweeter also than honey
        and drippings of the honeycomb.   R

11 Moreover by them is your servant warned;
        in keeping them there is great reward.
12 **But who can understand one's own errors?**
        Clear me from hidden faults.
13 Also keep your servant from the insolent;
        let them not have dominion over me!
    Then I shall be blameless,
        and innocent of great transgression.
14 **Let the words of my mouth / and the meditation of my heart**
        be acceptable in your sight,
        O Lord, my rock and my redeemer.   R

48 Psalm 22:1-18, 25-31

Response PASSION CHORALE (168)

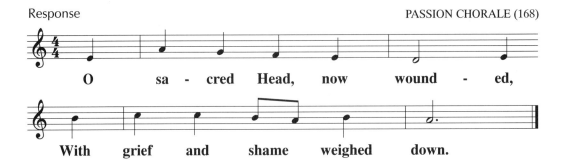

O sa - cred Head, now wound - ed,

With grief and shame weighed down.

R

1 My God, my God, why have you forsaken me?
   Why are you so far from helping me,
   from the words of my groaning?
2 O my God, I cry by day, but you do not answer;
   and by night, but find no rest.
3 Yet you, the praise of Israel,
   are enthroned in holiness.
4 **In you our forbears trusted;**
   they trusted and you delivered them.
5 To you they cried, and were saved;
   in you they trusted, and were not disappointed. R

6 But I am a worm, and not human;
   scorned by others, and despised by the people.
7 All who see me mock at me,
   they make mouths at me, they wag their heads;
8 "He committed his cause to the Lord;
      let the Lord deliver him.
      Let the Lord rescue him,
      for the Lord delights in him!"
9 **Yet it was you who took me from the womb;**
   you kept me safe upon my mother's breast.
10 Upon you I was cast from my birth,
   and since my mother bore me, you have been my God.
11 **Do not be far from me,**
   for trouble is near
   and there is none to help. R

12 Many bulls encompass me,
    strong bulls of Bashan surround me;
13 **they open wide their mouths at me,**
    like a ravening and roaring lion.
14 I am poured out like water
    and all my bones are out of joint;
my heart is like wax,
    it is melted within my breast;
15 my mouth is dried up like a potsherd,
    and my tongue cleaves to my jaws;
    you lay me in the dust of death.
16 Indeed, dogs surround me;
    a company of evildoers encircles me;
    they have pierced my hands and feet—
17 I can count all my bones—
    they stare and gloat over me;
18 they divide my garments among them,
    and for my raiment, they cast lots.   R

25 From you comes my praise in the great congregation;
    my vows I will pay before those who worship the Lord.
26 The poor shall eat and be satisfied;
    those who seek the Lord shall praise the Lord!
    May your hearts live for ever!
27 All the ends of the earth shall remember
    and turn to the Lord;
and all the families of the nations
    shall worship before the Lord.
28 For dominion belongs to the Lord
    who rules over the nations.
29 **All who sleep in the earth**
    shall bow down to the Lord.
All who go down to the dust shall bow before the Lord,
    and I shall live for God.
30 **Posterity shall serve the Lord;**
    each generation shall tell of the Lord,
31 and proclaim his deliverance to a people yet unborn.
    Surely the Lord has done it.   R

49   Psalm 23

Response   Joseph Gelineau

My shep-herd is the Lord, noth-ing in-deed shall I want.

R

1   The Lord is my shepherd;
> I shall not want.

2   **He maketh me to lie down in green pastures:**
> **he leadeth me beside the still waters.**

3   He restoreth my soul:
> he leadeth me in the paths of righteousness for his name's sake.

4   **Yea, though I walk through the valley of the shadow of death,**
> **I will fear no evil:**
> **For thou art with me;**
> **thy rod and thy staff they comfort me.   R**

5   Thou preparest a table before me
> in the presence of mine enemies:
thou anointest my head with oil;
> my cup runneth over.

6   **Surely goodness and mercy shall follow me**
> **all the days of my life:**
and I will dwell in the house of the Lord for ever.   R

Psalm 24

50

Response   TRURO (123)

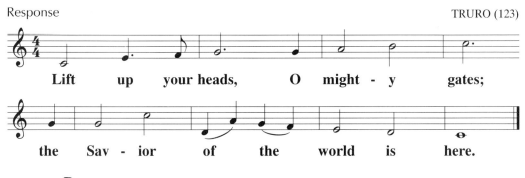

Lift up your heads, O might - y gates;

the Sav - ior of the world is here.

R

1   The earth is the Lord's and the fullness thereof,
       the world and those who dwell therein;
2   for God has founded it upon the seas,
       and established it upon the rivers.
3   Who shall ascend the hill of the Lord?
       And who shall stand in God's holy place?
4   Those who have clean hands and pure hearts,
       who do not lift up their souls to what is false,
       and do not swear deceitfully.
5   They will receive blessing from the Lord,
       and vindication from the God of their salvation.
6   Such is the generation of those who seek the Lord,
       who seek the face of the God of Jacob.   R

7   Lift up your heads, O gates!
       and be lifted up, O ancient doors!
       that the Ruler of glory may come in.
8   **Who is the Ruler of glory?**
       The Lord, strong and mighty,
       the Lord, mighty in battle!
9   **Lift up your heads, O gates!**
       and be lifted up, O ancient doors!
       that the Ruler of glory may come in.
10 Who is this Ruler of glory?
       The Lord of hosts,
       the Lord is the Ruler of glory!   R

51   Psalm 27

Response   NUN DANKET ALLE GOTT (358)

Sing praise to God our rock, in whom we take our ref - uge.

R

¹ The Lord is my light and my salvation;
   whom shall I fear?
   The Lord is the stronghold of my life;
   of whom shall I be afraid?
² When evildoers assail me,
   to devour my flesh,
   my adversaries and foes
   shall stumble and fall.
³ **Though a host encamp against me,**
   my heart shall not fear;
   though war arise against me,
   yet I will be confident.
⁴ One thing I asked of the Lord,
   that will I seek after:
   that I may dwell in the house of the Lord
   all the days of my life,
   to behold the beauty of the Lord,
   and to inquire in the Lord's temple. R

⁵ The Lord will hide me in his shelter
   in the day of trouble,
   will conceal me under the cover of his tent,
   and will set me high upon a rock.
⁶ **And now my head shall be lifted up**
   above my enemies round about me;
   and I will offer sacrifices in the Lord's tent
   with shouts of joy;
   I will sing and make melody to the Lord. R

7   Hear, O Lord, when I cry aloud,
        be gracious to me and answer me!
8   **"Come," my heart said, "seek the Lord's face."**
        Your face, O Lord, I seek.
9   Hide not your face from me.
        Turn not your servant away in anger,
        for you have been my help.
10 **Cast me not off, forsake me not,**
        O God of my salvation!
    If my father and mother should forsake me,
        the Lord would take me up.   R

11 Teach me your way, O Lord;
        and lead me on a level path
        because of my enemies.
12 **Give me not up to the will of my adversaries;**
        for false witnesses have risen against me,
        and they breathe out violence.
13 I believe that I shall see the goodness of the Lord
        in the land of the living!
14 **Wait for the Lord;**
        be strong, and let your heart take courage.
    Wait for the Lord!   R

52　　　　　　　　　　　**Psalm 46**

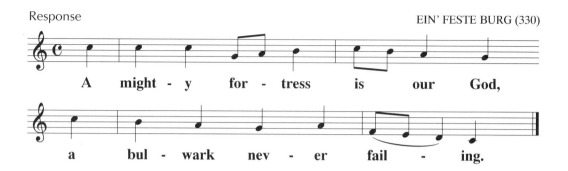

Response　　　　　　　　　　　　　　　　　　EIN' FESTE BURG (330)

A might-y for-tress is our God,

a bul-wark nev-er fail-ing.

R

1　God is our refuge and strength,
　　　a very present help in trouble.
2　**Therefore we will not fear though the earth should change,**
　　　though the mountains shake in the heart of the sea;
3　though its waters roar and foam,
　　　though the mountains tremble with its tumult.
4　**There is a river whose streams make glad the city of God,**
　　　the holy habitation of the Most High.
5　God is in the midst of the city which shall not be moved;
　　　God will help it at the dawn of the day.
6　**The nations rage, the kingdoms totter;**
　　　God's voice resounds, the earth melts.
7　The Lord of hosts is with us;
　　　the God of Jacob is our refuge.　R

8　Come, behold the works of the Lord,
　　　who has wrought desolations in the earth;
9　**who makes wars cease to the end of the earth,**
　　　breaks the bow, shatters the spear,
　　　and burns the shields with fire!
10　"Be still, and know that I am God.
　　　I am exalted among the nations,
　　　I am exalted in the earth!"
11　**The Lord of hosts is with us;**
　　　the God of Jacob is our refuge.　R

Psalm 51:1-17

Response　　　　　　　　　　　　　　　　　AUS TIEFER NOT (152)

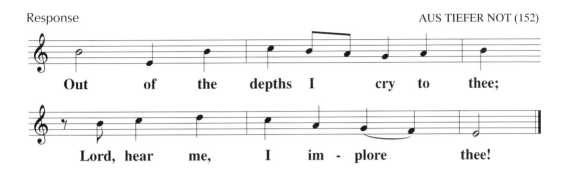

Out　　of　　the　　depths　I　　cry　to　　thee;

Lord,　hear　　me,　　　I　　im - plore　　　thee!

R

[1] Have mercy on me, O God,
according to your steadfast love;
**according to your abundant mercy
blot out my transgressions.**

[2] Wash me thoroughly from my iniquity,
and cleanse me from my sin!

[3] **For I know my transgressions,
and my sin is ever before me.**

[4] Against you, you only, have I sinned,
and done that which is evil in your sight,
so that you are justified in your sentence
and blameless in your judgment.

[5] **Behold, I was born into iniquity,
and I have been sinful since my mother conceived me. R**

[6] Behold, you desire truth in the inward being;
therefore teach me wisdom in my secret heart.

[7] **Purge me with hyssop, and I shall be clean;
wash me, and I shall be whiter than snow;**

[8] Make me hear with joy and gladness;
let the bones which you have broken rejoice.

[9] **Hide your face from my sins,
and blot out all my iniquities. R**

10   Create in me a clean heart, O God,
     and put a new and right spirit within me.
11   **Cast me not away from your presence,**
     and take not your holy Spirit from me.
12   Restore to me the joy of your salvation,
     and sustain in me a willing spirit.
13   **Then I will teach transgressors your ways,**
     and sinners will return to you.
14   Deliver me from death, O God, God of my salvation,
     and my tongue will sing aloud of your deliverance.
15   **O Lord, open my lips,**
     and my mouth shall show forth your praise.
16   For you have no delight in sacrifice;
     were I to give a burnt offering, you would not be pleased.
17   **The sacrifice acceptable to God is a broken spirit;**
     a broken and contrite heart, O God, you will not despise.   R

Psalm 62:5-12   **54**

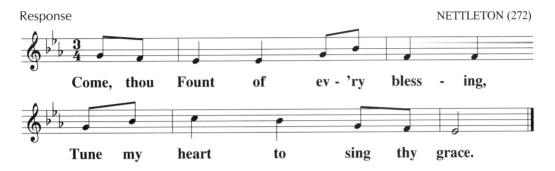

Response   NETTLETON (272)

Come, thou Fount of ev - 'ry bless - ing,

Tune my heart to sing thy grace.

R

5   For God alone my soul waits in silence,
        for my hope is from God,
6   **who alone is my rock and my salvation,**
        my fortress; I shall not be shaken.
7   On God rests my deliverance and my honor;
        my mighty rock, my refuge is God.
8   **Trust in God at all times, O people;**
        pour out your heart before God who is a refuge for us.   R

9   Those of low estate are but a breath,
        those of high estate are a delusion;
    in the balances they go up;
        they are together lighter than a breath.
10 **Put no confidence in extortion,**
        set no vain hopes on robbery;
        if riches increase, set not your heart on them.
11 Once God has spoken,
        twice have I heard this:
        power belongs to God;
12 **and to you, O Lord, belongs steadfast love,**
        for you repay all according to their work.   R

55   # Psalm 90

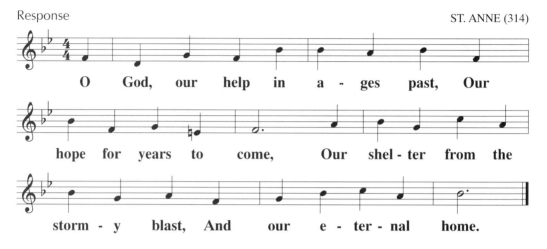

Response   ST. ANNE (314)

O God, our help in a - ges past, Our

hope for years to come, Our shel - ter from the

storm - y blast, And our e - ter - nal home.

R

1   Lord, you have been our dwelling place
        in all generations.

2   **Before the mountains were brought forth,**
            or ever you had formed the earth and the world,
            from everlasting to everlasting you are God.

3   You turn us back to the dust,
            and say, "Turn back, O mortal ones!"

4   **For a thousand years in your sight**
            are but as yesterday when it is past,
            or as a watch in the night.

5   You sweep them away; they are like a dream,
            like grass which is renewed in the morning:

6   **in the morning it flourishes and is renewed;**
            in the evening it fades and withers.   R

7   For we are consumed by your anger;
        by your wrath we are overwhelmed.

8   **You have set our iniquities before you,**
        our secret sins in the light of your countenance.

9   For all our days pass away under your wrath,
        our years come to an end like a sigh.

10   **The years of our life are threescore and ten,**
        or even by reason of strength fourscore;
    yet their span is but toil and trouble;
        they are soon gone, and we fly away.

11   Who considers the power of your anger,
        the awesomeness of your wrath?

12   **So teach us to number our days**
        that we may receive a heart of wisdom.   R

13   Return, O Lord! How long?
        Have pity on your servants!

14   **Satisfy us in the morning with your steadfast love,**
        that we may rejoice and be glad all our days.

15   Make us glad as many days as you have afflicted us,
        and as many years as we have seen evil.

16   **Let your work be manifest to your servants,**
        and your glorious power to their children.

17   Let the favor of the Lord our God be upon us,
        and establish the work of our hands;
    yes, establish the work of our hands.   R

56   Psalm 96

Response   ANTIOCH (145)

Joy   to the world! the Lord is   come: Let earth re-ceive her King.

R

1   O sing to the Lord a new song;
        sing to the Lord, all the earth!
2   **Sing to the Lord, bless God's name;**
        proclaim God's salvation from day to day.
3   Declare the Lord's glory among the nations,
        the Lord's marvelous works among all the peoples!
4   **For great is the Lord and greatly to be praised,**
        to be feared above all gods.
5   For all the gods of the peoples are idols;
        but the Lord made the heavens.
6   **Honor and majesty are before the Lord**
        in whose sanctuary are strength and beauty.   R

7   Ascribe to the Lord, O families of the peoples,
        ascribe to the Lord glory and strength!
8   **Ascribe to the Lord the glory of his name!**
        Bring an offering, and come into the courts of the Lord!
9   Worship the Lord in holy splendor;
        tremble before the Lord, all the earth!   R

10 Say among the nations, "The Lord reigns!
        The Lord has established the world,
        it shall never be moved.
        The Lord will judge the peoples with equity."
11 Let the heavens be glad, and let the earth rejoice;
        let the sea roar, and all that fills it;
12   let the field exult, and everything in it!
    Then shall all the trees of the wood sing for joy
13   **before the Lord, who comes to judge the earth.**
    The Lord will judge the world with righteousness,
        and the peoples with his truth.   R

Psalm 100

57

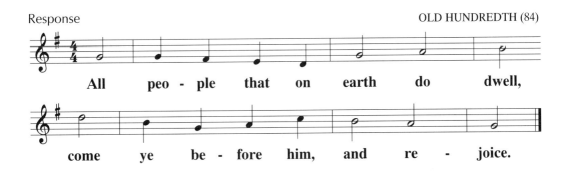

Response   OLD HUNDREDTH (84)

All peo - ple that on earth do dwell, come ye be - fore him, and re - joice.

R

1 Make a joyful noise to the Lord, all the lands!
2 **Serve the Lord with gladness!**
    Come into God's presence with singing!
3 Know that the Lord, who made us, is God.
    We are the Lord's;
    we are the people of God,
    the sheep of God's pasture.
4 Enter God's gates with thanksgiving,
    and God's courts with praise!
    Give thanks and bless God's name!
5 For the Lord is good;
    God's steadfast love endures for ever;
    God's faithfulness to all generations.   R

58   Psalm 103:1-18

Response   LAUDA ANIMA (100)

Praise, my soul, the King of heav - en;

Glo - rious in his faith - ful - ness.

R

1 Bless the Lord, O my soul!
        and all that is within me,
        bless God's holy name!
2 **Bless the Lord, O my soul,**
        and forget not all God's benefits,
3 who forgives all your iniquity,
        who heals all your diseases,
4 **who redeems your life from the pit,**
        who crowns you with steadfast love and mercy,
5 **who satisfies you with good as long as you live**
        so that your youth is renewed like the eagle's.   R

6 The Lord, who works vindication
        and justice for all who are oppressed,
7 has made known God's ways to Moses,
        God's acts to the people of Israel.
8 **The Lord is merciful and gracious,**
        slow to anger and abounding in steadfast love.
9 The Lord will not always chide,
        nor harbor anger for ever.
10 **The Lord does not deal with us according to our sins,**
        nor repay us according to our iniquities.
11 For as the heavens are high above the earth,
        so great is the Lord's steadfast love toward the faithful;
12 **as far as the east is from the west,**
        so far does the Lord remove our transgressions from us.

13 As a father shows compassion to his children,
    so the Lord shows compassion to the faithful.
14 **For the Lord knows our frame,**
    and remembers that we are dust.   R

15 As for mortals, their days are like grass;
    they flourish like a flower of the field;
16 for the wind passes over it, and it is gone,
    and its place knows it no more.
17 **But the steadfast love of the Lord**
    is from everlasting to everlasting upon the faithful,
and the righteousness of the Lord to children's children,
18   **to those who keep his covenant**
    and remember to do his commandments.   R

59   Psalm 104:1-13, 24-35

Response   LOBE DEN HERREN (99)

Praise to the Lord, the Al - might-y, who rules all cre - a - tion!

R

1   Bless the Lord, O my soul!
         O Lord my God, you are very great!
     You are clothed with honor and majesty,
2   and cover yourself with light as with a garment;
     you have stretched out the heavens like a tent,
3   **and have laid the beams of your chambers on the waters;**
     you make the clouds your chariot,
          and ride on the wings of the wind;
4   **you make the winds your messengers,**
          fire and flame your ministers.
5   You set the earth on its foundations,
          so that it should never be shaken.
6   **You covered it with the deep as with a garment;**
          the waters stood above the mountains.
7   At your rebuke they fled;
          at the sound of your thunder they took to flight.
8   They rose up to the mountains, ran down to the valleys,
          to the place which you appointed for them.
9   **You set a bound which they should not pass,**
          so that they might not again cover the earth.   R

10   You make springs gush forth in the valleys;
          they flow between the hills;
11   **they give drink to every beast of the field;**
          the wild asses quench their thirst.
12   Above the springs the birds of the air have their nests;
          they sing among the branches.
13   **From your lofty place you water the mountains;**
          with the fruit of your work the earth is satisfied.   R

24 O Lord, how manifold are your works!
 In wisdom you have made them all;
 the earth is full of your creatures.
25 Yonder is the sea, great and wide,
 creeping things innumerable are there,
 living things both small and great.
26 There go the ships,
 and Leviathan whom you formed to play in it.
27 **These all look to you,**
 to give them their food in due season.
28 When you give to them, they gather it;
 when you open your hand, they are filled with good things.
29 When you hide your face, they are dismayed;
 when you take away their breath, they die
 and return to their dust.
30 When you send forth your spirit, they are created;
 and you renew the face of the ground.
31 May the glory of the Lord endure for ever,
 may the Lord rejoice in his works,
32 **who looks on the earth and it trembles,**
 who touches the mountains and they smoke.
33 I will sing to the Lord as long as I live;
 I will sing praise to my God while I have being.
34 May my meditation be pleasing to the Lord
 in whom I rejoice.
35 **Let sinners be consumed from the earth,**
 and let the wicked be no more!
 Bless the Lord, O my soul!
 O praise the Lord!   R

60   Psalm 116

Response   LASST UNS ERFREUEN (83)

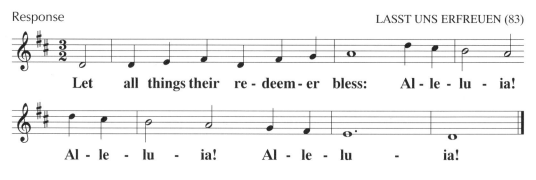

Let all things their re - deem - er bless: Al - le - lu - ia!

Al - le - lu - ia!   Al - le - lu - ia!

R

1 I love the Lord, who has heard
        my voice and my supplications,
2 and has inclined his ear to me
        whenever I called.
3 **The snares of death encompassed me;**
        the pangs of Sheol laid hold on me;
        I suffered distress and anguish.
4 Then I called on the name of the Lord:
        "O Lord, I beseech you, save my life!"   R

5 Gracious is the Lord, and righteous;
        our God is merciful.
6 **The Lord preserves the simple;**
        when I was brought low, the Lord saved me.
7 Return, O my soul, to your rest;
        for the Lord has dealt bountifully with you.
8 For you have delivered my soul from death,
        my eyes from tears,
        my feet from stumbling;
9 **I walk before the Lord**
        in the land of the living.
10 I kept my faith, even when I said,
        "I am greatly afflicted."
11 **I said in my consternation,**
        "All humans are a vain hope."   R

12 What shall I return tó the Lord
        for åll my benefits?
13 **I will lift up the cup óf salvation**
        and call on the name óf the Lord,
14 I will pay my vows tó the Lord,
        in the presence of åll his people.
15 **Precious in the sight óf the Lord**
        is the death óf his faithful ones.
16 O Lord, I am your servant;
        I am your servant, the child óf your handmaid.
        You have loósed my bonds.
17 **I will offer to you the sacrifice óf thanksgiving**
        and call on the name óf the Lord.
18 I will pay my vows tó the Lord,
        in the presence of åll his people,
19 **in the courts of the house of the Lord,**
        in your midst, O Jerúsalem.
    O praíse the Lord!   R

61   Psalm 118:14-29

Response   FOREST GREEN (77)

The Lord has done great things for us,

and we are filled with joy.

R

14   The Lord is my strength and my power;
        the Lord has become my salvation.
15   **There are joyous songs of victory**
        in the tents of the righteous:
     "The right hand of the Lord does valiantly,
16   the right hand of the Lord is exalted,
        the right hand of the Lord does valiantly!"
17   I shall not die, but I shall live,
        and recount the deeds of the Lord.
18   **The Lord has chastened me sorely,**
        but has not given me over to death.
19   Open to me the gates of righteousness,
        that I may enter through them
        and give thanks to the Lord.
20   **This is the gate of the Lord;**
        the righteous shall enter through it.   R

21   I thank you that you have answered me
        and have become my salvation.
22   **The stone which the builders rejected**
        has become the cornerstone.
23   This is the Lord's doing;
        it is marvelous in our eyes.
24   **This is the day which the Lord has made;**
        let us rejoice and be glad in it.   R

25 Save us, we beseech you, O Lord!
O Lord, we beseech you, give us success!
26 Blessed is the one who comes in the name of the Lord!
We bless you from the house of the Lord.
27 The Lord is God,
who has given us light.
**Lead the festal procession with branches,
up to the horns of the altar!**
28 You are my God, and I will give thanks to you;
you are my God, I will extol you.
29 **O give thanks to the Lord, who is good;
for God's steadfast love endures for ever! R**

62   Psalm 121

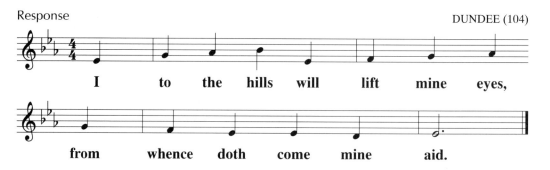

Response   DUNDEE (104)

I   to   the   hills   will   lift   mine   eyes,

from   whence   doth   come   mine   aid.

R

¹ I lift up my eyes to the hills.
From whence does my help come?

² **My help comes from the Lord,**
who made heaven and earth.

³ The Lord will not let your foot be moved,
the Lord who keeps you will not slumber.

⁴ **Behold, the One who keeps Israel**
will neither slumber nor sleep.

⁵ The Lord is your keeper;
the Lord is your shade
on your right hand.

⁶ The sun shall not smite you by day,
nor the moon by night.

⁷ The Lord will keep you from all evil,
and will keep your life.

⁸ **The Lord will keep**
your going out and your coming in
from this time forth and for evermore.   R

Psalm 130

Response   NEW BRITAIN (261)

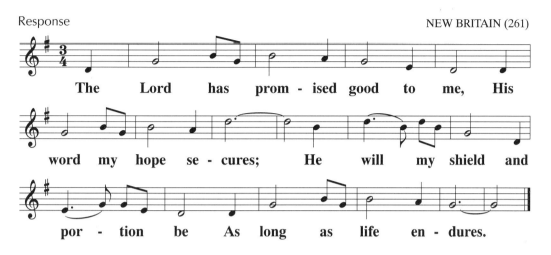

The Lord has prom - ised good to me, His
word my hope se - cures; He will my shield and
por - tion be As long as life en - dures.

R

¹ Out of the depths I cry to you, O Lord!
²   Lord, hear my voice!
Let your ears be attentive
    to the voice of my supplications!
³ If you, O Lord, should mark iniquities,
    Lord, who could stand?
⁴ **But there is forgiveness with you,**
    that you may be worshipped.
⁵ I wait for the Lord, my soul waits,
    in the Lord's word I hope;
⁶ **my soul waits for the Lord**
    more than those who watch for the morning,
    more than those who watch for the morning.
⁷ O Israel, hope in the Lord!
    For with the Lord there is steadfast love,
    with the Lord is plenteous redemption.
⁸ **And the Lord will redeem Israel**
    from all iniquities.   R

64　　　　　　　**Psalm 139**

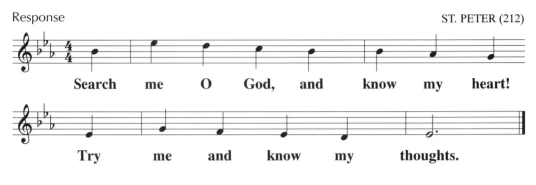

Response　　　　　　　　　　　　　　　　　　ST. PETER (212)

Search　me　O　God,　and　know　my　heart!

Try　　me　and　know　my　thoughts.

R

1　O Lord, you have searched me
　　and you have known me!
2　**You know when I sit down and when I rise up;**
　　you discern my thoughts from afar.
3　You search out my path and my lying down,
　　and are acquainted with all my ways.
4　**Even before a word is on my tongue, O Lord,**
　　you know it altogether.
5　You pursue me behind and before,
　　and lay your hand upon me.
6　**Such knowledge is too wonderful for me;**
　　it is high, I cannot attain it.　R

7　Whither shall I go from your spirit?
　　Or whither shall I flee from your presence?
8　If I ascend to heaven, you are there!
　　If I make my bed in Sheol, you are there!
9　**If I take the wings of the morning**
　　and dwell in the uttermost parts of the sea,
10　**even there your hand shall lead me,**
　　and your right hand shall hold me.
11　If I say, "Let only darkness cover me,
　　and the light about me be night,"
12　**even the darkness is not dark to you,**
　　the night is bright as the day;
　　for darkness is as light with you.　R

13 For it was you who formed my inward parts,
   you knit me together in my mother's womb.
14 I praise you, for you are fearful and wonderful.
   Wonderful are your works!
   You know me very well;
15   **my frame was not hidden from you,**
   when I was being made in secret,
   intricately wrought in the depths of the earth.
16 Your eyes beheld my unformed substance;
   in your book were written
   the days that were formed for me,
   every day, before they came into being.
17 How profound to me are your thoughts, O God!
   How vast is the sum of them!
18 **If I would count them, they are more than the sand.**
   When I awake, I am still with you.   R

19 O that you would slay the wicked, O God,
   and that the bloodthirsty would depart from me,
20 **those who maliciously defy you,**
   who lift themselves up against you for evil.
21 Do I not hate them that hate you, O Lord?
   And do I not loathe them that rise up against you?
22 **I hate them with perfect hatred;**
   I count them my enemies.
23 Search me, O God, and know my heart!
   Try me and know my thoughts;
24 **and see if there be any wicked way in me,**
   and lead me in the way everlasting!   R

Lord of Our Growing Years

65

PARENTI 6.6.6.6.8.8

David Mowbray (1982)

Richard Proulx (1996)

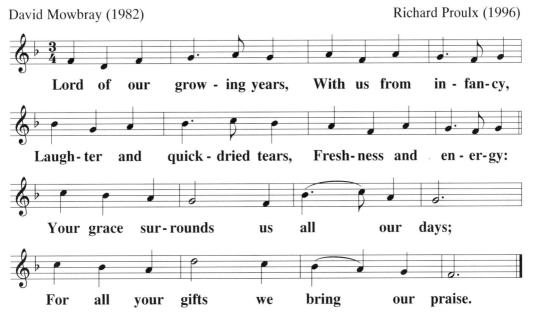

Lord of our grow-ing years, With us from in-fan-cy,

Laugh-ter and quick-dried tears, Fresh-ness and en-er-gy:

Your grace sur-rounds us all our days;

For all your gifts we bring our praise.

Lord of our strongest years,
Stretching our youthful pow'rs,
Lovers and pioneers
When all the world seems ours:
Your grace…

Lord of our middle years,
Giver of steadfastness,
Courage that perseveres
When there is small success:
Your grace…

Lord of our older years,
Steep though the road may be,
Rid us of foolish fears,
Bring us serenity:
Your grace…

Lord of our closing years,
Always your promise stands;
Hold us, when death appears,
Safely within your hands:
Your grace…

66   Holy God, We Praise Thy Name

GROSSER GOTT 7.8.7.8.7.7

Ignaz Franz (18th C.)
Trans. by Clarence Walworth (1853)

Katholisches Gesangbuch (c. 1774)

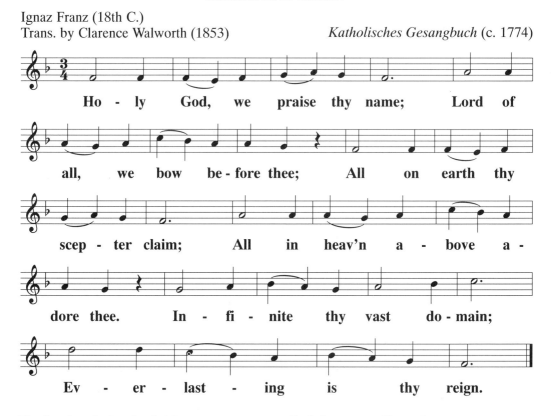

Ho - ly God, we praise thy name; Lord of
all, we bow be - fore thee; All on earth thy
scep - ter claim; All in heav'n a - bove a -
dore thee. In - fi - nite thy vast do - main;
Ev - er - last - ing is thy reign.

Hark, the glad celestial hymn
Angel choirs above are raising;
Cherubim and seraphim,
In unceasing chorus praising,
Fill the heav'ns with sweet accord:
Holy, holy, holy Lord.

Lo! the apostolic train
Joins thy sacred name to hallow;
Prophets swell the glad refrain,
And the white-robed martyrs follow.
And from morn to set of sun,
Through the church the song goes on.

Holy Father, Holy Son,
Holy Spirit: three we name thee,
Though in essence only one;
Undivided God we claim thee,
And adoring bend the knee
While we own the mystery.

We Believe in One True God   67

RATISBON 7.7.7.7.7.7

Tobias Clausnitzer (1668)   Werner's *Choralbuch* (1815)
Trans. by Catherine Winkworth (1863)   Arr. by William Henry Havergal (1861)

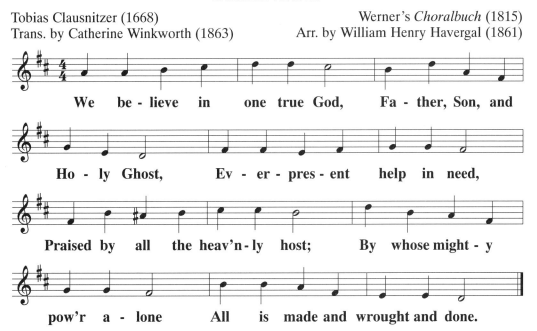

We be - lieve in one true God, Fa - ther, Son, and
Ho - ly Ghost, Ev - er - pres - ent help in need,
Praised by all the heav'n - ly host; By whose might - y
pow'r a - lone All is made and wrought and done.

We believe in Jesus Christ,
Son of God and Mary's Son,
Who descended from his throne
And for us salvation won;
By whose cross and death are we
Rescued from sin's misery.

We confess the Holy Ghost,
Who from both for e'er proceeds;
Who upholds and comforts us
In all trials, fears, and needs.
Blest and Holy Trinity,
Praise for ever be to thee!

68 Praise God, from Whom All Blessings Flow

OLD HUNDREDTH LM

Thomas Ken (1674)

Attr. to Louis Bourgeois (1551)

Praise God, from whom all bless - ings flow;

Praise him, all crea - tures here be - low;

Praise him a - bove, ye heav'n - ly host;

Praise Fa - ther, Son, and Ho - ly Ghost.

Come, Thou Almighty King   69

ITALIAN HYMN 6.6.4.6.6.6.4

Anonymous (c. 1757)   Felice de Giardini (1769)

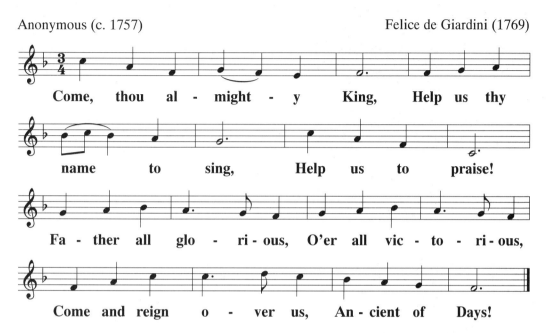

Come, thou al - might - y King, Help us thy

name to sing, Help us to praise!

Fa - ther all glo - ri - ous, O'er all vic - to - ri - ous,

Come and reign o - ver us, An - cient of Days!

Come, thou Incarnate Word,
Gird on thy mighty sword,
Our prayer attend!
Come, and thy people bless,
And give thy word success;
Spirit of holiness,
On us descend!

Come, holy Comforter,
Thy sacred witness bear
In this glad hour.
Thou who almighty art,
Now rule in ev'ry heart,
And ne'er from us depart,
Spirit of Pow'r!

To thee, great One-in-Three,
Eternal praises be,
Hence, evermore.
Thy sov'reign majesty
May we in glory see,
And to eternity
Love and adore!

70   Holy, Holy, Holy! Lord God Almighty

NICEA 11.12.12.10

Reginald Heber (1826)   John Bacchus Dykes (1861)

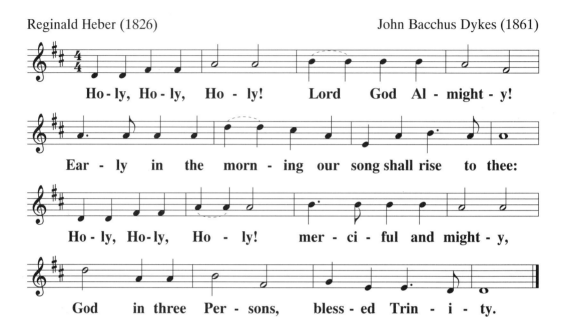

Ho - ly, Ho - ly, Ho - ly!   Lord   God   Al - might - y!

Ear - ly   in   the   morn - ing   our   song shall rise   to   thee:

Ho - ly, Ho-ly,   Ho - ly!   mer - ci - ful and might - y,

God   in three Per - sons,   bless - ed Trin - i - ty.

Holy, Holy, Holy! all the saints adore thee,
Casting down their golden crowns around the glassy sea;
Cherubim and seraphim falling down before thee,
God everlasting through eternity.

Holy, Holy, Holy! though the darkness hide thee,
Though the eye made blind by sin thy glory may not see,
Only thou art holy; there is none beside thee,
Perfect in pow'r, in love, and purity.

Holy, Holy, Holy! Lord God Almighty!
All thy works shall praise thy Name in earth, and sky, and sea;
Holy, Holy, Holy! merciful and mighty,
God in three Persons, blesséd Trinity.

Glory Be to the Father

GREATOREX Irregular

71

Lesser Doxology (3rd-4th C.)

Henry Wellington Greatorex (1851)

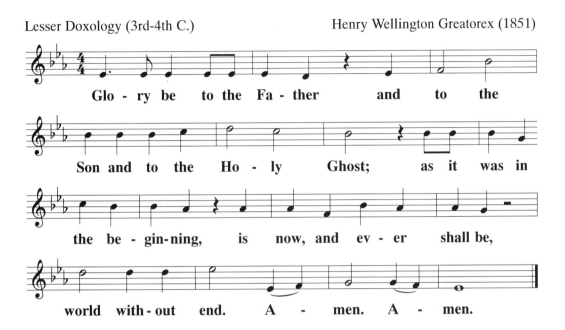

72 Ancient of Days, Who Sittest Throned in Glory
ANCIENT OF DAYS 11.10.11.10

William C. Doane (1886, 1892)   J. Albert Jeffery (1886)

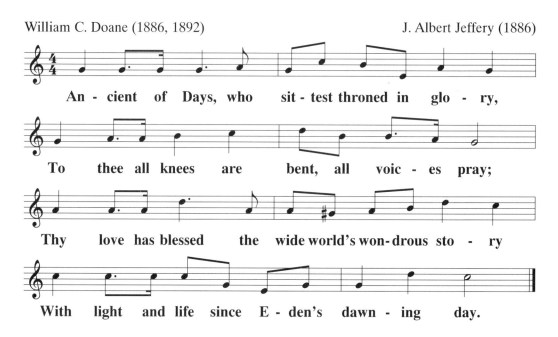

An - cient of Days, who sit - test throned in glo - ry,

To thee all knees are bent, all voic - es pray;

Thy love has blessed the wide world's won- drous sto - ry

With light and life since E - den's dawn - ing day.

O Holy Father, who hast led thy children
In all the ages, with the fire and cloud,
Through seas dryshod, through weary wastes bewild'ring;
To thee, in rev'rent love, our hearts are bowed.

O Holy Jesus, Prince of Peace and Savior,
To thee we owe the peace that still prevails,
Stilling the rude wills of men's wild behavior,
And calming passion's fierce and stormy gales.

O Holy Ghost, the Lord and the Life Giver,
Thine is the quick'ning pow'r that gives increase;
From thee have flowed, as from a pleasant river,
Our plenty, wealth, prosperity, and peace.

O Triune God, with heart and voice adoring,
Praise we the goodness that doth crown our days;
Pray we that thou wilt hear us, still imploring
Thy love and favor, kept to us always.

Now Praise the Hidden God of Love 73

O WALY WALY LM

English folk melody
Harm. by John Weaver (1988)

Fred Pratt Green (1975)

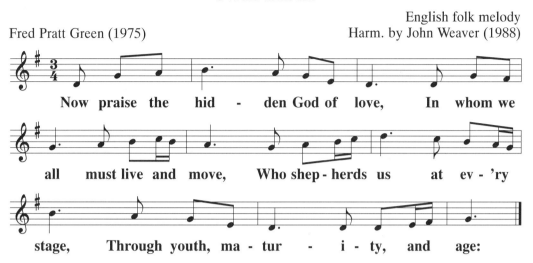

Now praise the hid - den God of love, In whom we
all must live and move, Who shep - herds us at ev - 'ry
stage, Through youth, ma - tur - i - ty, and age:

Who challenged us, when we were young,
To storm the citadels of wrong;
In care for others taught us how
God's true community must grow:

Who bids us never lose our zest,
Though age is urging us to rest,
But proves to us that we have still
A work to do, a place to fill.

74   Immortal, Invisible, God Only Wise
ST. DENIO 11.11.11.11

1 Timothy 1:17
Walter Chalmers Smith (1867)   Robert's *Canaidau y Cyssegr* (1839)

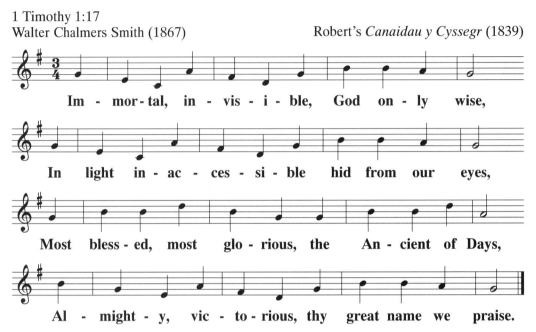

Im - mor - tal, in - vis - i - ble, God on - ly wise,

In light in - ac - ces - si - ble hid from our eyes,

Most bless - ed, most glo - rious, the An - cient of Days,

Al - might - y, vic - to - rious, thy great name we praise.

Unresting, unhasting, and silent as light,
Nor wanting, nor wasting, thou rulest in might;
Thy justice like mountains high soaring above
Thy clouds, which are fountains of goodness and love.

To all, life thou givest, to both great and small;
In all life thou livest, the true life of all;
We blossom, and flourish like leaves on the tree,
Then wither and perish; but naught changeth thee.

All praise we would render; O help us to see
'Tis only the splendor of light hideth thee!
And now let thy glory to our gaze unroll
Through Christ in the story, and Christ in the soul.

O Worship the King   75

LYONS 10.10.11.11

Psalm 104
Robert Grant (1833)

Attr. to Johann Michael Haydn
Arr. by William Gardiner (1815)

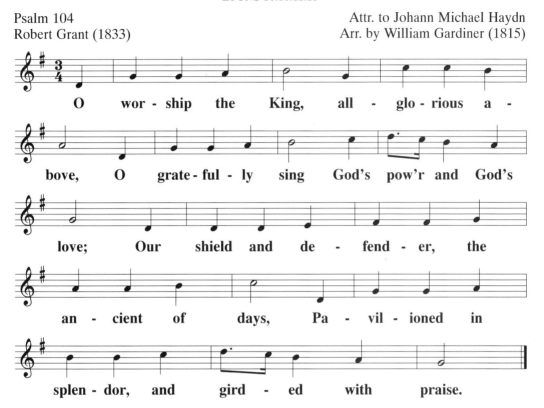

O wor-ship the King, all-glo-rious a-
bove, O grate-ful-ly sing God's pow'r and God's
love; Our shield and de-fend-er, the
an-cient of days, Pa-vil-ioned in
splen-dor, and gird-ed with praise.

O tell of God's might, O sing of God's grace,
Whose robe is the light, whose canopy space,
Whose chariots of wrath the deep thunderclouds form,
And dark is God's path on the wings of the storm.

The earth with its store of wonders untold,
Almighty, thy pow'r hath founded of old;
Hath stablished it fast by a changeless decree,
And round it hath cast, like a mantle, the sea.

Thy bountiful care, what tongue can recite?
It breathes in the air, it shines in the light;
It streams from the hills, it descends to the plain,
And sweetly distills in the dew and the rain.

Frail children of dust, and feeble as frail,
In thee do we trust, nor find thee to fail;
Thy mercies how tender, how firm to the end,
Our maker, defender, redeemer, and friend.

76 God, Who Stretched the Spangled Heavens

HOLY MANNA 8.7.8.7 D

Catherine Cameron (1967)

William Moore (1825)
Harm. by Charles Anders (1969)

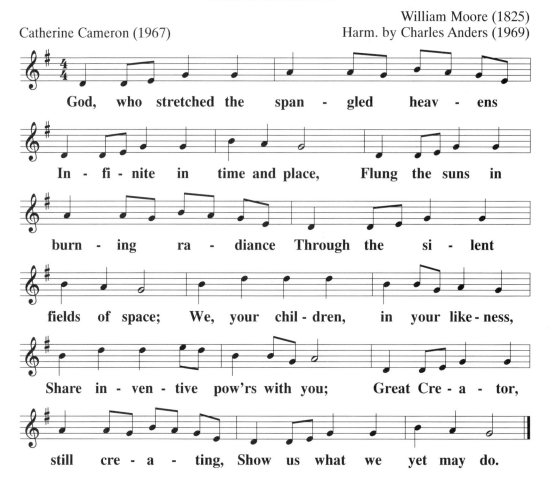

God, who stretched the span - gled heav - ens

In - fi - nite in time and place, Flung the suns in

burn - ing ra - diance Through the si - lent

fields of space; We, your chil - dren, in your like - ness,

Share in - ven - tive pow'rs with you; Great Cre - a - tor,

still cre - a - ting, Show us what we yet may do.

Proudly rise our modern cities,
Stately buildings, row on row;
Yet their windows, blank, unfeeling,
Stare on canyoned streets below,
Where the lonely drift unnoticed
In the city's ebb and flow,
Lost to purpose and to meaning,
Scarcely caring where they go.

We have ventured worlds undreamed of
Since the childhood of our race;
Known the ecstasy of winging
Through untraveled realms of space;
Probed the secrets of the atom,
Yielding unimagined pow'r,
Facing us with life's destruction
Or our most triumphant hour.

As each far horizon beckons,
May it challenge us anew,
Children of creative purpose,
Serving others, hon'ring you.
May our dreams prove rich with promise,
Each endeavor, well begun:
Great Creator, give us guidance
Till our goals and yours are one.

77 All Beautiful the March of Days
FOREST GREEN CMD

English folk melody
Frances Whitmarsh Wile (1912)
Arr. by Ralph Vaughan Williams (1906)

All beau-ti-ful the march of days, As
sea-sons come and go; The hand that shaped the
rose hath wrought The crys-tal of the snow;
Hath sent the hoar-y frost of heav'n, The
flow-ing wa-ters sealed, And laid a si-lent
love-li-ness On hill and wood and field.

O'er white expanses sparkling pure
The radiant morns unfold;
The solemn splendors of the night
Burn brighter through the cold;
Life mounts in ev'ry throbbing vein,
Love deepens round the hearth,
And clearer sounds the angel hymn,
"Good will to all on earth."

O thou from whose unfathomed law
The year in beauty flows,
Thyself the vision passing by
In crystal and in rose,
Day unto day doth utter speech,
And night to night proclaim,
In everchanging words of light,
The wonder of thy name.

O God beyond All Praising

78

THAXTED 13.13.13.13.13.13

Michael Perry (1982)   Gustav Holst

O God be-yond all prais - ing, we wor-ship you to-day And sing the love a - maz - ing that songs can - not re - pay; For we can on - ly won - der at ev - 'ry gift you send, At bless - ings with - out num - ber and mer - cies with - out end: We lift our hearts be - fore you and wait up - on your word, We hon - or and a - dore you, our great and might - y Lord.

Then hear, O gracious Savior, accept the love we bring,
That we who know your favor may serve you as our king;
And whether our tomorrows be filled with good or ill,
We'll triumph through our sorrows and rise to bless you still:
To marvel at your beauty and glory in your ways,
And make a joyful duty our sacrifice of praise.

79   Creating God, Your Fingers Trace

KEDRON LM

Jeffery Rowthorn (1974)   Attr. to Elkanah Kelsay Dare (1799)

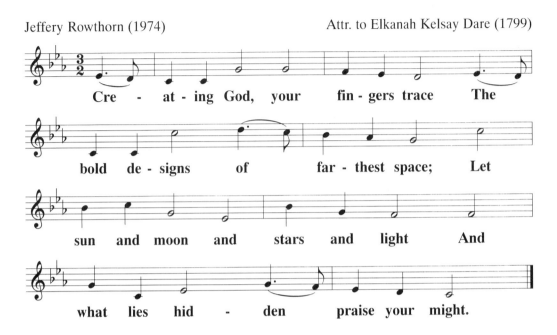

Cre - at - ing God, your fin - gers trace The
bold de - signs of far - thest space; Let
sun and moon and stars and light And
what lies hid - den praise your might.

Sustaining God, your hands uphold
Earth's myst'ries known or yet untold;
Let water's fragile blend with air,
Enabling life, proclaim your care.

Redeeming God, your arms embrace
All now despised for creed or race;
Let peace, descending like a dove,
Make known on earth your healing love.

Indwelling God, your gospel claims
One fam'ly with a billion names;
Let ev'ry life be touched by grace
Until we praise you face to face.

O For a Thousand Tongues to Sing   80

AZMON CM

Charles Wesley (1738), alt.

Carl Gotthilf Gläser (1828)
Adapt. and arr. by Lowell Mason (1839)

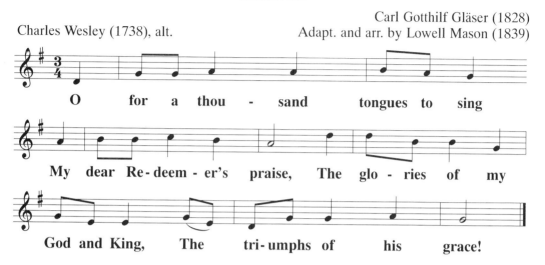

O for a thou - sand tongues to sing

My dear Re - deem - er's praise, The glo - ries of my

God and King, The tri- umphs of his grace!

My gracious master and my God,
Assist me to proclaim
And spread through all the earth abroad
The honors of thy name.

Jesus! the Name that charms our fears
And bids our sorrows cease;
'Tis music in the sinner's ears,
'Tis life and health and peace.

He speaks; and, list'ning to his voice,
New life the dead receive,
The mournful broken hearts rejoice,
The humble poor believe.

Hear him, ye deaf; ye voiceless ones,
Your loosened tongues employ;
Ye blind, behold, your Savior comes;
And leap, ye lame, for joy!

Glory to God and praise and love
Be now and ever giv'n
By saints below and saints above,
The church in earth and heav'n.

81   When, in Our Music, God Is Glorified

ENGELBERG 10.10.10 with alleluia

Mark 14:26
Fred Pratt Green (1972)   Charles Villiers Stanford (1904)

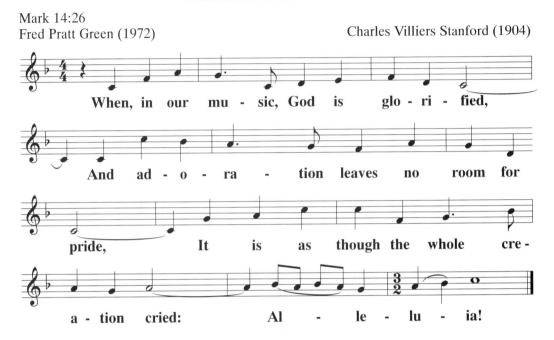

When, in our music, God is glorified,
And adoration leaves no room for pride,
It is as though the whole creation cried: Alleluia!

How often, making music, we have found
A new dimension in the world of sound,
As worship moved us to a more profound
Alleluia!

So has the Church, in liturgy and song,
In faith and love, through centuries of wrong,
Borne witness to the truth in ev'ry tongue:
Alleluia!

And did not Jesus sing a psalm that night
When utmost evil strove against the Light?
Then let us sing, for whom he won the fight:
Alleluia!

Let ev'ry instrument be tuned for praise!
Let all rejoice who have a voice to raise!
And may God give us faith to sing always:
Alleluia!

Praise to God, Immortal Praise

DIX 7.7.7.7.7.7

82

Conrad Kocher (1838)
Arr. by William Henry Monk (1861)

Anna Laetitia Barbauld (1772)

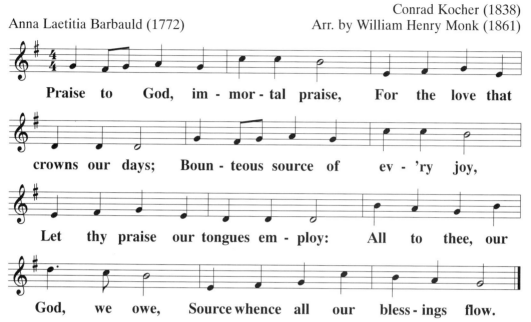

Praise to God, im - mor - tal praise, For the love that

crowns our days; Boun - teous source of ev - 'ry joy,

Let thy praise our tongues em - ploy: All to thee, our

God, we owe, Source whence all our bless - ings flow.

All the plenty summer pours;
Autumn's rich o'erflowing stores;
Flocks that whiten all the plain;
Yellow sheaves of ripened grain:
Lord, for these our souls shall raise
Grateful vows and solemn praise.

As thy prosp'ring hand hath blessed,
May we give thee of our best;
And by deeds of kindly love
For thy mercies grateful prove;
Singing thus through all our days
Praise to God, immortal praise.

83   Ye Watchers and Ye Holy Ones

LASST UNS ERFREUEN LM with alleluias

Geistliche Kirchengesänge (1623)

Athelstan Laurie Riley (1906)

Harm. by Ralph Vaughan Williams (1906)

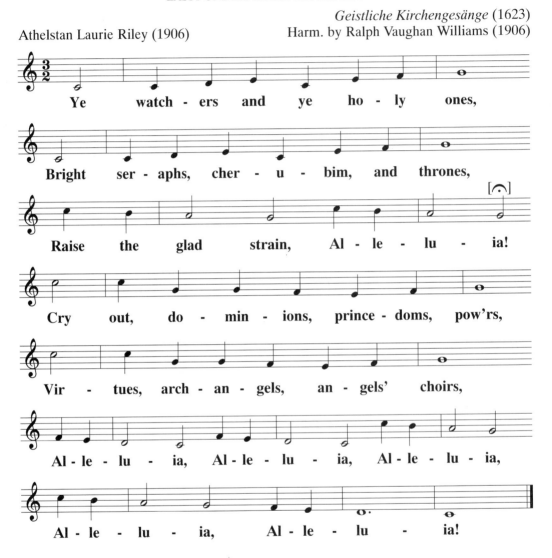

Ye watch-ers and ye ho-ly ones,

Bright ser-aphs, cher-u-bim, and thrones,

Raise the glad strain, Al-le-lu-ia!

Cry out, do-min-ions, prince-doms, pow'rs,

Vir-tues, arch-an-gels, an-gels' choirs,

Al-le-lu-ia, Al-le-lu-ia, Al-le-lu-ia,

Al-le-lu-ia, Al-le-lu-ia!

O higher than the cherubim,
More glorious than the seraphim,
Lead their praises, Alleluia!
O bearer of the eternal Word,
Most gracious, magnify the Lord, *Alleluia...*

Respond, ye souls in endless rest,
Ye patriarchs and prophets blest,
Alleluia, Alleluia!
Ye holy Twelve, ye martyrs strong,
All saints triumphant, raise in song, *Alleluia...*

O friends, in gladness let us sing,
Supernal anthems echoing,
Alleluia, Alleluia!
To God the Father, God the Son,
And God the Spirit, Three in One, *Alleluia...*

84 All People That on Earth Do Dwell
OLD HUNDREDTH LM

Psalm 100
William Kethe (1561)

Louis Bourgeois (c. 1510-1561)

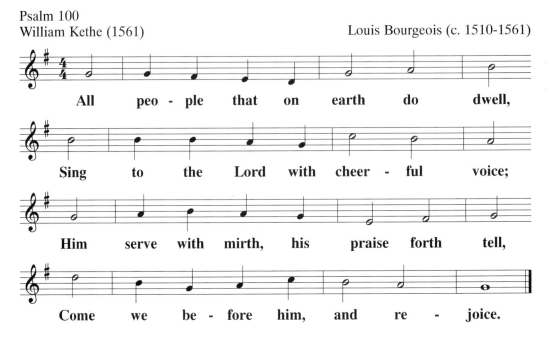

All peo - ple that on earth do dwell,

Sing to the Lord with cheer - ful voice;

Him serve with mirth, his praise forth tell,

Come we be - fore him, and re - joice.

Know that the Lord is God indeed;
Without our aid he did us make;
We are his folk, he does us feed,
And for his sheep he does us take.

O enter then his gates with praise;
Approach with joy his courts unto;
Praise, laud, and bless his Name always,
For it is seemly so to do.

For why? the Lord our God is good:
His mercy is for ever sure;
His truth at all times firmly stood,
And shall from age to age endure.

To Father, Son, and Holy Ghost,
The God whom heav'n and earth adore,
From us and from the angel host
Be praise and glory evermore.

From All That Dwell below the Skies   85

DUKE STREET LM

Psalm 117
St. 1-2, Isaac Watts (1719); st. 3-4, anonymous   John Hatton (c. 1710-1793)

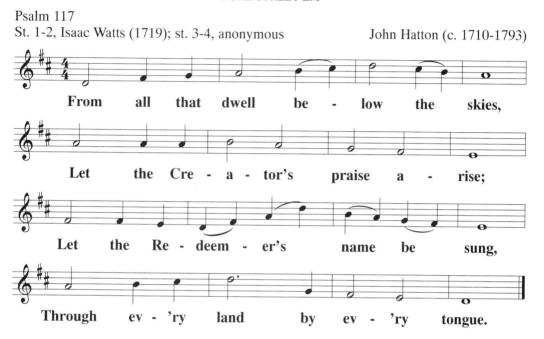

From all that dwell be - low the skies,

Let the Cre - a - tor's praise a - rise;

Let the Re - deem - er's name be sung,

Through ev - 'ry land by ev - 'ry tongue.

Eternal are your mercies, Lord;
Eternal truth attends your word:
Your praise shall sound from shore to shore,
Till suns shall rise and set no more.

Your lofty themes, all mortals, bring;
In songs of praise divinely sing;
The great salvation loud proclaim,
And shout for joy the Savior's name.

In ev'ry land begin the song;
To ev'ry land the strains belong;
In cheerful sounds all voices raise,
And fill the world with loudest praise.

86 **Blest Are They**

Matthew 5:3-12
David Haas (1985)

David Haas (1985)

Verses 1-3

1. Blest are they, the poor in spir - it,
theirs is the king - dom of God.
Blest are they, full of sor - row,
they shall be con - soled.

2. Blest are they, the low - ly ones,
they shall in - her - it the earth.
Blest are they who hun - ger and thirst,
they shall have their fill.

3. Blest are they who show mer - cy,
mer - cy shall be theirs.
Blest are they, the pure of heart,
they shall see God!

Refrain 𝄋

Re - joice and be glad! Bless-ed are you,
ho - ly are you! Re - joice and be glad!
Yours is the king-dom of God!

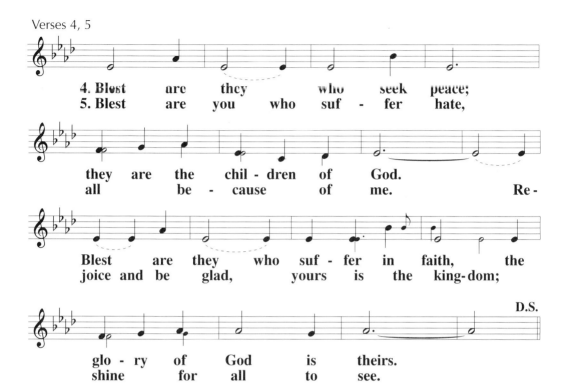

4. Blest are they who seek peace;
5. Blest are you who suf - fer hate,

they are the chil - dren of God.
all be - cause of me. Re -

Blest are they who suf - fer in faith, the
joice and be glad, yours is the king - dom;

D.S.

glo - ry of God is theirs.
shine for all to see.

87 All Glory Be to God on High

ALLEIN GOTT IN DER HOH' 8.7.8.7.8.8.7

Nikolaus Decius (1522)
Trans. by F. Bland Tucker (1977)

Attr. to Nikolaus Decius (1539)
Harm. by Michael Praetorius

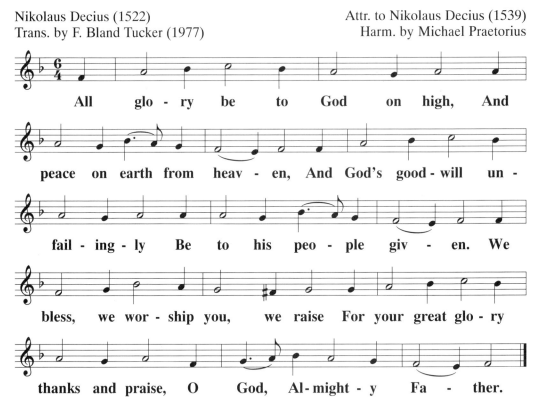

All glo - ry be to God on high, And
peace on earth from heav - en, And God's good - will un -
fail - ing - ly Be to his peo - ple giv - en. We
bless, we wor - ship you, we raise For your great glo - ry
thanks and praise, O God, Al - might - y Fa - ther.

O Lamb of God, Lord Jesus Christ,
Whom God the Father gave us,
Who for the world was sacrificed
Upon the cross to save us;
And as you sit at God's right hand,
And we for judgment there must stand,
Have mercy, Lord, upon us.

You only are the Holy One,
Who came for our salvation,
And only you are God's true Son,
The first born of creation.
You only, Christ, as Lord we own
And, with the Spirit, you alone
Share in the Father's glory.

All Things Bright and Beautiful   88

ROYAL OAK 7.6.7.6 with refrain

Genesis 1:31   English melody (17th C.)
Cecil Frances Alexander (1848)   Adapt. by Martin Shaw (1915)

The purple-headed mountains,
The river running by,
The sunset, and the morning
That brightens up the sky. *Ref.*

The cold wind in the winter,
The pleasant summer sun,
The ripe fruits in the garden:
God made them ev'ry one. *Ref.*

God gave us eyes to see them,
And lips that we might tell
How great is God Almighty,
Who has made all things well. *Ref.*

89 All Creatures of Our God and King
LASST UNS ERFREUEN LM with alleluias

Francis of Assisi (1225)
Trans. by William H. Draper (c. 1910), alt.

Geistliche Kirchengesänge (1623)
Harm. by Ralph Vaughan Williams (1906)

O rushing wind and breezes soft,
O clouds that ride the winds aloft:
Alleluia! Alleluia!
O rising morn, in praise rejoice,
O lights of evening, find a voice.
Alleluia! Alleluia!
Alleluia, alleluia, alleluia!

O flowing waters, pure and clear,
Make music for your Lord to hear.
Alleluia! Alleluia!
O fire so masterful and bright,
Providing us with warmth and light,
Alleluia! Alleluia!
Alleluia, alleluia, alleluia!

Dear mother earth, who day by day
Unfolds rich blessings on our way,
Alleluia! Alleluia!
The fruits and flow'rs that verdant grow,
Let them his praise abundant show.
Alleluia! Alleluia!
Alleluia, alleluia, alleluia!

O ev'ry one of tender heart,
Forgiving others, take your part,
Alleluia! Alleluia!
All you who pain and sorrow bear,
Praise God and lay on him your care.
Alleluia! Alleluia!
Alleluia, alleluia, alleluia!

And you, most kind and gentle death,
Waiting to hush our final breath,
Alleluia! Alleluia!
You lead to heav'n the child of God,
Where Christ our Lord the way has trod.
Alleluia! Alleluia!
Alleluia, alleluia, alleluia!

Let all things their Creator bless,
And worship him in humbleness,
Alleluia! Alleluia!
Oh praise the Father, praise the Son,
And praise the Spirit, Three in One!
Alleluia! Alleluia!
Alleluia, alleluia, alleluia!

90 God of the Sparrow God of the Whale
ROEDER 5.4.6.7.7

Jaroslav J. Vajda (1983)   Carl F. Schalk (1983)

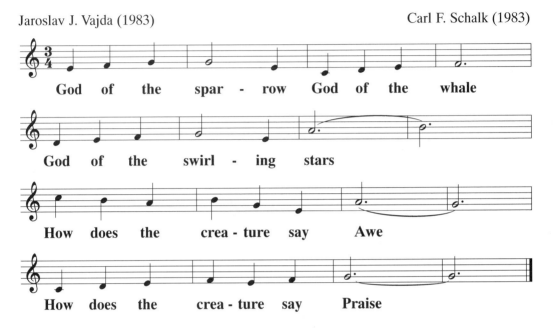

God of the spar - row   God of the whale

God of the swirl - ing   stars

How does the crea - ture say   Awe

How does the crea - ture say   Praise

God of the earthquake / God of the storm
God of the trumpet blast / How does the creature cry Woe
How does the creature cry Save

God of the rainbow / God of the cross
God of the empty grave / How does the creature say Grace
How does the creature say Thanks

God of the hungry / God of the sick
God of the prodigal / How does the creature say Care
How does the creature say Life

God of the neighbor / God of the foe
God of the pruning hook / How does the creature say Love
How does the creature say Peace

God of the ages / God near at hand
God of the loving heart / How do your children say Joy
How do your children say Home

Sing a New Song   91

Dan Schutte (1972)   Dan Schutte (1972)

Refrain

Sing a new song un-to the Lord; let your song be sung from moun-tains high. Sing a new song un-to the Lord, sing-ing al-le-lu-ia.

Verse

Yah-weh's peo-ple dance for joy. O come be-fore the Lord. And play for him on glad tam-bou-rines, and let your trum-pet sound.

Rise, O children, from your sleep; your Savior now has come.
He has turned your sorrow to joy, and filled your soul with song. *Ref.*

Glad my soul for I have seen the glory of the Lord.
The trumpet sounds; the dead shall be raised. I know my Savior lives. *Ref.*

92   Joyful, Joyful, We Adore Thee

HYMN TO JOY 8.7.8.7 D

Ludwig van Beethoven (1824)
Adapt. by Edward Hodges (1864), alt.

Henry Van Dyke (1907)

Joy - ful, joy - ful, we a - dore thee, God of glo - ry,

Lord of love; Hearts un - fold like flow'rs be - fore thee,

Prais - ing thee, their sun a - bove. Melt the clouds of

sin and sad - ness; Drive the dark of doubt a - way; Giv -

er of im - mor - tal glad - ness, Fill us with the light of day.

All thy works with joy surround thee,
Earth and heav'n reflect thy rays,
Stars and angels sing around thee,
Center of unbroken praise.
Field and forest, vale and mountain,
Blooming meadow, flashing sea,
Chanting bird and flowing fountain,
Call us to rejoice in thee.

Thou art giving and forgiving,
Ever blessing, ever blest,
Wellspring of the joy of living,
Ocean-depth of happy rest!
Thou our Father, Christ our Brother:
All who live in love are thine;
Teach us how to love each other,
Lift us to the joy divine.

For the Fruits of This Creation   93

EAST ACKLAM 8.4.8.4.8.8.8.4

Fred Pratt Green (1970)   Francis Jackson

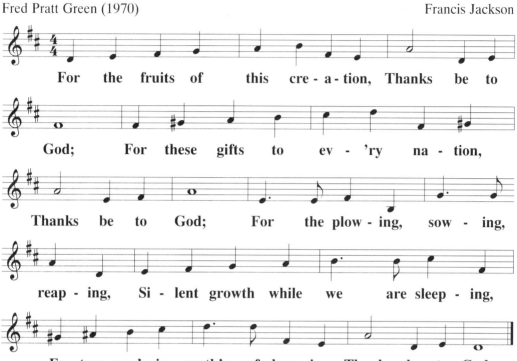

For the fruits of this cre-a-tion, Thanks be to
God; For these gifts to ev-'ry na-tion,
Thanks be to God; For the plow-ing, sow-ing,
reap-ing, Si-lent growth while we are sleep-ing,
Fu-ture needs in earth's safe keep-ing, Thanks be to God.

In the just reward of labor,
God's will is done;
In the help we give our neighbor,
God's will is done;
In our world-wide task of caring
For the hungry and despairing,
In the harvests we are sharing,
God's will is done.

For the harvests of the Spirit,
Thanks be to God;
For the good we all inherit,
Thanks be to God;
For the wonders that astound us,
For the truths that still confound us,
Most of all, that love has found us,
Thanks be to God.

94 I'll Praise My Maker

OLD 113th 8.8.8.8.8.8

Psalm 146; Isaac Watts (1719)
Alt. by John Wesley (1737), alt. (1989)

Attr. to Matthäus Greiter (1525)
Harm. by V. Earle Copes (1963)

I'll praise my Mak-er while I've breath; And when my voice is lost in death, Praise shall em-ploy my no-bler pow'rs. My days of praise shall ne'er be past, While life, and thought, and be-ing last, Or im-mor-tal-i-ty en-dures.

Happy are they whose hopes rely
On Israel's God, who made the sky
And earth and seas, with all their train;
Whose truth for ever stands secure,
Who saves th'oppressed and
　feeds the poor,
For none shall find God's promise vain.

The Lord pours eyesight on the blind;
The Lord supports the fainting mind
And sends the lab'ring conscience peace.
God helps the stranger in distress,
The widow and the fatherless,
And grants the pris'ner sweet release.

I'll praise my God who lends me breath;
And when my voice is lost in death,
Praise shall employ my nobler pow'rs.
My days of praise shall ne'er be past,
While life, and thought, and being last,
Or immortality endures.

For the Beauty of the Earth   95
DIX 7.7.7.7.7.7

Conrad Kocher (1838)
Arr. by William Henry Monk (1861)

Folliot S. Pierpoint (1864)

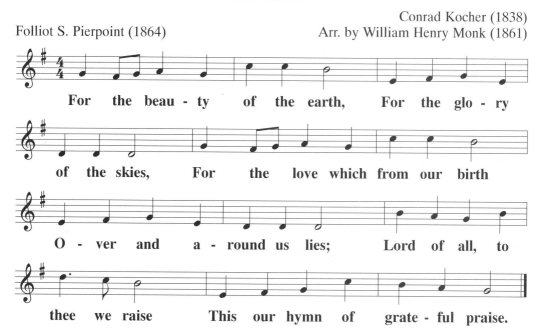

For the beau-ty of the earth, For the glo-ry

of the skies, For the love which from our birth

O - ver and a - round us lies; Lord of all, to

thee we raise This our hymn of grate-ful praise.

For the beauty of each hour
Of the day and of the night,
Hill and vale, and tree and flow'r,
Sun and moon, and stars of light;
  Lord of all...

For the joy of ear and eye,
For the heart and mind's delight,
For the mystic harmony
Linking sense to sound and sight;
  Lord of all...

For the joy of human love,
Brother, sister, parent, child,
Friends on earth and friends above,
For all gentle thoughts and mild; *Lord of all...*

For thy church, that evermore
Lifteth holy hands above,
Off'ring upon ev'ry shore
Her pure sacrifice of love; *Lord of all...*

For thyself, best Gift Divine,
To the world so freely giv'n,
For that great, great love of thine,
Peace on earth, and joy in heav'n: *Lord of all...*

96   The God of Abraham Praise

LEONI 6.6.8.4 D

Yigdal Elohim Hai of Daniel ben Judah (c. 1400)   Hebrew melody
Para. by Thomas Olivers (1760), alt.   Trans. by Meyer Lyon (1770)

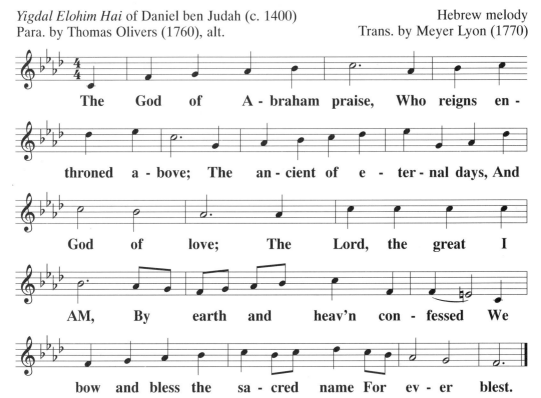

The God of A-braham praise, Who reigns en-throned a-bove; The an-cient of e-ter-nal days, And God of love; The Lord, the great I AM, By earth and heav'n con-fessed We bow and bless the sa-cred name For ev-er blest.

The Lord, our God has sworn:
I on that oath depend;
I shall, on eaglewings upborne,
To heav'n ascend:
I shall behold God's face,
I shall God's pow'r adore,
And sing the wonders of God's grace
For evermore.

There dwells the Lord, our King,
The Lord, our Righteousness,
Triumphant o'er the world and sin,
The Prince of Peace;
On Zion's sacred height
The kingdom God maintains,
And, glorious with the saints in light,
For ever reigns.

The God who reigns on high
The great archangels sing,
And "Holy, Holy, Holy," cry,
"Almighty King!
Who was, and is, the same,
For all eternity,
Immortal Father, great I AM,
All glory be."

I Sing the Almighty Power of God 97
FOREST GREEN CMD

Traditional English melody
Adapt. and harm. by Ralph Vaughan Williams (1906)

Isaac Watts (1715), alt.

I sing the al-might-y pow'r of God, That made the moun-tains rise, That spread the flow-ing seas a-broad And built the lof-ty skies. I sing the wis-dom that or-dained The sun to rule the day; The moon shines full at his com-mand, And all the stars o-bey.

I sing the goodness of the Lord,
That filled the earth with food;
He formed the creatures with his Word,
And then pronounced them good.
Lord, how thy wonders are displayed,
Where'er I turn my eye,
If I survey the ground I tread,
Or gaze upon the sky!

There's not a plant or flow'r below,
But makes thy glories known;
And clouds arise, and tempests blow,
By order from thy throne;
While all that borrows life from thee
Is ever in thy care,
And ev'rywhere that I could be,
Thou, God, art present there.

98   Seek Ye First the Kingdom of God

SEEK YE FIRST Irregular

Matthew 6:33, 7:7
St. 1 adapt. by Karen Lafferty (1972)
Sts. 2-3, anonymous

Karen Lafferty (1972)

Canon

1. Seek ye first the king - dom of God
2. Man shall not live by bread a - lone,
3. Ask, and it shall be giv - en un - to you,

and His right - eous - ness,
but by ev - 'ry word
seek, and ye shall find,

and all these things shall be add - ed un - to you;
that pro - ceeds from the mouth of God;
knock, and the door shall be o - pened un - to you;

Al - le - lu, al - le - lu - ia. Al - le -

lu - ia, al - le - lu - ia, al - le -

lu - ia, al - le - lu, al - le - lu - ia.

Praise to the Lord, the Almighty 99

LOBE DEN HERREN 14.14.4.7.8

Joachim Neander (1680)
Trans. by Catherine Winkworth (1863), alt.

Straslund Gesangbuch (1665)

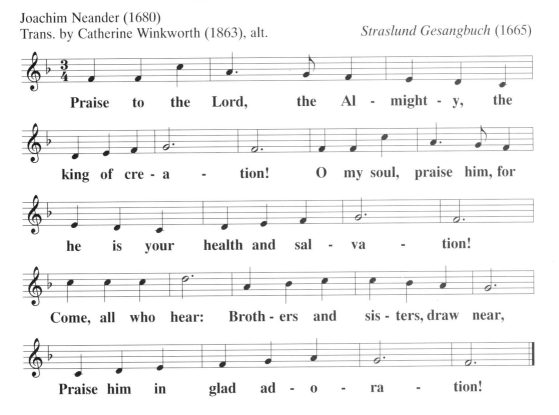

Praise to the Lord, the Al - might - y, the
king of cre - a - tion! O my soul, praise him, for
he is your health and sal - va - tion!
Come, all who hear: Broth - ers and sis - ters, draw near,
Praise him in glad ad - o - ra - tion!

Praise to the Lord, above all things so mightily reigning;
Keeping us safe at his side, and so gently sustaining.
Have you not seen
All you have needed has been
Met by his gracious ordaining?

Praise to the Lord, who shall prosper our work and defend us;
Surely his goodness and mercy shall daily attend us.
Ponder anew
What the Almighty can do,
Who with his love will befriend us.

Praise to the Lord— O let all that is in us adore him!
All that has life and breath come now with praises before him!
Let the "Amen!"
Sound from his people again—
Gladly with praise we adore him!

100   Praise, My Soul, the King of Heaven

LAUDA ANIMA 8.7.8.7.8.7

Psalm 103
Henry F. Lyte (1834), alt.

John Goss (1869)

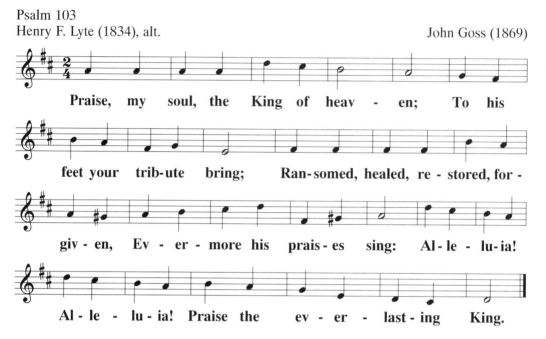

Praise, my soul, the King of heav - en; To his feet your trib-ute bring; Ran-somed, healed, re - stored, for - giv - en, Ev - er - more his prais - es sing: Al - le - lu - ia! Al - le - lu - ia! Praise the ev - er - last - ing King.

Praise him for his grace and favor	Fatherlike he tends and spares us;
To his people in distress;	Well our feeble frame he knows;
Praise him still the same as ever,	In his hands he gently bears us,
Slow to chide, and swift to bless:	Rescues us from all our foes.
Alleluia! Alleluia!	Alleluia! Alleluia!
Glorious in his faithfulness.	Widely yet his mercy flows.

Frail as summer's flow'r we flourish,
Blows the wind and it is gone;
But while mortals rise and perish,
God endures unchanging on:
Alleluia! Alleluia!
Praise the high eternal one!

Angels, help us to adore him;
You behold him face to face;
Sun and moon, bow down before him,
Dwellers all in time and space:
Alleluia! Alleluia!
Praise with us the God of grace.

Children of the Heavenly Father 101

TRYGGARE KAN INGEN VARA LM

Caroline V. Sandell Berg (1855)
Trans. by Ernest W. Olson (1925), alt.

Swedish melody

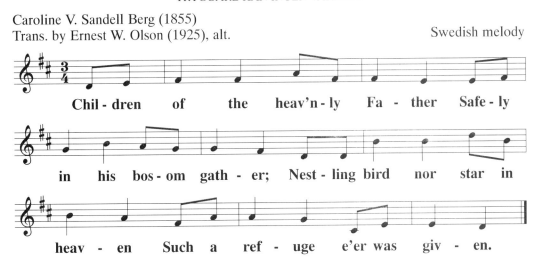

Chil - dren of the heav'n - ly Fa - ther Safe - ly

in his bos - om gath - er; Nest - ling bird nor star in

heav - en Such a ref - uge e'er was giv - en.

God his own shall tend and nourish;
In his holy courts they flourish.
From all evil pow'rs he spares them;
In his mighty arms he bears them.

Neither life nor death shall ever
From the Lord his children sever;
For to them his grace revealing,
He turns sorrow into healing.

God has given, he has taken,
But his children ne'er forsaken;
His the loving purpose solely
To preserve them pure and holy.

102   If Thou But Trust in God to Guide Thee

WER NUR DEN LIEBEN GOTT 9.8.9.8.8.8

Psalm 55:22; Georg Neumark (1657)
Trans. by Catherine Winkworth (1863)

Georg Neumark (1657)

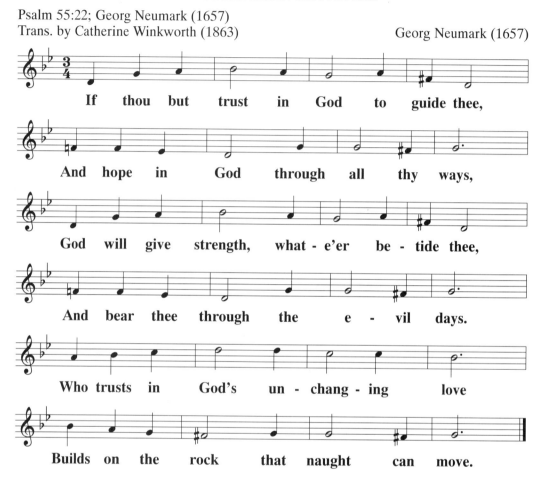

If thou but trust in God to guide thee,

And hope in God through all thy ways,

God will give strength, what-e'er be-tide thee,

And bear thee through the e-vil days.

Who trusts in God's un-chang-ing love

Builds on the rock that naught can move.

Only be still, and wait God's leisure
In cheerful hope, with heart content
To take whate'er thy Maker's pleasure
And all-discerning love hath sent;
We know our inmost wants are known,
For we are called to be God's own.

Sing, pray, and keep God's ways unswerving;
So do thine own part faithfully,
And trust God's word; though undeserving,
Thou yet shalt find it true for thee.
God never yet forsook at need
The soul that trusted God indeed.

The Lord's My Shepherd

103

BROTHER JAMES' AIR 8.6.8.6.8.6

Psalm 23
Scottish Psalter (1650)

J. L. Macbeth Bain
Harm. by Gordon Jacob (1934), alt.

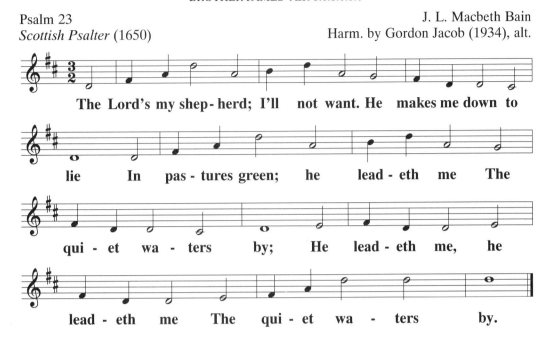

The Lord's my shep-herd; I'll not want. He makes me down to
lie In pas-tures green; he lead-eth me The
qui-et wa-ters by; He lead-eth me, he
lead-eth me The qui-et wa-ters by.

My soul he doth restore again,
And me to walk doth make
Within the paths of righteousness
E'en for his own name's sake;
Within the paths of righteousness,
E'en for his own name's sake.

Yea, though I walk in death's dark vale,
Yet will I fear no ill;
For thou art with me, and thy rod
And staff me comfort still;
For thou art with me, and thy rod
And staff me comfort still.

My table thou hast furnishéd
In presence of my foes;
My head thou dost with oil anoint,
And my cup overflows;
My head thou dost with oil anoint,
And my cup overflows.

Goodness and mercy all my life
Shall surely follow me,
And in God's house for evermore
My dwelling place shall be;
And in God's house for evermore
My dwelling place shall be.

104   God Moves in a Mysterious Way

DUNDEE CM

Scottish Psalter (1615)

William Cowper (1774)

Harm. by Thomas Ravenscroft (1621)

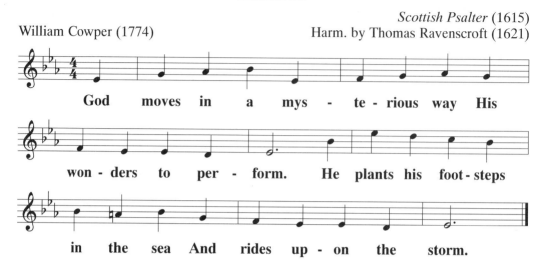

God moves in a mys - te - rious way His won - ders to per - form. He plants his foot - steps in the sea And rides up - on the storm.

Deep in unfathomable mines
Of neverfailing skill,
He treasures up his bright designs
And works his sov'reign will.

You fearful saints, fresh courage take;
The clouds you so much dread
Are big with mercy and shall break
In blessings on your head.

His purposes will ripen fast,
Unfolding ev'ry hour.
The bud may have a bitter taste,
But sweet will be the flow'r.

Blind unbelief is sure to err
And scan his work in vain.
God is his own interpreter,
And he will make it plain.

He Leadeth Me: O Blessed Thought   105

HE LEADETH ME LM with refrain

Psalm 23
Joseph H. Gilmore (1862)   William B. Bradbury (1864)

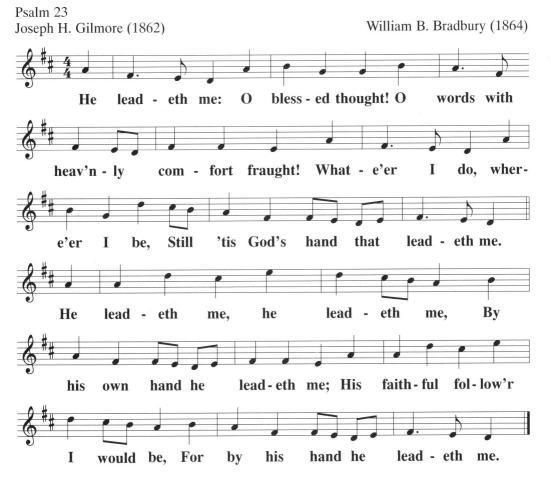

He lead - eth me: O bless - ed thought! O words with heav'n - ly com - fort fraught! What - e'er I do, wher - e'er I be, Still 'tis God's hand that lead - eth me.

He lead - eth me, he lead - eth me, By his own hand he lead - eth me; His faith - ful fol - low'r I would be, For by his hand he lead - eth me.

Sometimes mid scenes of deepest gloom,
Sometimes where Eden's bowers bloom,
By waters still, o'er troubled sea,
Still 'tis his hand that leadeth me.
   He leadeth me….

Lord, I would place my hand in thine,
Nor ever murmur nor repine;
Content, whatever lot I see,
Since 'tis my God that leadeth me.
   He leadeth me….

And when my task on earth is done,
When by thy grace the vict'ry's won,
E'en death's cold wave I will not flee,
Since God through Jordan leadeth me.
   He leadeth me….

106   On Eagle's Wings

Psalm 91
Michael Joncas (1979)

Michael Joncas (1979)

Verse 1

1. You who dwell in the shel-ter of the Lord, who a-bide in his shad-ow for life, say to the Lord: "My ref-uge, my rock in whom I trust!"

Refrain

And he will raise you up on ea-gle's wings, bear you on the breath of dawn, make you to shine like the

Last time to coda   *To verses*

sun, and hold you in the palm of his hand. 2. The

Verse 2

snare of the fowl-er will nev-er cap-ture you, and

fam-ine will bring you no fear: un-der his wings your

D.S.

ref - uge, his faith - ful - ness your shield.

Verse 3

3

3. You need not fear the ter - ror of the night, nor the

ar - row that flies by day; though thou - sands fall a -

D.S.

bout you, near you it shall not come.

Verse 4

3

4. For to his an - gels he's giv - en a com - mand to

guard you in all of your ways; up - on their hands they will

D.S.

bear you up, lest you dash your foot a - gainst a stone.

Coda

And hold you, hold you in the

palm of his hand.

107   The King of Love My Shepherd Is

ST. COLUMBA 8.7.8.7

Psalm 23   Irish melody
Henry Williams Baker (1868)   Harm. by A. Gregory Murray, OSB

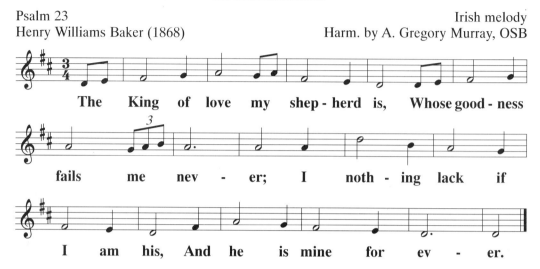

The King of love my shep-herd is, Whose good-ness
fails me nev-er; I noth-ing lack if
I am his, And he is mine for ev-er.

Where streams of living water flow
My ransomed soul he's leading,
And where the verdant pastures grow
With food celestial feeding.

Confused and foolish oft I strayed,
But yet in love he sought me;
And on his shoulder gently laid,
And home, rejoicing, brought me.

In death's dark vale I fear no ill
With you, dear Lord, beside me,
Your rod and staff my comfort still,
Your cross before to guide me.

You spread a table in my sight;
Your saving grace bestowing;
And O what transport of delight
From your pure chalice flowing!

As so through all the length of days
Your goodness fails me never;
Good Shepherd, may I sing your praise
Within your house for ever.

The Care the Eagle Gives Her Young   108

ST. ANNE CM

CRimond

Psalm 90   Attr. to William Croft (1708)
Isaac Watts (1719)   Harm. by William Henry Monk (1861)

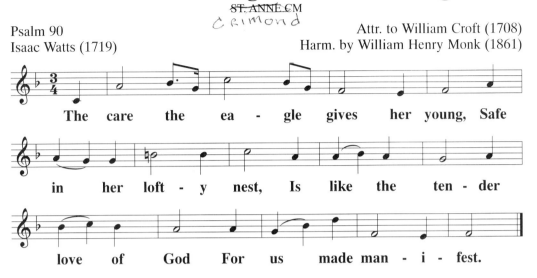

The care the ea - gle gives her young, Safe
in her loft - y nest, Is like the ten - der
love of God For us made man - i - fest.

As when the time to venture comes,   And if we flutter helplessly,
She stirs them out to flight,   As fledgling eagles fall,
So we are pressed to boldly try,   Beneath us lift God's mighty wings
To strive for daring height.   To bear us, one and all.

109   Glory and Praise to Our God

Daniel L. Schutte (1976)
Acc. by Sr. Theophane Hytrek, OSF, alt.

Daniel L. Schutte (1976)

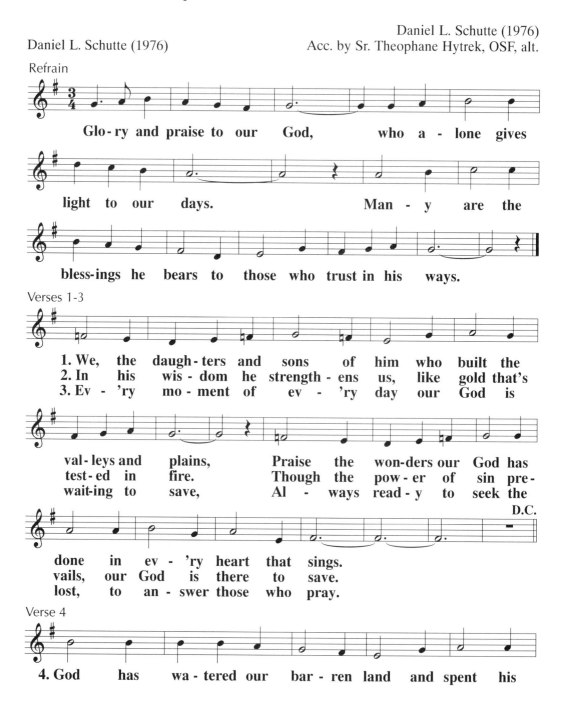

Refrain

Glo - ry and praise to our God, who a - lone gives light to our days. Man - y are the bless-ings he bears to those who trust in his ways.

Verses 1-3

1. We, the daugh-ters and sons of him who built the val - leys and plains, Praise the won-ders our God has done in ev - 'ry heart that sings.
2. In his wis - dom he strength - ens us, like gold that's test - ed in fire. Though the pow - er of sin pre - vails, our God is there to save.
3. Ev - 'ry mo - ment of ev - 'ry day our God is wait-ing to save, Al - ways read - y to seek the lost, to an - swer those who pray.

D.C.

Verse 4

4. God has wa - tered our bar - ren land and spent his

mer - ci - ful   rain.   Now the   riv - ers of   life run

D.C.

full   for   an - y - one   to   drink.

110 Sing Praise to God Who Reigns Above

MIT FREUDEN ZART 8.7.8.7.8.8.7

Deuteronomy 32:3
Johann J. Schütz (1675)
Trans. by Frances E. Cox (1864)

Bohemian Brethren's *Kirchengesange* (1566)

Sing praise to God who reigns a-bove, The
God of all cre - a - tion, The
God of pow'r, the God of love, The
God of our sal - va - tion; With
heal - ing balm my soul he fills, And
ev - 'ry faith - less mur - mur stills: To
God all praise and glo - ry.

What God's almighty pow'r has made,
His gracious mercy keeping;
By morning glow or evening shade
His watchful eye ne'er sleeping;
Within the kingdom of his might,
Lo! all is just and all is right:
To God all praise and glory.

Then all my gladsome way along,
I sing aloud your praises,
That all may hear the grateful song
My voice unwearied raises;
Be joyful in the Lord, my heart,
Both soul and body sing your part:
To God all praise and glory.

Let all who name Christ's holy name,
Give God all praise and glory;
All you who own his pow'r, proclaim
Aloud the wondrous story!
Cast each false idol from its throne,
The Lord is God, and he alone:
To God all praise and glory.

111   Guide Me, O Thou Great Jehovah

CWM RHONDDA 8.7.8.7.8.7.7

William Williams (1745)
Trans. by Peter Williams and William Williams (1771), alt.   John Hughes (1907)

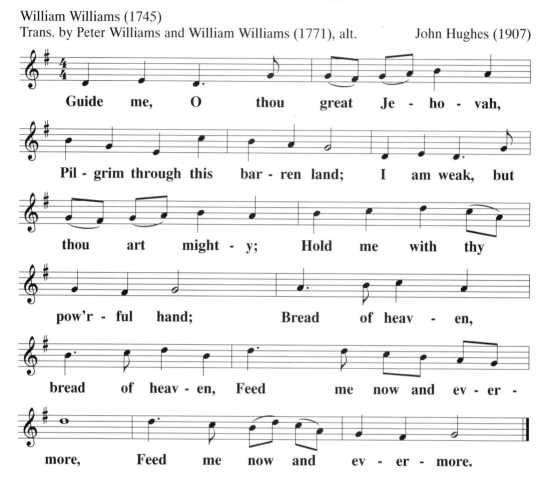

Guide me, O thou great Je - ho - vah,
Pil - grim through this bar - ren land; I am weak, but
thou art might - y; Hold me with thy
pow'r - ful hand; Bread of heav - en,
bread of heav - en, Feed me now and ev - er -
more, Feed me now and ev - er - more.

Open now the crystal fountain,	When I tread the verge of Jordan,
Whence the healing stream doth flow;	Bid my anxious fears subside;
Let the fire and cloudy pillar	Death of death, and hell's destruction,
Lead me all my journey through;	Land me safe on Canaan's side;
Strong deliv'rer, strong deliv'rer,	Songs of praises, songs of praises,
Be thou still my strength and shield,	I will ever give to thee,
Be thou still my strength and shield.	I will ever give to thee.

There's a Wideness in God's Mercy   112
IN BABILONE 8.7.8.7 D

Dutch melody
Arr. by Julius Röntgen (1906)

Frederick William Faber (1854), alt.

There's a wide-ness in God's mer - cy Like the wide-ness

of the sea; There's a kind-ness in God's jus - tice

Which is more than lib - er - ty. There is plen - ti -

ful re - demp - tion In the blood that has been shed;

There is joy for all the mem - bers

In the sor - rows of the Head.

For the love of God is broader
Than the measures of our mind,
And the heart of the Eternal
Is most wonderfully kind.
If our love were but more simple
We should take him at his word,
And our lives would be thanksgiving
For the goodness of our Lord.

Troubled souls, why will you scatter
Like a crowd of frightened sheep?
Foolish hearts, why will you wander
From a love so true and deep?
There is welcome for the sinner
And more graces for the good;
There is mercy with the Savior,
There is healing in his blood.

113   Great Is Thy Faithfulness

FAITHFULNESS 11.10.11.10 with refrain

Lamentations 3:22-23
Thomas O. Chisholm (1923)   William M. Runyan (1923)

Great is thy faith - ful-ness, O God my Fa-ther;

There is no shad - ow of turn - ing with thee;

Thou chang - est not, thy com - pas - sions, they fail not;

As thou hast been, thou for ev - er wilt be.

Great is thy faith - ful-ness! Great is thy faith - ful-ness!

Morn-ing by morn - ing new mer - cies I see;

All I have need - ed thy hand hath pro - vid-ed;

Great is thy faith - ful-ness, Lord, un - to me!

Summer and winter and springtime and harvest,
Sun, moon, and stars in their courses above
Join with all nature in manifold witness
To thy great faithfulness, mercy, and love.
Great is thy faithfulness! Great is thy faithfulness!
Morning by morning new mercies I see;
All I have needed thy hand hath provided;
Great is thy faithfulness, Lord, unto me!

Pardon for sin and a peace that endureth,
Thine own dear presence to cheer and to guide;
Strength for today and bright hope for tomorrow,
Blessings all mine, with ten thousand beside!
Great is thy faithfulness! Great is thy faithfulness!
Morning by morning new mercies I see;
All I have needed thy hand hath provided;
Great is thy faithfulness, Lord, unto me!

114 This Is My Father's World

TERRA BEATA SMD

Maltbie D. Babcock (1901), alt.
St. 2 rev. by Mary Babcock Crawford (1972)

English melody
Adapt. by Franklin L. Sheppard (1915)

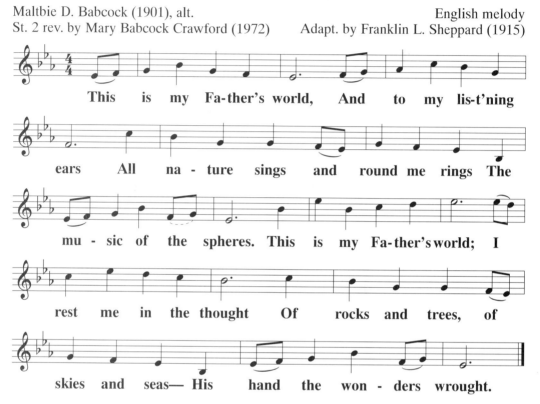

This is my Fa-ther's world, And to my lis-t'ning ears All na-ture sings and round me rings The mu-sic of the spheres. This is my Fa-ther's world; I rest me in the thought Of rocks and trees, of skies and seas— His hand the won-ders wrought.

This is our Father's world:
O let us not forget
That though the wrong is great and strong,
God is the ruler yet.
He trusts us with his world,
To keep it clean and fair—
All earth and trees, all skies and seas,
All creatures ev'rywhere.

This is my Father's world:
He shines in all that's fair;
In rustling grass I hear him pass—
He speaks to me ev'rywhere.
This is my Father's world:
Why should my heart be sad?
The Lord is King, let heaven ring!
God reigns; let earth be glad.

He's Got the Whole World in His Hands   115

WHOLE WORLD Irregular

African-American spiritual   African-American spiritual

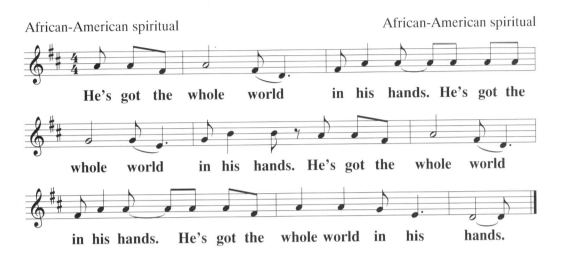

He's got the whole world in his hands. He's got the

whole world in his hands. He's got the whole world

in his hands. He's got the whole world in his hands.

He's got the wind and the rain in his hands. *Sing three times.*
He's got the whole world in his hands.

He's got the little tiny baby in his hands...
He's got the whole world in his hands.

He's got you and me, brother, in his hands...
He's got the whole world in his hands.

He's got you and me, sister, in his hands...
He's got the whole world in his hands.

He's got everybody here in his hands...
He's got the whole world in his hands.

116   On Jordan's Bank

WINCHESTER NEW LM

Charles Coffin (1736)   *Musikalisches Handbuch* (1690)
Trans. by John Chandler (1837)   Harm. by William Henry Monk (1847), alt.

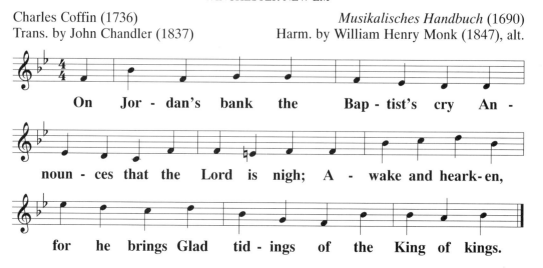

On Jordan's bank the Baptist's cry
Announces that the Lord is nigh;
Awake and hearken, for he brings
Glad tidings of the King of kings.

Then cleansed be ev'ry heart from sin;
Make straight the way of God within,
And let each heart prepare a home
Where such a mighty guest may come.

For you are our salvation, Lord,
Our refuge, and our great reward;
Without your grace we waste away
Like flow'rs that wither and decay.

To heal the sick stretch out your hand,
And bid the fallen sinner stand;
Shine forth, and let your light restore
Earth's own true loveliness once more.

All praise the Son eternally,
Whose advent sets his people free;
Whom with the Father we adore
And Spirit blest for evermore.

Hail to the Lord's Anointed　　117

ELLACOMBE 7.6.7.6 D

Psalm 72　　　　　　　　　　　*Gesangbuch der Herzogl,* Wirtermberg (1784), alt.
James Montgomery (1821)　　　　　　Harm. by William Henry Monk (1868)

Hail to the Lord's A - noint - ed, Great
Da - vid's great - er Son! Hail in the time ap -
point - ed, His reign on earth be - gun! He
comes to break op - pres - sion, To
set the cap - tive free; To take a - way trans -
gres - sion, And rule in eq - ui - ty.

He comes with succor speedy
To those who suffer wrong;
To help the poor and needy,
And bid the weak be strong;
To give them songs for sighing,
Their darkness turn to light,
Whose souls, condemned and dying,
Are precious in his sight.

He shall come down like showers
Upon the fruitful earth;
Love, joy, and hope, like flowers,
Spring in his path to birth.
Before him, on the mountains,
Shall peace, the herald, go,
And righteousness, in fountains,
From hill to valley flow.

To him shall prayer unceasing
And daily vows ascend;
His kingdom still increasing,
A kingdom without end.
The tide of time shall never
His covenant remove;
His name shall stand for ever;
That name to us is love.

118 Savior of the Nations, Come
NUN KOMM DER HEIDEN HEILAND 7.7.7.7

Attr. to St. Ambrose (4th C.)
Sts. 1-3a trans. by William Reynolds (1851)
Sts. 3b-5 trans. by Martin L. Seltz (1969), alt.   *Geystliche gesangk Buchleyn* (1524)

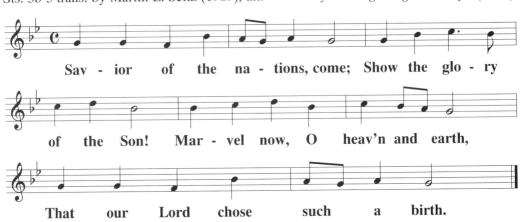

Sav - ior of the na - tions, come; Show the glo - ry

of the Son! Mar - vel now, O heav'n and earth,

That our Lord chose such a birth.

Not by human flesh and blood,
By the Spirit of our God
Was the word of God made flesh—
Woman's offspring, pure and fresh.

Wondrous birth! O wondrous child
Of the Virgin undefiled!
Mighty God and man in one,
Eager now his race to run!

God Creator is his source,
Back to God he runs his course,
Down to death and hell descends,
God's high throne he reascends.

Now your lowly manger bright
Hallows night with newborn light;
Let no night this light subdue,
Let our faith shine ever new.

Lo, How a Rose E'er Blooming   **119**

ES IST EIN' ROS' ENTSPRUNGEN 7.6.7.6.6.7.6

Isaiah 11:1, sts. 1-2 (15th C.)
Trans. by Theodore Baker (1894)
St. 3, *The Hymnal 1940*

Geistliche Kirchengesang (1599)
Harm. by Michael Praetorius (1609)

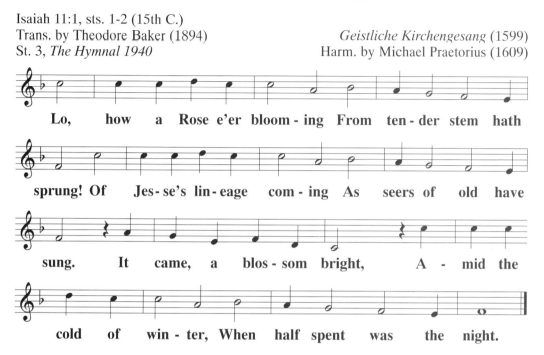

Lo, how a Rose e'er bloom-ing From ten-der stem hath sprung! Of Jes-se's lin-eage com-ing As seers of old have sung. It came, a blos-som bright, A-mid the cold of win-ter, When half spent was the night.

Isaiah 'twas foretold it,
The Rose I have in mind,
With Mary we behold it,
The Virgin Mother kind.
To show God's love aright,
She bore to us a Savior,
When half spent was the night.

O Flow'r, whose fragrance tender
With sweetness fills the air,
Dispel in glorious splendor
The darkness ev'rywhere;
True man, yet very God,
From sin and death now save us,
And share our ev'ry load.

120 Tell Out, My Soul, the Greatness of the Lord

WOODLANDS 10.10.10.10

Luke 1:46b-55
Timothy Dudley-Smith (1961)

Walter Greatorex (1919)

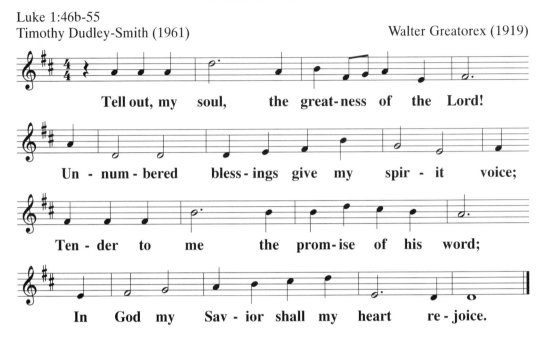

Tell out, my soul, the great-ness of the Lord!

Un - num - bered bless - ings give my spir - it voice;

Ten - der to me the prom-ise of his word;

In God my Sav - ior shall my heart re - joice.

Tell out, my soul, the greatness of his name!
Make known his might, the deeds his arm has done;
His mercy sure, from age to age the same;
His holy name— the Lord, the mighty One.

Tell out, my soul, the greatness of his might!
Pow'rs and dominions lay their glory by;
Proud hearts and stubborn wills are put to flight,
The hungry fed, the humble lifted high.

Tell out, my soul, the glories of his word!
Firm is his promise, and his mercy sure.
Tell out, my soul, the greatness of the Lord
To children's children and for evermore!

O Come, O Come, Emmanuel 121

VENI EMMANUEL LM with refrain

Processionale (15th C.)

Latin (9th C.)

Adapt. by Thomas Helmore (1854)

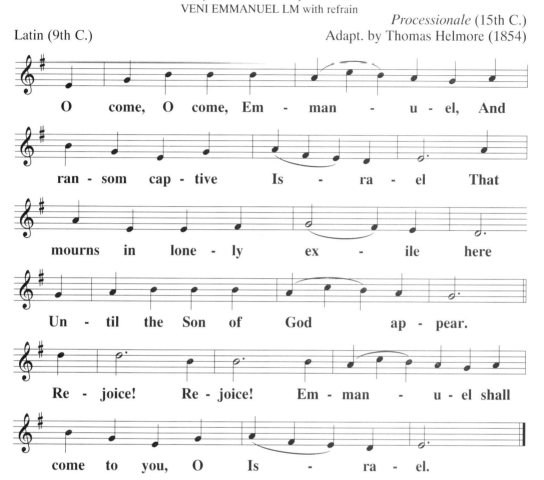

O come, O come, Em - man - u - el, And
ran - som cap - tive Is - ra - el That
mourns in lone - ly ex - ile here
Un - til the Son of God ap - pear.
Re - joice! Re - joice! Em - man - u - el shall
come to you, O Is - ra - el.

O come, O Wisdom from on high, / Who ordered all things mightily;
To us the path of knowledge show / And teach us in its ways to go. *Rejoice!...*

O come, O come, great Lord of might, / Who to your tribes on Sinai's height
In ancient times did give the law / In cloud and majesty and awe. *Rejoice!...*

O come, O Branch of Jesse's stem, / Unto your own and rescue them!
From depths of hell your people save, / And give them vict'ry o'er the grave. *Rejoice!...*

O come, O Key of David, come / And open wide our heav'nly home.
Make safe for us the heav'nward road / And bar the way to death's abode. *Rejoice!...*

O come, O Bright and Morning Star, / And bring us comfort from afar!
Dispel the shadows of the night / And turn our darkness into light. *Rejoice!...*

O come, O King of nations, bind / In one the hearts of all mankind.
Bid all our sad divisions cease / And be yourself our King of Peace. *Rejoice!...*

122   Come, Thou Long-expected Jesus

STUTTGART 8.7.8.7

Psalmodia Sacra (1715)

Charles Wesley (1744)

Adapt. and harm. by William Henry Havergal, alt.

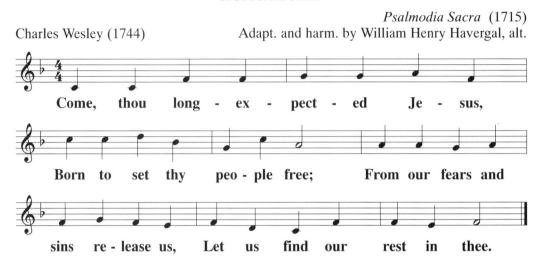

Come, thou long - ex - pect - ed Je - sus,

Born to set thy peo - ple free; From our fears and

sins re - lease us, Let us find our rest in thee.

Israel's strength and consolation,	Born thy people to deliver,
Hope of all the earth thou art:	Born a child, and yet a king,
Dear desire of ev'ry nation,	Born to reign in us for ever,
Joy of ev'ry longing heart.	Now thy gracious kingdom bring.

By thine own eternal Spirit
Rule in all our hearts alone;
By thine all-sufficient merit
Raise us to thy glorious throne.

Lift Up Your Heads, O Mighty Gates   123

TRURO LM

Based on Psalm 24; Georg Weissel (1642)
Trans. by Catherine Winkworth (1855)   Williams' *Psalmodia Evangelica* (1789)

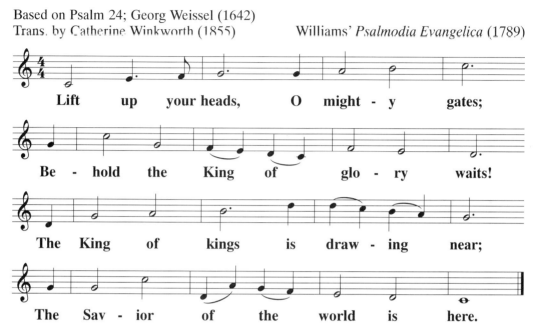

Lift up your heads, O might - y gates;

Be - hold the King of glo - ry waits!

The King of kings is draw - ing near;

The Sav - ior of the world is here.

O blest the land, the city blest,
Where Christ the ruler is confest!
O happy hearts and happy homes
To whom this King of triumph comes!

Fling wide the portals of your heart;
Make it a temple, set apart
From earthly use for heav'n's employ,
Adorned with prayer and love and joy.

Come, Savior, come with us abide;
Our hearts to you we open wide:
Your Holy Spirit guide us on,
Until our glorious goal is won.

124 Wake, O Wake, and Sleep No Longer

WACHET AUF 8.9.8.8.9.8.6.6.4.4.4.8

Philipp Nicolai (1599)
Trans. and adapt. by Christopher Idle (1982)

Philipp Nicolai (1599)
Harm. by Johann Sebastian Bach (1731)

Wake, O wake, and sleep no long - er, For
he who calls you is no stran - ger: A -
wake, God's own Je - ru - sa - lem! Hear, the mid - night
bells are chim - ing The sig - nal for his
roy - al com - ing: Let voice to voice an -
nounce his name! We feel his foot - step near, The
Bride - groom at the door— Al - le - lu - ia! The
lamps will shine With light di - vine
As Christ the Sav - ior comes to reign.

Zion hears the sound of singing;
Her heart is thrilled with sudden longing:
She stirs, and wakes, and stands prepared.
Christ, her friend, and lord, and lover,
Her star and sun and strong redeemer—
At last his mighty voice is heard.
The Son of God has come
To make with us his home:
Sing Hosanna!
The fight is won,
The feast begun;
We fix our eyes on Christ alone.

Glory, glory, sing the angels,
While music sounds from strings and cymbals;
All humankind, with songs arise!
Twelve the gates into the city,
Each one a pearl of shining beauty;
The streets of gold ring out with praise.
All creatures round the throne
Adore the holy One
With rejoicing:
Amen be sung
By ev'ry tongue
To crown their welcome to the King.

Advent

125   Comfort, Comfort, O My People
GENEVA 42 8.7.8.7.7.7.8.8

Isaiah 40:1-8; Johann Olearius (1671)   *Genevan Psalter* (1551)
Trans. by Catherine Winkworth (1863), alt.   Harm. adapt. from Claude Goudimel (1565)

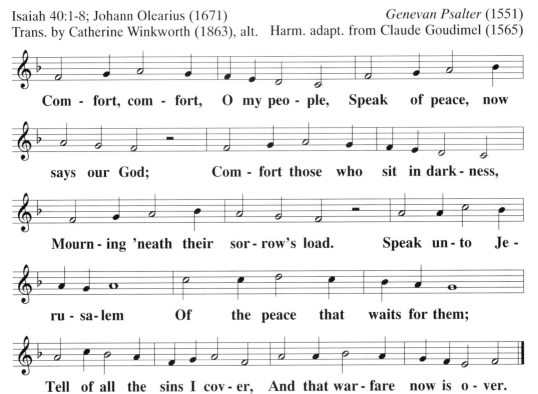

Com - fort, com - fort, O my peo - ple, Speak of peace, now
says our God; Com - fort those who sit in dark - ness,
Mourn - ing 'neath their sor - row's load. Speak un - to Je -
ru - sa-lem Of the peace that waits for them;
Tell of all the sins I cov- er, And that war - fare now is o - ver.

Hark, the voice of one who's crying
In the desert far and near,
Bidding all to full repentance
Since the kingdom now is here.
O that warning cry obey!
Now prepare for God a way;
Let the valleys rise to meet him
And the hills bow down to greet him.

O make straight what long was crooked,
Make the rougher places plain;
Let your hearts be true and humble,
As befits his holy reign.
For the glory of the Lord
Now o'er earth is shed abroad;
And all flesh shall see the token
That his word is never broken.

Infant Holy, Infant Lowly   126

W ZLOBIE LEZY 4.4.7.4.4.7.4.4.4.4.7

Luke 2:6-20; Polish carol   Polish carol
Trans. by Edith M. G. Reed (1925)   Harm. by A. E. Rusbridge

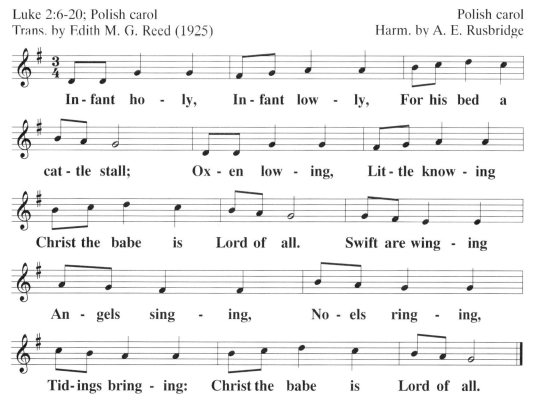

In - fant ho - ly, In - fant low - ly, For his bed a
cat - tle stall; Ox - en low - ing, Lit - tle know - ing
Christ the babe is Lord of all. Swift are wing - ing
An - gels sing - ing, No - els ring - ing,
Tid - ings bring - ing: Christ the babe is Lord of all.

Flocks were sleeping:
Shepherds keeping
Vigil till the morning new.
Saw the glory,
Heard the story,
Tidings of a gospel true.
Thus rejoicing,
Free from sorrow,
Praises voicing
Greet the morrow:
Christ the babe was born for you.

127 Let All Mortal Flesh Keep Silence
PICARDY 8.7.8.7.8.7

Liturgy of St. James (4th C.)
Trans. by Gerard Moultrie (1864)

French carol (17th C.)

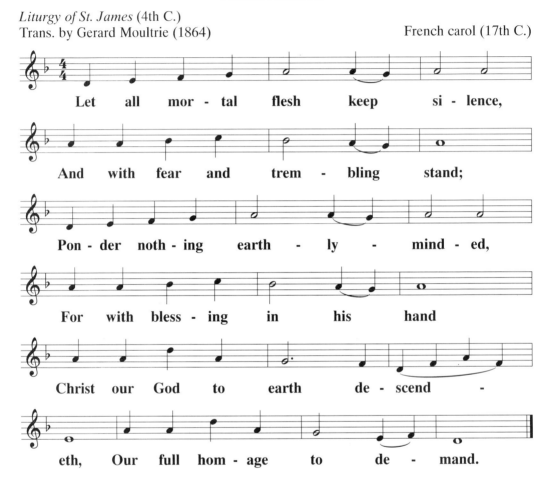

Let all mor - tal flesh keep si - lence,
And with fear and trem - bling stand;
Pon - der noth - ing earth - ly - mind - ed,
For with bless - ing in his hand
Christ our God to earth de - scend -
eth, Our full hom - age to de - mand.

King of kings, yet born of Mary,
As of old on earth he stood,
Lord of lords in human vesture,
In the Body and the Blood
He will give to all the faithful
His own self for heav'nly food.

Rank on rank the host of heaven
Spreads its vanguard on the way,
As the Light of Light descendeth
From the realms of endless day,
That the pow'rs of hell may vanish
As the darkness clears away.

At his feet the six-winged seraph;
Cherubim with sleepless eye,
Veil their faces to the Presence
As with ceaseless voice they cry,
"Alleluia, alleluia!
Alleluia, Lord, Most High!"

The First Nowell

128

THE FIRST NOWELL Irregular with refrain

English carol (17th C.)

English carol
Harm. from *Christmas Carols New and Old* (1871)

The first Now - ell, the an - gel did say, Was to
cer - tain poor shep - herds in fields as they lay; In
fields where they lay keep - ing their sheep, On a
cold win - ter's night that was so deep.
Now - ell, Now - ell, Now - ell, Now - ell,
Born is the King of Is - ra - el.

They looked up and saw a star / Shining in the east, beyond them far,
And to the earth it gave great light, / And so it continued both day and night.
Nowell …

And by the light of that same star / Three wise men came from country far;
To seek for a king was their intent, / And to follow the star wherever it went.
Nowell…

This star drew nigh to the northwest, / O'er Bethlehem it took its rest;
And there it did both stop and stay, / Right over the place where Jesus lay.
Nowell…

Then entered in those wise men three, / Full rev'rently upon their knee,
And offered there, in his presence, / Their gold and myrrh and frankincense.
Nowell…

Then let us all with one accord / Sing praises to our heav'nly Lord;
Who with the Father we adore / And Spirit blest for evermore.
Nowell…

129   The Snow Lay on the Ground

VENITE ADOREMUS 10.10.10.10 with refrain

English melody
Adapt. by Charles Winfred Douglas
Harm. by Leo Sowerby (1941)

Anglo-Irish carol (19th C.)

The snow lay on the ground, the stars shone bright, When Christ our Lord was born on Christ-mas night. Ve-ni-te a-do-re-mus Do-mi-num. Ve-ni-te a-do-re-mus Do-mi-num. Ve-ni-te a-do-re-mus Do-mi-num. Ve-ni-te a-do-re-mus Do-mi-num.

'Twas Mary, daughter pure of holy Anne,
That brought into this world the God made man.
She laid him in a stall at Bethlehem;
The ass and oxen shared the roof with them.
    Venite…

Saint Joseph, too, was by to tend the child;
To guard him, and protect his mother mild;
The angels hovered round, and sang this song,
Venite adoremus Dominum.
    Venite…

Tune: Harm. copyright © 1941, used by permission of Ronald Stalford, executor of the estate of Leo Sowerby

And thus that manger poor became a throne;
For he whom Mary bore was God the Son.
O come, then, let us join the heav'nly host;
To praise the Father, Son, and Holy Ghost.
  Venite…

130   Away in a Manger

CRADLE SONG 11.11.11.11

St. 1-2, anonymous
St. 3, John T. McFarland (1885)

William J. Kirkpatrick (1895)

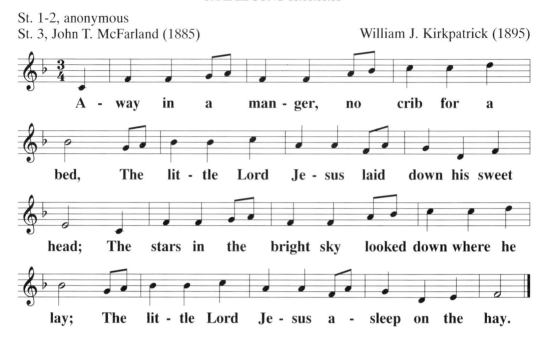

A - way in a man - ger, no crib for a
bed, The lit - tle Lord Je - sus laid down his sweet
head; The stars in the bright sky looked down where he
lay; The lit - tle Lord Je - sus a - sleep on the hay.

The cattle are lowing, the baby awakes,
But little Lord Jesus, no crying he makes.
I love you, Lord Jesus: look down from on high
And stay by my side until morning is nigh.

Be near me, Lord Jesus; I ask you to stay
Close by me for ever and love me, I pray.
Bless all the dear children in your tender care;
Prepare us for heaven to live with you there.

Away in a Manger

131

MUELLER 11.11.11.11

St. 1-2, anonymous
St. 3, John T. McFarland (1885)

James R. Murray (1887)

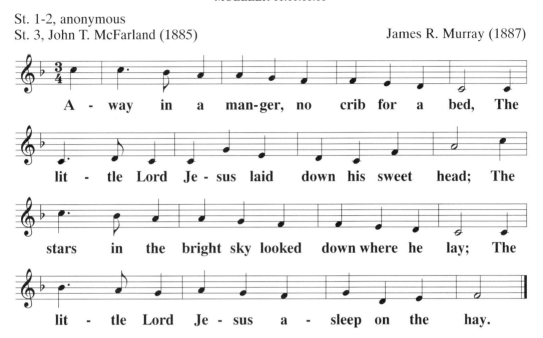

A - way in a man-ger, no crib for a bed, The

lit - tle Lord Je - sus laid down his sweet head; The

stars in the bright sky looked down where he lay; The

lit - tle Lord Je - sus a - sleep on the hay.

The cattle are lowing, the baby awakes,
But little Lord Jesus, no crying he makes.
I love you, Lord Jesus: look down from on high
And stay by my side until morning is nigh.

Be near me, Lord Jesus; I ask you to stay
Close by me for ever and love me, I pray.
Bless all the dear children in your tender care;
Prepare us for heaven to live with you there.

132 O Little Town of Bethlehem

ST. LOUIS 8.6.8.6.7.6.8.6

Phillips Brooks (1868)   Lewis Henry Redner (1868)

O lit - tle town of Beth - le - hem, How

still we see thee lie! A - bove thy deep and

dream - less sleep The si - lent stars go by;

Yet in the dark streets shin - eth The

ev - er - last - ing Light; The hopes and fears of

all the years Are met in thee to - night.

**For Christ is born of Mary,
And gathered all above,
While mortals sleep, the angels keep
Their watch of wond'ring love.
O morning stars, together
Proclaim the holy birth!
And praises sing to God the King
And peace to all on earth.**

How silently, how silently,
The wondrous gift is giv'n!
So God imparts to human hearts
The blessings of his heav'n.
No ear may hear his coming,
But in this world of sin,
Where meek souls will receive him, still
The dear Christ enters in.

O holy Child of Bethlehem!
Descend to us we pray;
Cast out our sin and enter in,
Be born in us today.
We hear the Christmas angels
The great glad tidings tell;
O come to us, abide with us,
Our Lord Emmanuel!

133   O Come, All Ye Faithful

ADESTE FIDELES Irregular with refrain

John F. Wade (c. 1743)
Trans. by Frederick Oakeley (1841)

John F. Wade (c. 1743)

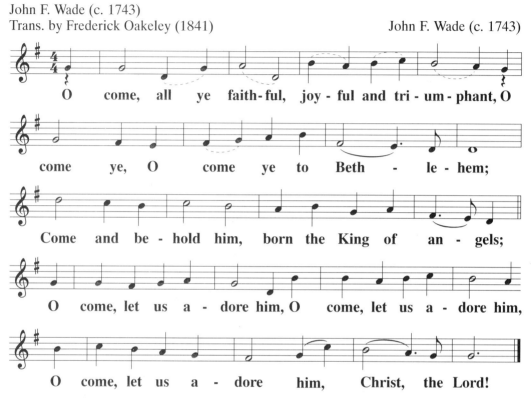

O come, all ye faith-ful, joy-ful and tri-um-phant, O come ye, O come ye to Beth-le-hem; Come and be-hold him, born the King of an-gels; O come, let us a-dore him, O come, let us a-dore him, O come, let us a-dore him, Christ, the Lord!

God of God,
Light of Light,
Lo! He comes forth
  from the Virgin's womb.
Our very God,
Begotten not created,
  O come...

Sing, choirs of angels,
Sing in exultation,
Sing, all ye citizens
  of heav'n above!
Glory to God,
All glory in the highest;
  O come...

Yea, Lord, we greet thee,
Born this happy morning,
Jesus, to thee be all glory giv'n;
Word of the Father,
Now in flesh appearing;
  O come...

Angels, from the Realms of Glory   134

REGENT SQUARE 8.7.8.7.8.7

St. 1-3, James Montgomery (1816)
St. 4, *Christmas Box* (1825)

Henry Thomas Smart (1867)

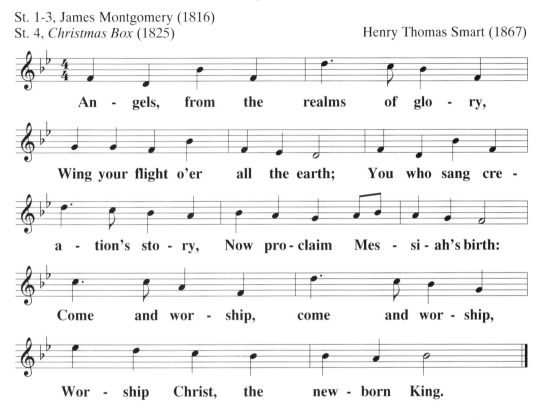

An - gels, from the realms of glo - ry,

Wing your flight o'er all the earth; You who sang cre -

a - tion's sto - ry, Now pro - claim Mes - si - ah's birth:

Come and wor - ship, come and wor - ship,

Wor - ship Christ, the new - born King.

Shepherds, in the fields abiding,
Watching o'er your flocks by night,
God on earth is now residing,
Yonder shines the infant light:
  Come and worship…

Sages, leave your contemplations,
Brighter visions beam afar;
Seek the great Desire of nations,
You have seen his morning star:
  Come and worship…

Though an infant now we view him,
He shall fill his heav'nly throne,
Gather all the nations to him;
Ev'ry knee shall then bow down:
  Come and worship…

135   Once in Royal David's City

IRBY 8.7.8.7.7.7

Henry John Gauntlett (1849)

Cecil Frances Alexander (1848)

Harm. by Arthur Henry Mann (1919)

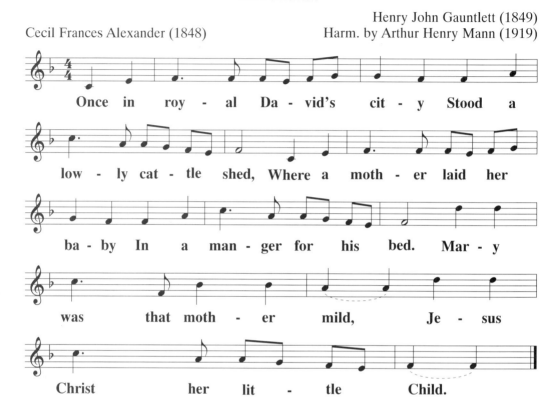

Once in roy - al Da - vid's cit - y Stood a
low - ly cat - tle shed, Where a moth - er laid her
ba - by In a man - ger for his bed. Mar - y
was that moth - er mild, Je - sus
Christ her lit - tle Child.

He came down to earth from heaven / Who is God and Lord of all,
And his shelter was a stable, / And his cradle was a stall.
With the poor and mean and lowly / Lived on earth our Savior holy.

And through all his wondrous childhood / He would honor and obey,
Love and watch the lowly maiden / In whose gentle arms he lay.
Christian children all should be / Kind, obedient, good as he.

For he is our childhood's pattern, / Day by day like us he grew;
He was little, weak, and helpless, / Tears and smiles like us he knew:
And he feels for all our sadness, / And he shares in all our gladness.

And our eyes at last shall see him, / Through his own redeeming love;
For that child so dear and gentle / Is our Lord in heav'n above;
And he leads his children on / To the place where he has gone.

What Child Is This   136

GREENSLEEVES 8.7.8.7 with refrain

English melody (16th C.)
Harm. by John Stainer

William Chatterton Dix (1865)

What child is this, who, laid to rest, On
Mar-y's lap is sleep-ing? Whom an-gels greet with
an-thems sweet, While shep-herds watch are keep-ing?
This, this is Christ the King, Whom shep-herds
guard and an-gels sing; Haste, haste to
bring him laud, The Babe, the Son of Mar-y.

Why lies he in such low estate
Where ox and ass are feeding?
Good Christian, fear; for sinners here
The silent Word is pleading.
  This…

So bring him incense, gold and myrrh,
Come, peasant, king to own him;
The King of kings salvation brings,
Let loving hearts enthrone him.
  This…

137 While Shepherds Watched Their Flocks

WINCHESTER OLD CM

Thomas Est (1592)

Nahum Tate (1700)

Harm. from *Hymns Ancient and Modern* (1922)

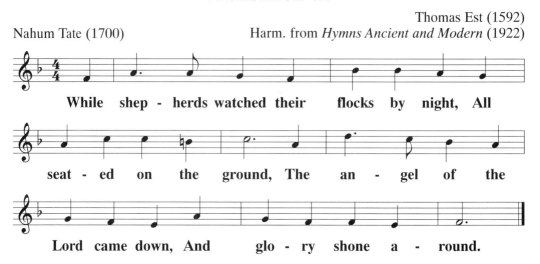

While shep - herds watched their flocks by night, All

seat - ed on the ground, The an - gel of the

Lord came down, And glo - ry shone a - round.

"Fear not," said he, for mighty dread
Had seized their troubled mind;
"Glad tidings of great joy I bring
To you and all mankind."

"To you, in David's town, this day
Is born of David's line
The Savior, who is Christ the Lord;
And this shall be the sign:

"The heav'nly babe you there shall find
To human view displayed,
All meanly wrapped in swathing bands,
And in a manger laid."

Thus spake the seraph, and forthwith
Appeared a shining throng
Of angels praising God, who thus
Addressed their joyful song:

"All glory be to God on high
And on the earth be peace;
Good will henceforth from heav'n to men
Begin and never cease."

God Rest You Merry, Gentlemen 138

GOD REST YOU MERRY 8.6.8.6.8.6 with refrain

English carol (18th C.)
Harm. by John Stainer

English carol (18th C.)

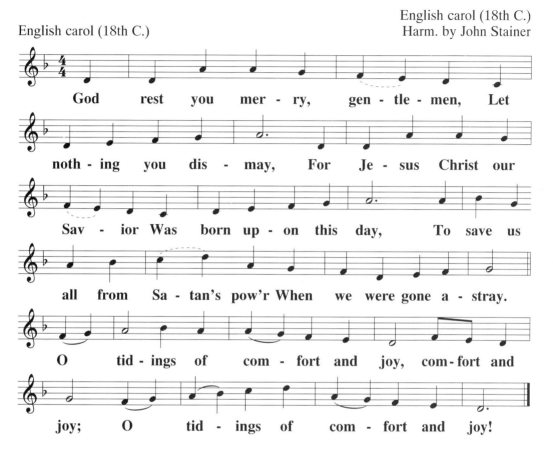

God rest you mer - ry, gen - tle - men, Let
noth - ing you dis - may, For Je - sus Christ our
Sav - ior Was born up - on this day, To save us
all from Sa - tan's pow'r When we were gone a - stray.
O tid - ings of com - fort and joy, com - fort and
joy; O tid - ings of com - fort and joy!

In Bethlehem in Judah / This blessèd babe was born,
And laid within a manger / Upon this blessèd morn:
For which his mother Mary / Did nothing take in scorn. *O tidings…*

From God our great Creator / A blessèd angel came,
And unto certain shepherds / Brought tidings of the same,
How that in Bethlehem was born / The Son of God by name. *O tidings…*

The shepherds at those tidings / Rejoicèd much in mind,
And left their flocks a-feeding / In tempest, storm and wind,
And went to Bethlehem straight-way, / The blessèd babe to find. *O tidings…*

Now to the Lord sing praises, / All you within this place,
And with true love and charity / Each other now embrace;
This holy tide of Christmas / All others shall replace. *O tidings…*

139   Angels We Have Heard on High
GLORIA 7.7.7.7 with refrain

French (c. 18th C.)
Trans. from *Crown of Jesus Music*, London (1862)   French traditional

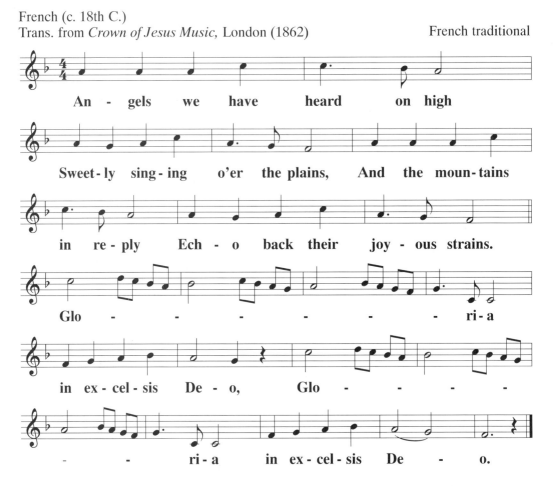

An - gels   we   have   heard   on   high

Sweet - ly sing - ing   o'er   the plains,   And   the moun - tains

in   re - ply   Ech - o   back   their   joy - ous strains.

Glo - - - - - - ri - a

in   ex - cel - sis   De - o,   Glo - - - -

- - ri - a   in   ex - cel - sis   De - o.

Shepherds, why this jubilee?
Why your joyous strains prolong?
Say what may the tidings be,
Which inspire your heav'nly song.
  Gloria…

Come to Bethlehem and see
Him whose birth the angels sing;
Come adore, on bended knee,
Christ, the Lord, the newborn King.
  Gloria…

See him in a manger laid,
Whom the choirs of angels praise;
Mary, Joseph, lend your aid,
While our hearts in love we raise.
    Gloria…

Go Tell It on the Mountain

140

GO TELL IT ON THE MOUNTAIN 7.6.7.6 with refrain

African-American spiritual
Adapt. by John W. Work, Jr. (1907)

African-American spiritual
Harm. by Paul Sjolund

Refrain

Go tell it on the moun - tain, O - ver the
hills and ev - 'ry - where; Go tell it on the
moun - tain That Je - sus Christ is born!

Verse

While shep - herds kept their watch - ing O'er
si - lent flocks by night, Be - hold through - out the
heav - ens There shone a ho - ly light.

The shepherds feared and trembled
When lo! above the earth
Rang out the angel chorus
That hailed our Savior's birth. *Ref.*

Down in a lowly manger
The humble Christ was born,
And God sent us salvation
That blesséd Christmas morn. *Ref.*

141   It Came upon the Midnight Clear

CAROL CMD

Luke 2:8-14
Edmund H. Sears (1849)   Richard Storrs Willis (1850)

It came up-on the mid-night clear, That

glo - rious song of old, From

an - gels bend - ing near the earth To

touch their harps of gold: "Peace

on the earth, good will to all From

heav'n's all gra - cious King"; The

world in sol - emn still - ness lay, To

hear the an - gels sing.

Still through the cloven skies they come,
With peaceful wings unfurled,
And still their heav'nly music floats
O'er all the weary world:
Above its sad and lowly plains
They bend on hov'ring wing,
And ever o'er its Babel sounds
The blessèd angels sing.

Yet with the woes of sin and strife,
The world has suffered long;
Beneath the heav'nly hymn have rolled
Two thousand years of wrong;
And warring humankind hears not
The tidings which they bring;
O hush the noise and cease your strife
And hear the angels sing.

For lo, the days are hast'ning on,
By prophets seen of old,
When with the ever-circling years
Shall come the time foretold,
When peace shall over all the earth
Its ancient splendors fling,
And all the world give back the song
Which now the angels sing.

142   Good Christian Friends, Rejoice

IN DULCI JUBILO 6.6.7.7.7.7.5.5

Latin and German (14th C.)
Trans. by John Mason Neale (1853)

Klug's *Geistliche Lieder* (1535)
Harm. by Robert L. Pearsall

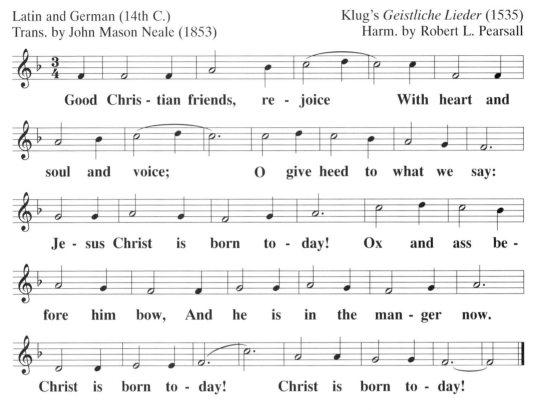

Good Chris - tian friends, re - joice With heart and
soul and voice; O give heed to what we say:
Je - sus Christ is born to - day! Ox and ass be -
fore him bow, And he is in the man - ger now.
Christ is born to - day! Christ is born to - day!

Good Christian friends, rejoice
With heart and soul and voice;
Now you hear of endless bliss:
Jesus Christ was born for this!
He has opened heaven's door,
And we are blest for evermore.
Christ was born for this!
Christ was born for this!

Good Christian friends, rejoice
With heart and soul and voice;
Now you need not fear the grave:
Jesus Christ was born to save!
Calls you one and calls you all
To gain his everlasting hall.
Christ was born to save!
Christ was born to save!

Hark! The Herald Angels Sing   143

MENDELSSOHN 7.7.7.7 D with refrain

Charles Wesley (1739), alt.   Felix Mendelssohn (1840)

Hark! the her-ald an-gels sing, "Glo-ry to the new-born King; Peace on earth, and mer-cy mild God and sin-ners rec-on-ciled!" Joy-ful, all you na-tions, rise, Join the tri-umph of the skies; With the an-gel-ic host pro-claim, "Christ is born in Beth-le-hem!" Hark! the her-ald an-gels sing, "Glo-ry to the new-born King!"

Christ, by highest heav'n adored,
Christ the everlasting Lord:
Late in time behold him come,
Offspring of the Virgin's womb.
Veiled in flesh the Godhead see:
Hail the incarnate Deity,
Pleased as man with us to dwell,
Jesus, our Emmanuel.
  Hark!...

Hail the heav'n-born Prince of Peace!
Hail the Sun of Righteousness!
Light and life to all he brings,
Ris'n with healing in his wings.
Mild he lays his glory by,
Born that we no more may die,
Born to raise us from the earth,
Born to give us second birth.
  Hark!...

144   From Heaven Above
VOM HIMMEL HOCH LM

Schumann's *Geistliche Lieder* (1539)
Vom Himmel hoch da komm ich her; Martin Luther
Harm. by Hans Leo Hassler

From heav'n a - bove   to   earth   I   come   To bring good news
to   ev - 'ry - one!   Glad tid - ings   of   great   joy   I   bring
To   all   the   world,   and   glad - ly   sing:

To you this night is born a child
Of Mary, chosen virgin mild;
This newborn child of lowly birth
Shall be the joy of all the earth.

This is the Christ, God's Son most high,
Who hears your sad and bitter cry;
He will himself your Savior be
And from all sin will set you free.

The blessing which the Father planned
The Son holds in his infant hand,
That in his kingdom bright and fair,
You may with us his glory share.

These are the signs which you will see
To let you know that it is he:
In manger-bed, in swaddling clothes
The child who all the earth upholds.

*How glad we'll be to find it so!
Then with the shepherds let us go
To see what God for us had done
In sending us his own dear Son.

*Look, look, dear friends, look over there!
What lies within that manger bare?
Who is that lovely little one?
The baby Jesus, God's dear Son.

*Welcome to earth, O noble Guest,
Through whom this sinful world is blest!
You turned not from our needs away!
How can our thanks such love repay?

*O Lord, you have created all!
How did you come to be so small,
To sweetly sleep in manger-bed
Where lowing cattle lately fed?

*Were earth a thousand times as fair
And set with gold and jewels rare,
Still such a cradle would not do
To rock a prince so great as you.

*For velvets soft and silken stuff
You have but hay and straw so rough
On which as king so rich and great
To be enthroned in humble state.

*O dearest Jesus, holy child,
Prepare a bed, soft, undefiled,
A holy shrine, within my heart,
That you and I need never part.

*My heart for very joy now leaps;
My voice no longer silence keeps;
I too must join the angel-throng
To sing with joy his cradle-song:

"Glory to God in highest heav'n,
 Who unto us his Son has giv'n."
 With angels sing in pious mirth:
 A glad new year to all the earth!

*Stanzas 6-13 may be omitted.

145   Joy to the World

ANTIOCH CM with repeat

Psalm 98:4-9
Isaac Watts (1719)

George Frederick Handel (1742)
Arr. by Lowell Mason (1836)

Joy to the world! the Lord is come: Let earth receive her King; Let ev-'ry heart prepare him room, And heav'n and na-ture
sing, And heav'n and na-ture sing, And
heav'n, and heav'n and na-ture sing.

Joy to the world! the Savior reigns:
Let us, our songs employ;
While fields and floods, rocks,
   hills, and plains
Repeat the sounding joy,
Repeat the sounding joy,
Repeat, repeat the sounding joy.

No more let sin and sorrows grow,
Nor thorns infest the ground;
He comes to make his blessings flow
Far as the curse is found,
Far as the curse is found,
Far as, far as the curse is found.

He rules the world with truth and grace,
And makes the nations prove
The glories of his righteousness,
And wonders of his love,
And wonders of his love,
And wonders, wonders of his love.

Silent Night, Holy Night   **146**

STILLE NACHT 6.6.8.9.6.6

Joseph Mohr (1818)
Trans. by John F. Young (1863)   Franz X. Gruber (1818)

Si - lent night, ho - ly night, All is calm, all is bright Round yon Vir - gin Moth- er and Child, Ho - ly In - fant so ten - der and mild, Sleep in heav- en- ly peace, Sleep in heav - en - ly peace.

Silent night, holy night,	Silent night, holy night,
Shepherds quake at the sight;	Son of God, love's pure light
Glories stream from heaven afar,	Radiant beams from thy holy face,
Heav'nly hosts sing alleluia;	With the dawn of redeeming grace,
Christ, the Savior, is born!	Jesus, Lord, at thy birth,
Christ, the Savior, is born!	Jesus, Lord, at thy birth.

147   As with Gladness Men of Old

DIX 7.7.7.7.7.7

Conrad Kocher (1838)
Arr. by William Henry Monk (1861)

William Chatterton Dix (1860)

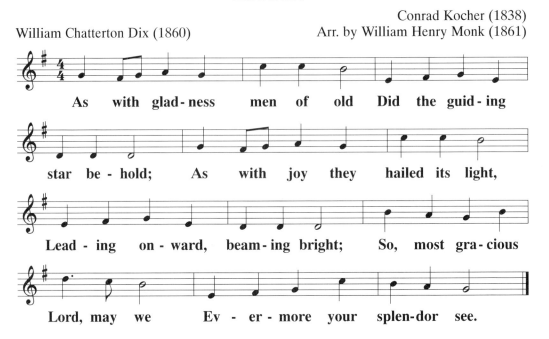

As with glad-ness men of old Did the guid-ing
star be-hold; As with joy they hailed its light,
Lead-ing on-ward, beam-ing bright; So, most gra-cious
Lord, may we Ev-er-more your splen-dor see.

As with joyful steps they sped
To that lowly manger-bed,
There to bend the knee before
Christ whom heav'n and earth adore;
So may we with hurried pace
Run to seek your throne of grace.

As they offered gifts most rare
At that manger crude and bare;
So may we this holy day,
Drawn to you without delay,
All our costliest treasures bring,
Christ, to you, our heav'nly King.

Christ Redeemer, with us stay,
Help us live your holy way;
And when earthly things are past,
Bring our ransomed souls at last
Where they need no star to guide,
Where no clouds your glory hide.

In the heav'nly city bright
None shall need created light;
You, its light, its joy, its crown,
You, its sun which goes not down;
There for ever may we sing
Alleluias to our King.

We Three Kings of Orient Are

148

KINGS OF ORIENT 8.8.4.4.6 with refrain

Matthew 2:1-11
John Henry Hopkins, Jr. (1857)   John Henry Hopkins, Jr. (1857)

We three kings of O - ri - ent are, Bear - ing
gifts we trav - erse a - far Field and foun - tain,
Moor and moun - tain, Fol - low - ing yon - der star.
O star of won - der, star of night, Star with
roy - al beau - ty bright, West - ward lead - ing,
still pro - ceed - ing, Guide us to the per - fect Light.

Born a babe on Bethlehem's plain, / Gold we bring to crown him again;
King for ever, Ceasing never, / Over us all to reign. *O…*

Frankincense to offer have I; / Incense owns a Deity nigh,
Prayer and praising, Gladly raising, / Worshiping God on high. *O…*

Myrrh is mine: its bitter perfume / Breathes a life of gath'ring gloom;
Sorrowing, sighing, Bleeding, dying, / Sealed in the stone cold tomb. *O…*

Glorious now behold him rise, / King and God and sacrifice:
Heav'n sings, "Hallelujah!" / "Hallelujah!" earth replies. *O…*

149   How Brightly Beams the Morning Star

WIE SCHÖN LEUCHTET 8.8.7.8.8.7.4.4.4.4.8

Philipp Nicolai (1599)   Philipp Nicolai (1599)
Trans. from *Lutheran Book of Worship* (1978), alt.   Harm. by Johann Sebastian Bach

How bright - ly beams the morn - ing star! What

sud - den ra - diance from a - far A - glow with grace and

mer - cy! Of Ja - cob's race, King Da - vid's Son, Our

Lord and mas - ter, you have won Our hearts to serve you

on - ly! Low - ly, ho - ly! Great and glo - rious,

All vic - to - rious, Rich in bless - ing!

Rule and might o'er all pos - sess - ing!

Come, heav'nly bridegroom, light divine,
And deep within our hearts now shine;
There light a flame undying!
In you one body let us be
As living branches of a tree
Your life our lives supplying.
Now, though daily
Earth's deep sadness
May perplex us
And distress us,
Yet with heav'nly joy you bless us.

O let the harps break forth in sound!
Our joy be all with music crowned,
Our voices richly blending!
For Christ goes with us all the way—
Today, tomorrow, ev'ry day!
His love is never ending!
Sing out! Ring out!
Jubilation!
Exultation!
Tell the story!
Great is he, the King of glory!

150 Your Hands, O Lord, in Days of Old
MOZART CMD

Matthew 14:35-36
Edward H. Plumptre, alt.

Adapt. from Wolfgang Amadeus Mozart

Your hands, O Lord, in days of old Were
strong to heal and save; They tri-umphed o-ver
pain and death, Fought dark-ness and the grave. To
you they went, the blind, the mute, The
pal-sied, and the lame, The lep-er set a-
part and shunned The sick and those in shame.

And then your touch brought
  life and health,
Gave speech, and strength,
  and sight;
And youth renewed
  and health restored,
Claimed you, the Lord of light:
And so, O Lord, be near to bless,
Almighty now as then,
In ev'ry street, in ev'ry home,
In ev'ry troubled friend.

O be our mighty healer still,
O Lord of life and death;
Restore and strengthen,
  soothe and bless,
With your almighty breath:
On hands that work
  and eyes that see,
Your healing wisdom pour,
That whole and sick,
  and weak and strong,
May praise you evermore.

Swiftly Pass the Clouds of Glory   151

GENEVA 8.7.8.7 D

Thomas H. Troeger (1985)   George Henry Day (1940)

Swift - ly pass the clouds of glo - ry,
Heav - en's voice, the daz - zling light; Mo - ses and E -
li - jah van - ish; Christ a - lone com - mands the height!
Pe - ter, James, and John fall si - lent,
Turn - ing from the sum - mit's rise Down - ward toward the
shad - owed val - ley Where their Lord has fixed his eyes.

Glimpsed and gone the revelation,
They shall gain and keep its truth,
Not by building on the mountain
Any shrine or sacred booth,
But by following the Savior
Through the valley to the cross
And by testing faith's resilience
Through betrayal, pain, and loss.

Lord, transfigure our perception
With the purest light that shines,
And recast our life's intentions
To the shape of your designs,
Till we seek no other glory
Than what lies past Calv'ry's hill
And our living and our dying
And our rising by your will.

152 Out of the Depths I Cry to You

AUS TIEFER NOT 8.7.8.7.8.8.7

Psalm 120:1-2, 130
Martin Luther (1524)
Trans. by Gracia Grindal (1978)

Attr. to Martin Luther (1524)
Harm. by Austin C. Lovelace (1963)

Out of the depths I cry to you; O Lord, now hear me call - ing. In - cline your ear to my dis - tress In spite of my re - bel - ling. Do not re - gard my sin - ful deeds. Send me the grace my spir - it needs; With - out it I am noth - ing.

All things you send are full of grace;
You crown our lives with favor.
All our good works are done in vain
Without our Lord and Savior.
We praise the God who gives us faith
And saves us from the grip of death;
Our lives are in God's keeping.

It is in God that we shall hope,
And not in our own merit;
We rest our fears in God's good Word
And trust the Holy Spirit,
Whose promise keeps us strong and sure;
We trust the holy signature
Inscribed upon our temples.

My soul is waiting for the Lord
As one who longs for morning;
No watcher waits with greater hope
Than I for Christ's returning.
I hope as Israel in the Lord,
Who sends redemption through the Word.
Praise God for endless mercy.

Wilt Thou Forgive   **153**

SO GIEBST DU NUN 10.10.10.10.8.4

Geist und Lehr-reiches Kirchen und Haus Buch (1694)

John Donne (1573-1631)   Harm. by Johann Sebastian Bach

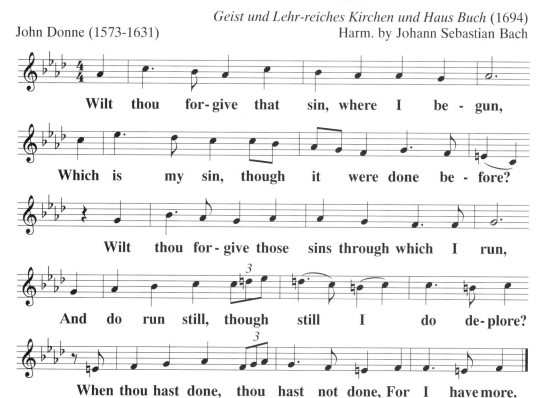

Wilt thou for-give that sin, where I be - gun,

Which is my sin, though it were done be - fore?

Wilt thou for-give those sins through which I run,

And do run still, though still I do de-plore?

When thou hast done, thou hast not done, For I have more.

Wilt thou forgive that sin, by which I won
Others to sin, and made my sin their door?
Wilt thou forgive that sin which I did shun
A year or two, but wallowed in a score?
When thou hast done, thou hast not done,
For I have more.

I have a sin of fear that when I've spun
My last thread, I shall perish on the shore;
Swear by thyself, that at my death thy Son
Shall shine as he shines now, and heretofore.
And having done that, thou hast done,
I fear no more.

154 My Faith Looks Up to Thee

OLIVET 6.6.4.6.6.6.4

Ray Palmer (1875)

Lowell Mason (1831)

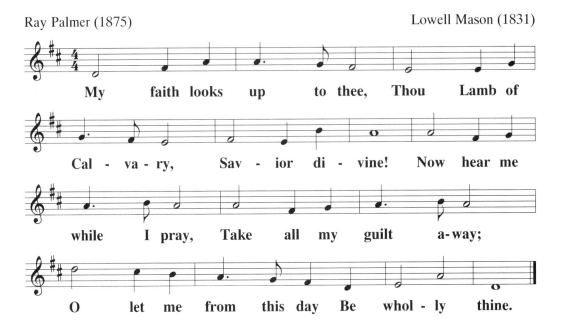

My faith looks up to thee, Thou Lamb of
Cal - va - ry, Sav - ior di - vine! Now hear me
while I pray, Take all my guilt a-way;
O let me from this day Be whol - ly thine.

May thy rich grace impart
Strength to my fainting heart,
My zeal inspire;
As thou hast died for me,
O may my love to thee
Pure, warm, and changeless be,
A living fire.

While life's dark maze I tread,
And griefs around me spread,
Be thou my guide;
Bid darkness turn to day;
Wipe sorrow's tears away,
Nor let me ever stray
From thee aside.

O Saving Victim

DUGUET LM

155

Attr. to Thomas Aquinas (13th C.)
Trans. by Edward Caswall, alt.

Dieu donne Duguet

O Sav - ing Vic - tim, o - p'ning wide The
gate of heav'n to us be - low! Our foes press on from
ev - 'ry side: Your aid sup - ply, your strength be - stow.

To your great name be endless praise,
Immortal Godhead, One-in-Three;
O grant us endless length of days
When our true native land we see.

156 Lord, Who throughout These Forty Days

ST. FLAVIAN CM

Day's *Psalter* (1562)

Claudia Frances Hernaman (1873)

Adapt. and harm. by Richard Redhead

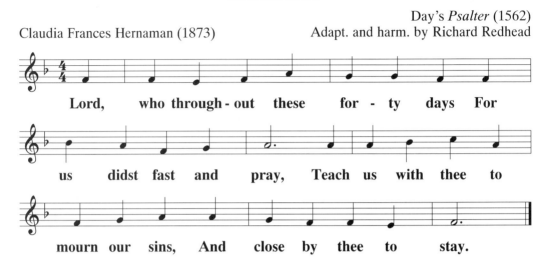

Lord, who through-out these for - ty days For

us didst fast and pray, Teach us with thee to

mourn our sins, And close by thee to stay.

As thou with Satan didst contend
And didst the vict'ry win,
O give us strength in thee to fight,
In thee to conquer sin.

As thou didst hunger bear and thirst,
So teach us, gracious Lord,
To die to self, and chiefly live
By thy most holy word.

And through these days of penitence,
And through thy Passiontide,
Yea, evermore, in life and death,
Jesus! with us abide.

Abide with us, that so, this life
Of suff'ring overpast,
An Easter of unending joy
We may attain at last!

Jesus, Keep Me Near the Cross   157

NEAR THE CROSS 7.6.7.6 with refrain

Fanny J. Crosby (1869)   William H. Doane (1869)

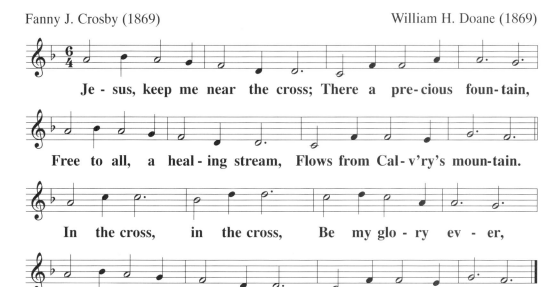

Je - sus, keep me near the cross; There a pre-cious foun-tain,

Free to all, a heal - ing stream, Flows from Cal- v'ry's moun-tain.

In the cross, in the cross, Be my glo - ry ev - er,

Till my rap-tured soul shall find Rest be-yond the riv - er.

Near the cross, a trembling soul,
Love and mercy found me;
There the bright and morning star
Sheds its beams around me.
   In the cross…

Near the cross! O Lamb of God,
Bring its scenes before me;
Help me walk from day to day
With its shadow o'er me.
   In the cross…

Near the cross I'll watch and wait,
Hoping, trusting ever,
Till I reach the golden strand
Just beyond the river.
   In the cross…

158   By the Babylonian Rivers

KAS DZIEDAJA 8.7.8.7

Latvian folk melody
Acc. by Robert J. Batastini (1995)

Psalm 137

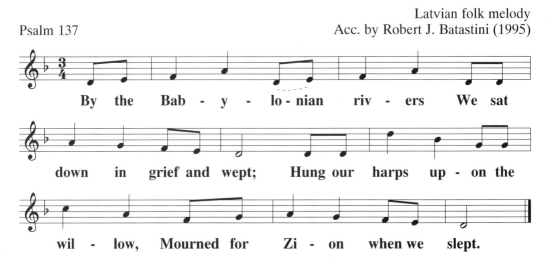

By the Bab - y - lo - nian riv - ers We sat

down in grief and wept; Hung our harps up - on the

wil - low, Mourned for Zi - on when we slept.

There our captors in derision
Did require of us a song;
So we sat with staring vision,
And the days were hard and long.

How shall we sing the Lord's song
In a strange and bitter land;
Can our voices veil the sorrow?
Lord God, hold your holy band.

Let the Cross be benediction
For those bound in tyranny;
By the pow'r of resurrection
Loose them from captivity.

Forty Days and Forty Nights   159

HEINLEIN 7.7.7.7

George H. Smyttan (1856), alt.

Attr. to Martin Herbst (1676), alt.
Harm. by William Henry Monk

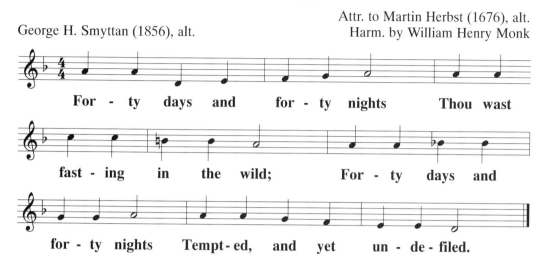

For - ty days and for - ty nights Thou wast

fast - ing in the wild; For - ty days and

for - ty nights Tempt - ed, and yet un - de - filed.

Should not we thy sorrow share
And from worldly joys abstain,
Fasting with unceasing prayer,
Strong with thee to suffer pain?

Then if Satan on us press,
Jesus, Savior, hear our call!
Victor in the wilderness,
Grant we may not faint nor fall!

So shall we have peace divine:
Holier gladness ours shall be;
Round us, too, shall angels shine,
Such as ministered to thee.

Keep, O keep us, Savior dear,
Ever constant by thy side;
That with thee we may appear
At the eternal Eastertide.

160   Beneath the Cross of Jesus

ST. CHRISTOPHER 7.6.8.6.8.6.8.6

Elizabeth C. Clephane (1872)   Frederick C. Maker (1881)

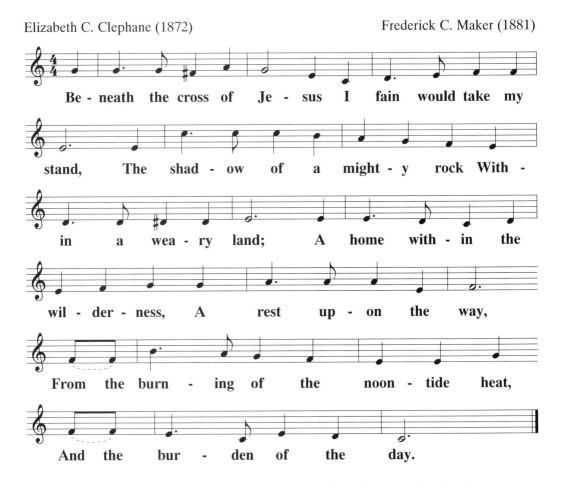

Be - neath the cross of Je - sus I fain would take my
stand, The shad - ow of a might - y rock With -
in a wea - ry land; A home with - in the
wil - der - ness, A rest up - on the way,
From the burn - ing of the noon - tide heat,
And the bur - den of the day.

Upon that cross of Jesus
Mine eye at times can see
The very dying form of One
Who suffered there for me;
And from my stricken heart
  with tears
Two wonders I confess:
The wonders of redeeming love
And my unworthiness.

I take, O cross, thy shadow
For my abiding place;
I ask no other sunshine than
The sunshine of his face;
Content to let the world go by,
To know no gain nor loss,
My sinful self my only shame,
My glory all the cross.

Lord Jesus, Think on Me

SOUTHWELL SM

161

Synesius of Cyrene (c. 370-414)
Trans. by Allen W. Chatfield (1876)

Daman's *Psalmes* (1579), alt.

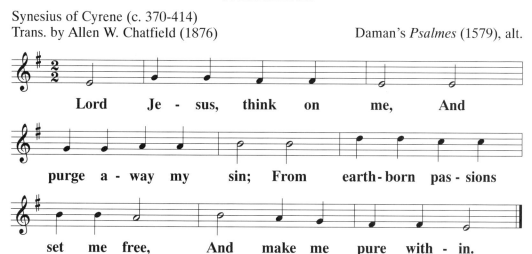

Lord Je - sus, think on me, And purge a - way my sin; From earth-born pas - sions set me free, And make me pure with - in.

Lord Jesus, think on me,
Amid the battle's strife;
In all my pain and misery
Be thou my health and life.

Lord Jesus, think on me,
Nor let me go astray;
Through darkness and perplexity
Point thou the heav'nly way.

Lord Jesus, think on me,
That, when this life is past,
I may the eternal brightness see,
And share thy joy at last.

162   Go to Dark Gethsemane

REDHEAD 76 7.7.7.7.7.7

James Montgomery (1825)   Richard Redhead (1853)

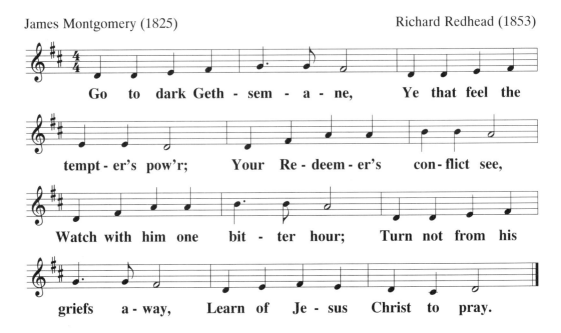

Go to dark Geth - sem - a - ne, Ye that feel the
tempt - er's pow'r; Your Re - deem - er's con - flict see,
Watch with him one bit - ter hour; Turn not from his
griefs a - way, Learn of Je - sus Christ to pray.

Follow to the judgment hall;	Calv'ry's mournful mountain climb;
View the Lord of life arraigned;	There, adoring at his feet,
O the wormwood and the gall!	Mark the miracle of time,
O the pangs his soul sustained!	God's own sacrifice complete;
Shun not suff'ring, shame, or loss;	"It is finished!" hear him cry;
Learn of him to bear the cross.	Learn of Jesus Christ to die.

What Wondrous Love Is This   163

WONDROUS LOVE 12.9.12.12.9

Alexander Means (1823)

Southern Harmony (1835)
Harm. from *Cantate Domino* (1980)

What won-drous love is this, O my soul, O my soul?

What won-drous love is this, O my soul?

What won-drous love is this that caused the Lord of bliss

To bear the dread-ful curse for my soul, for my soul;

To bear the dread - ful curse for my soul?

To God and to the Lamb I will sing, I will sing;
To God and to the Lamb, I will sing;
To God and to the Lamb who is the great I AM,
While millions join the theme, I will sing, I will sing;
While millions join the theme, I will sing.

And when from death I'm free, I'll sing on, I'll sing on;
And when from death I'm free, I'll sing on;
And when from death I'm free, I'll sing and joyful be,
And through eternity I'll sing on, I'll sing on!
And through eternity I'll sing on.

164 All Glory, Laud, and Honor

ST. THEODULPH 7.6.7.6 D

Theodulph of Orleans (c. 820)
Trans. by John Mason Neale (1851), alt.

Melchior Teschner (1615)

The company of angels / Are praising you on high;
And mortals, joined with all things / Created, make reply. *Ref.*

The people of the Hebrews / With palms before you went:
Our praise and prayers and anthems / Before you we present. *Ref.*

To you before your passion / They sang their hymns of praise:
To you, now high exalted, / Our melody we raise. *Ref.*

Their praises you accepted, / Accept the prayers we bring,
Great source of love and goodness, / Our Savior and our King. *Ref.*

Ah, Holy Jesus

HERZLIEBSTER JESU 11.11.11.5

165

Johann Heermann (1630)
Trans. by Robert Seymour Bridges (1899)

Johann Crüger (1640), alt.

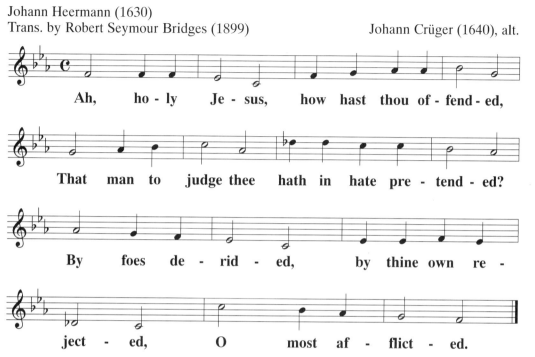

Ah, ho-ly Je-sus, how hast thou of-fend-ed,

That man to judge thee hath in hate pre-tend-ed?

By foes de-rid-ed, by thine own re-

ject-ed, O most af-flict-ed.

Who was the guilty? Who brought this upon thee?
Alas, my treason, Jesus, hath undone thee.
'Twas I, Lord Jesus, I it was denied thee:
I crucified thee.

Lo, the Good Shepherd for the sheep is offered;
The slave hath sinnéd, and the Son hath suffered;
For our atonement, while we nothing heeded,
God interceded.

For me, kind Jesus, was thy incarnation,
Thy mortal sorrow, and thy life's oblation;
Thy death of anguish and thy bitter passion,
For my salvation.

Therefore, kind Jesus, since I cannot pay thee,
I do adore thee, and will ever pray thee,
Think on thy pity and thy love unswerving,
Not my deserving.

166   There Is a Green Hill Far Away

HORSLEY CM

Cecil Frances Alexander, alt.

William Horsley

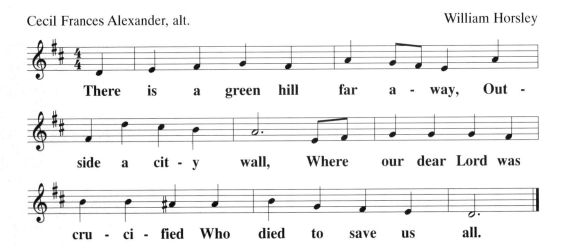

There is a green hill far a-way, Out-side a cit-y wall, Where our dear Lord was cru-ci-fied Who died to save us all.

We may not know, we cannot tell,
What pains he had to bear,
But we believe it was for us
He hung and suffered there.

He died that we might be forgiv'n,
He died to make us good,
That we might go at last to heav'n,
Saved by his precious blood.

There was no other good enough
To pay the price of sin,
He only could unlock the gate
Of heav'n and let us in.

O dearly, dearly has he loved!
And we must love him too,
And trust in his redeeming blood,
And try his works to do.

Alas! and Did My Savior Bleed   **167**
MARTYRDOM CM

Isaac Watts (1707)   Attr. to Hugh Wilson (1827)

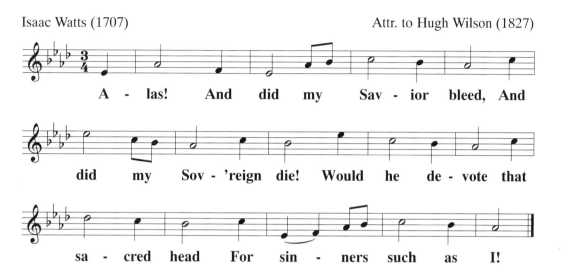

A - las! And did my Sav - ior bleed, And

did my Sov - 'reign die! Would he de - vote that

sa - cred head For sin - ners such as I!

Was it for sins that I have done   Well might the sun in darkness hide,
He suffered on the tree?   And shut its glories in,
Amazing pity! Grace unknown!   When Christ, the great Redeemer, died
And love beyond degree!   For human creatures' sin.

But drops of grief can ne'er repay
The debt of love I owe;
Here, Lord, I give myself away;
'Tis all that I can do.

168   O Sacred Head, Now Wounded

PASSION CHORALE 7.6.7.6 D

Matthew 27:27-31; Mark 15:16-20; John 19:1-5
Anonymous Latin
Trans. by Paul Gerhardt (1656) and   Hans Leo Hassler (1601)
    James W. Alexander (1830)   Harm. by Johann Sebastian Bach (1729), alt.

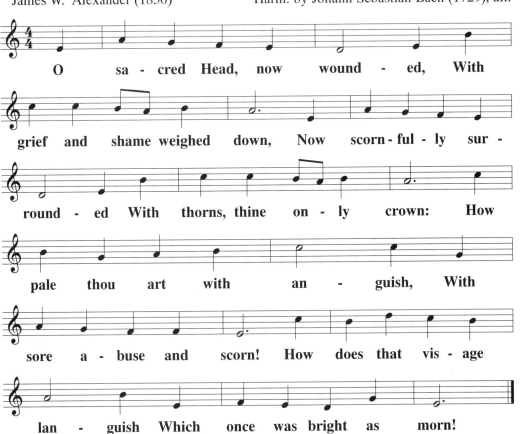

O sa - cred Head, now wound - ed, With
grief and shame weighed down, Now scorn - ful - ly sur -
round - ed With thorns, thine on - ly crown: How
pale thou art with an - guish, With
sore a - buse and scorn! How does that vis - age
lan - guish Which once was bright as morn!

What thou, my Lord, hast suffered
Was all for sinners' gain;
Mine, mine was the transgression,
But thine the deadly pain.
Lo, here I fall, my Savior!
'Tis I deserve thy place;
Look on me with thy favor,
Vouchsafe to me thy grace.

What language shall I borrow
To thank thee, dearest friend,
For this thy dying sorrow,
Thy pity without end?
O make me thine for ever;
And should I fainting be,
Lord, let me never, never
Outlive my love to thee.

Were You There   169

WERE YOU THERE 10.10 with refrain

African-American spiritual
Harm. by Charles Winfred Douglas (1940)

African-American spiritual

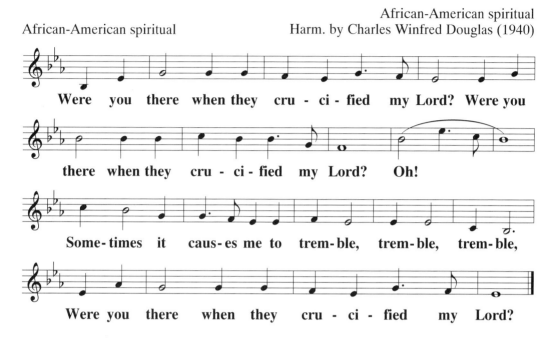

Were you there when they cru-ci-fied my Lord? Were you
there when they cru-ci-fied my Lord? Oh!
Some-times it caus-es me to trem-ble, trem-ble, trem-ble,
Were you there when they cru-ci-fied my Lord?

Were you there when they nailed him to the tree?...

Were you there when they pierced him in the side?...

Were you there when the sun refused to shine?...

Were you there when they laid him in the tomb?...

Were you there when they rolled the stone away?...

170   When I Survey the Wondrous Cross

ROCKINGHAM LM

Galatians 6:14   *Second Supplement to Psalmody in Miniature* (1783)
Isaac Watts (1707)   Adapt. by Edward Miller (1790)

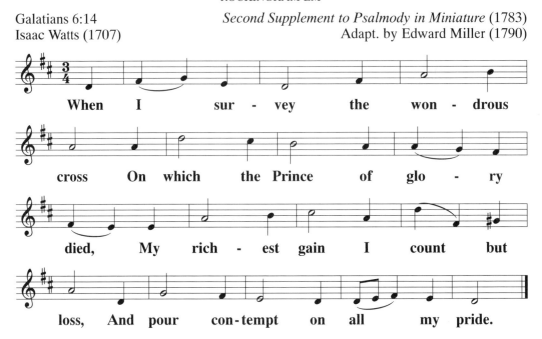

When I sur-vey the won-drous cross On which the Prince of glo-ry died, My rich-est gain I count but loss, And pour con-tempt on all my pride.

Forbid it, Lord, that I should boast,
Save in the death of Christ, my God;
All the vain things that charm me most,
I sacrifice them to his blood.

See, from his head, his hands, his feet,
Sorrow and love flow mingled down.
Did e'er such love and sorrow meet,
Or thorns compose so rich a crown?

Were the whole realm of nature mine,
That were an off'ring far too small;
Love so amazing, so divine,
Demands my soul, my life, my all.

When I Survey the Wondrous Cross **171**

HAMBURG LM

Galatians 6:14
Isaac Watts (1707)

Lowell Mason (1824)

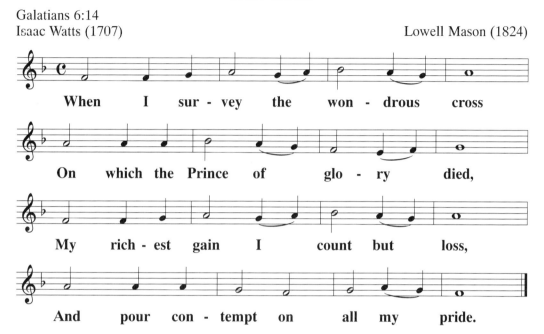

When I sur - vey the won - drous cross

On which the Prince of glo - ry died,

My rich - est gain I count but loss,

And pour con - tempt on all my pride.

Forbid it, Lord, that I should boast,
Save in the death of Christ, my God;
All the vain things that charm me most,
I sacrifice them to his blood.

See, from his head, his hands, his feet,
Sorrow and love flow mingled down.
Did e'er such love and sorrow meet,
Or thorns compose so rich a crown?

Were the whole realm of nature mine,
That were an off'ring far too small;
Love so amazing, so divine,
Demands my soul, my life, my all.

172 Ride On! Ride On in Majesty!

ST. DROSTANE LM

Henry Hart Milman (1827)

John Bacchus Dykes (1862)

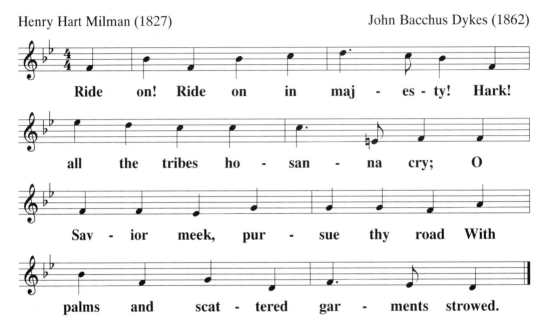

Ride on! Ride on in maj - es - ty! Hark!
all the tribes ho - san - na cry; O
Sav - ior meek, pur - sue thy road With
palms and scat - tered gar - ments strowed.

Ride on! Ride on in majesty!
In lowly pomp ride on to die:
O Christ, thy triumphs now begin
O'er captive death
    and conquered sin.

Ride on! Ride on in majesty!
The wingéd squadrons of the sky
Look down with sad
    and wond'ring eyes
To see the approaching sacrifice.

Ride on! Ride on in majesty!
In lowly pomp ride on to die;
Bow thy meek head to mortal pain,
Then take, O God, thy pow'r, and reign.

That Easter Day with Joy Was Bright 173

PUER NOBIS LM

Claro paschali gaudio, Latin (5th C.) Trier ms (15th C.)
Trans. by John Mason Neale (1851), alt. Adapt. by Michael Praetorius (1609)

That Eas - ter day with joy was bright, The sun shone
out with fair - er light, When to their long - ing
eyes re - stored, The a - pos - tles saw their ris - en Lord.

His risen flesh with radiance glowed;
His wounded hands and feet he showed;
Those scars their solemn witness gave
That Christ was risen from the grave.

O Jesus, King of gentleness,
Who with your grace our hearts possess
That we may give you all our days
The willing tribute of our praise.

O Lord of all, with us abide
In this our joyful Eastertide;
From ev'ry weapon death can wield
Your own redeemed for ever shield.

All praise, to you, O risen Lord,
Now both by heav'n and earth adored;
To God the Father equal praise,
And Spirit blest, our songs we raise.

174 Good Christians All, Rejoice and Sing

GELOBT SEI GOTT 8.8.8 with alleluias

Cyril A. Alington (1925), alt.   Melchior Vulpius (1609)

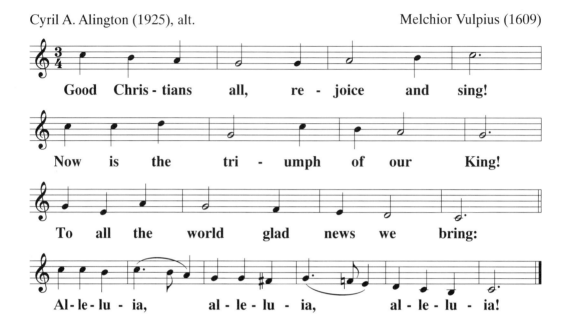

Good Chris - tians all, re - joice and sing!

Now is the tri - umph of our King!

To all the world glad news we bring:

Al - le - lu - ia, al - le - lu - ia, al - le - lu - ia!

The Lord of life is ris'n today.
Sing songs of praise along his way.
Let all the world rejoice and say:
Alleluia, alleluia, alleluia!

Praise we in songs of victory
That love, that life which cannot die,
And sing with hearts uplifted high:
Alleluia, alleluia, alleluia!

Your name we bless, O risen Lord,
And sing today with one accord
The life laid down, the life restored:
Alleluia, alleluia, alleluia!

The Strife Is O'er

175

VICTORY 8.8.8 with alleluias

Anonymous Latin (12th C.)   Giovanni da Palestrina (1591)
Trans. by Francis Pott (1861), alt.   Adapt. by William Henry Monk (1861)

Refrain

Al - le - lu - ia! Al - le - lu - ia! Al - le - lu - ia!

Verse

The strife is o'er, the bat - tle done; Now is the

Vic - tor's tri - umph won; Now be the song of

praise be - gun: Al - le - lu - ia!

Death's mightiest pow'rs have done their worst
And Jesus has his foes dispersed;
Let shouts of praise and joy outburst:
Alleluia! *Ref.*

He closed the yawning gates of hell;
The bars from heav'n's high portals fell;
Let hymns of praise his triumph tell:
Alleluia! *Ref.*

On the third morn he rose again
Glorious in majesty to reign;
O let us swell the joyful strain:
Alleluia! *Ref.*

176 Hail Thee, Festival Day

SALVE FESTA DIES Irregular with refrain

Venantius Honorius Fortunatus (c. 530-609)   Ralph Vaughan Williams (1906)

Hail thee, fes - ti - val day! Blest day that art

hal - lowed for ev - er; Day when our Lord was

First time only | *All other times*

raised, break - ing the king - dom of death. death.

1. All   the fair beau - ty of earth   from the
3. God   the Al - might - y, the Lord,   the
5. Spir - it of life and of pow'r,   now

death of the win - ter a - ris - ing! Ev - 'ry good
rul - er of earth and the heav - ens, Guard us from
flow in us, fount of our be - ing, Light that en -

D.C.

gift of the year   now with its mas - ter re - turns.
harm with - out;   cleanse us from e - vil with - in.
light - ens us all,   life that in all may a - bide.

2. Rise from the grave now, O Lord, the au - thor of
4. Je - sus, the health of the world, en - light - en our
6. Praise to the giv - er of good! O Lov - er and

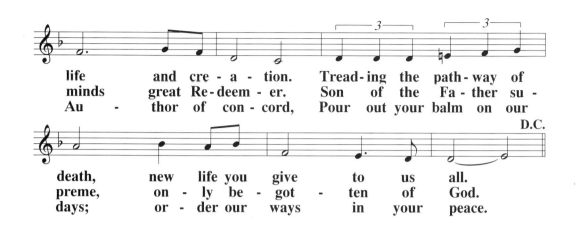

life	and cre - a - tion.	Tread-ing the path-way of
minds	great Re-deem - er.	Son of the Fa - ther su -
Au -	thor of con - cord,	Pour out your balm on our

D.C.

death,	new life you give	to us all.
preme,	on - ly be - got - ten	of God.
days;	or - der our ways	in your peace.

177   Christ Is Alive

TRURO LM

Romans 6:5-11
Brian Wren (1975)   Williams' *Psalmodia Evangelica* (1789)

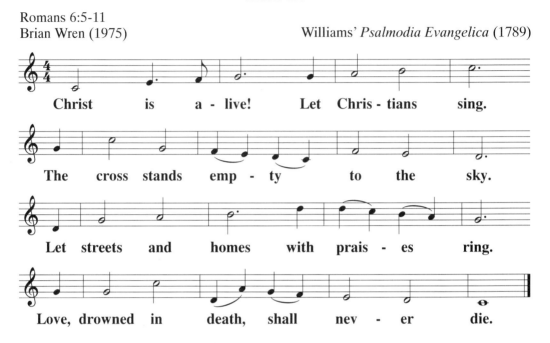

Christ is a - live! Let Chris - tians sing.

The cross stands emp - ty to the sky.

Let streets and homes with prais - es ring.

Love, drowned in death, shall nev - er die.

Christ is alive! No longer bound
To distant years in Palestine,
But saving, healing, here and now,
And touching ev'ry place and time.

In ev'ry insult, rift, and war,
Where color, scorn or wealth divide,
Christ suffers still, yet loves the more,
And lives, where even hope has died.

Women and men, in age and youth,
Can feel the Spirit, hear the call,
And find the way, the life, the truth,
Revealed in Jesus, freed for all.

Christ is alive, and comes to bring
Good news to this and ev'ry age,
Till earth and sky and ocean ring
With joy, with justice, love and praise.

The Day of Resurrection 178

ELLACOMBE 7.6.7.6 D

John of Damascus (8th C.) *Gesangbuch der Herzogl,* Wirtemberg (1784)
Trans. by John Mason Neale (1862) Harm. by William Henry Monk (1868)

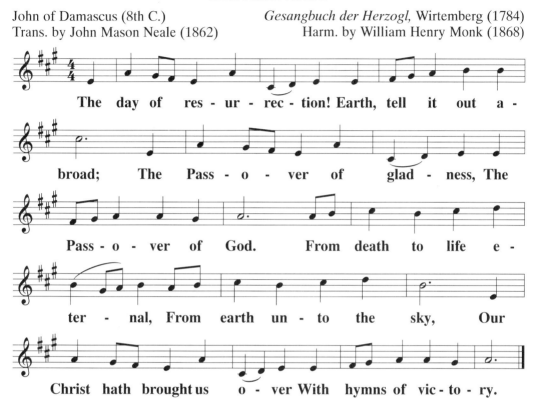

The day of res - ur - rec - tion! Earth, tell it out a -
broad; The Pass - o - ver of glad - ness, The
Pass - o - ver of God. From death to life e -
ter - nal, From earth un - to the sky, Our
Christ hath brought us o - ver With hymns of vic - to - ry.

Our hearts be pure from evil,
That we may see aright
The Lord in rays eternal
Of resurrection light;
And, list'ning to his accents,
May hear so calm and plain
His own "All hail!" and, hearing,
May raise the victor strain.

Now let the heav'ns be joyful,
Let earth her song begin,
The round world keep high triumph,
And all that is therein;
Let all things seen and unseen
Their notes together blend,
For Christ the Lord is risen,
Our joy that hath no end.

179 At the Lamb's High Feast We Sing

SALZBURG 7.7.7.7 D

Ad regias agni dapes; Latin (4th C.)
Trans. by Robert Campbell (1850), alt.

Jakob Hintze (1678)
Harm. by Johann Sebastian Bach

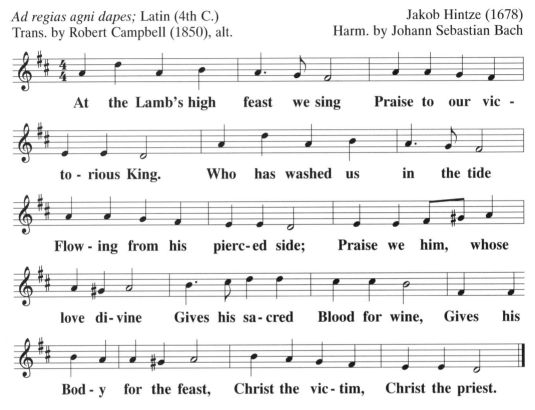

At the Lamb's high feast we sing Praise to our vic-
to-rious King. Who has washed us in the tide
Flow-ing from his pierc-ed side; Praise we him, whose
love di-vine Gives his sa-cred Blood for wine, Gives his
Bod-y for the feast, Christ the vic-tim, Christ the priest.

Where the Paschal blood is poured,
Death's dark angel sheathes his sword;
Israel's hosts triumphant go
Through the wave that drowns the foe.
Praise we Christ, whose blood was shed,
Paschal victim, Paschal bread;
With sincerity and love
Eat we manna from above.

Mighty victim from the sky,
Hell's fierce pow'rs beneath you lie;
You have conquered in the fight,
You have brought us life and light:
Now no more can death appall,
Now no more the grave enthrall;
You have opened paradise,
And in you your saints shall rise.

Easter triumph, Easter joy,
This alone can sin destroy;
From sin's pow'r, Lord, set us free
Newborn souls in you to be.
Father, who the crown shall give,
Savior, by whose death we live,
Spirit, guide through all our days,
Three in One, your name we praise.

O Sons and Daughters, Let Us Sing!   180

O FILII ET FILIAE 8.8.8 with alleluias

Attr. to Jean Tisserand   French tune (15th C.)
Trans. by John Mason Neale (1852)   *Airs sur les hymnes sacrez, odes et nöels* (1623)

That Easter morn, at break of day, / The faithful women went their way
To seek the tomb where Jesus lay. / Alleluia! Alleluia!

An angel clad in white they see, / Who sat, and spoke unto the three,
"Your Lord goes on to Galilee." / Alleluia! Alleluia!

That night the apostles met in fear; / Among them came their Lord most dear,
And said, "My peace be with you here." / Alleluia! Alleluia!

On this most holy day of days, / To God your hearts and voices raise,
In laud and jubilee and praise. / Alleluia! Alleluia!

181   Hail, Thou Once Despised Jesus

IN BABILONE 8.7.8.7 D

Revelation 4:2-11
Attr. to John Bakewell (1757)   Traditional Dutch melody
    and Martin Madan (1760), alt.   Arr. by Julius Röntgen (1906)

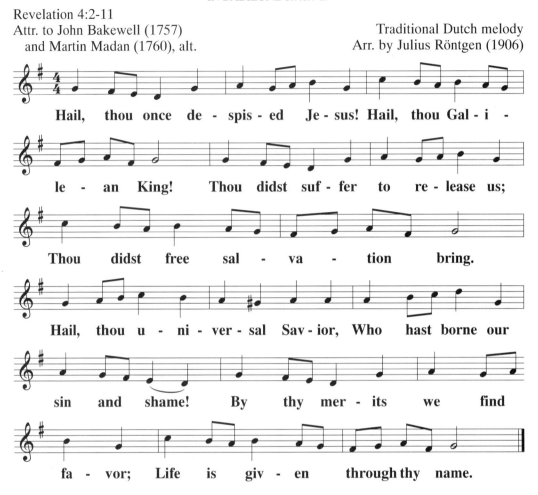

Hail, thou once de - spis - ed Je - sus! Hail, thou Gal - i -
le - an King! Thou didst suf - fer to re - lease us;
Thou didst free sal - va - tion bring.
Hail, thou u - ni - ver - sal Sav - ior, Who hast borne our
sin and shame! By thy mer - its we find
fa - vor; Life is giv - en through thy name.

Paschal Lamb, by God appointed,
All our sins on thee were laid;
By almighty love anointed,
Thou hast full atonement made.
Ev'ry sin may be forgiven
Through the virtue of thy blood;
Opened is the gate of heaven,
Reconciled are we with God.

Jesus, hail! enthroned in glory,
There for ever to abide;
All the heav'nly hosts adore thee,
Seated at thy Father's side.
There for sinners thou art pleading;
There thou dost our place prepare;
Thou for saints art interceding
Till in glory they appear.

Worship, honor, pow'r, and blessing
Christ is worthy to receive;
Loudest praises, without ceasing,
Right it is for us to give.
Help, ye bright angelic spirits,
Bring your sweetest, noblest lays;
Help to sing of Jesus' merits,
Help to chant Emmanuel's praise!

182 Welcome, Happy Morning
FORTUNATUS 11.11.11.11.11

Venantius Honorius Fortunatus (7th C.)
Trans. by John Ellerton, alt.

Arthur Seymour Sullivan (1871)

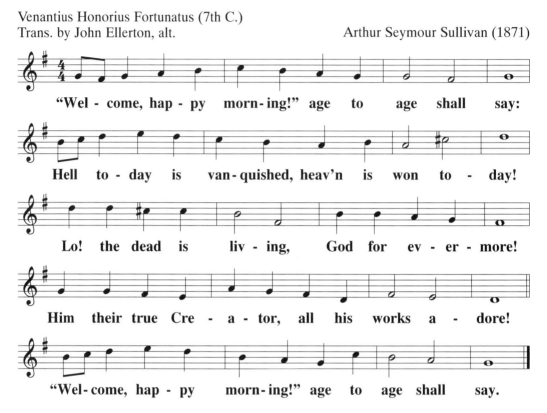

"Wel - come, hap - py morn- ing!" age to age shall say:

Hell to - day is van- quished, heav'n is won to - day!

Lo! the dead is liv - ing, God for ev - er - more!

Him their true Cre - a - tor, all his works a - dore!

"Wel- come, hap - py morn- ing!" age to age shall say.

Earth her joy confesses, clothing her for spring,
All fresh gifts returned with her returning King:
Bloom in ev'ry meadow, leaves on ev'ry bough,
Speak his sorrow ended, hail his triumph now.
    "Welcome…

Months in due succession, days of length'ning light,
Hours and passing moments praise thee in their flight.
Brightness of the morning, sky and fields and sea,
Vanquisher of darkness, bring their praise to thee.
    "Welcome…

Maker and Redeemer, life and health of all,
Thou from heav'n beholding human nature's fall,
Of the Father's Godhead true and only Son,
Mankind to deliver, manhood didst put on.
    "Welcome…

Thou, of life the author, death didst undergo,
Tread the path of darkness, saving strength to show;
Come then, true and faithful, now fulfill thy word,
'Tis thine own third morning! rise, O buried Lord!
  "Welcome...

Loose the souls long prisoned, bound with Satan's chain;
All that now is fallen raise to life again;
Show thy face in brightness, bid the nations see;
Bring again our daylight: day returns with thee!
  "Welcome...

183 Christ Jesus Lay in Death's Strong Bands

CHRIST LAG IN TODESBANDEN 8.7.8.7.7.8.7.4

Geystliche gesangk Buchleyn (1524)

Martin Luther (1524)
Trans. by Richard Massie (1854), alt.

Adapt. and harm. by
Johann Sebastian Bach (c. 1707)

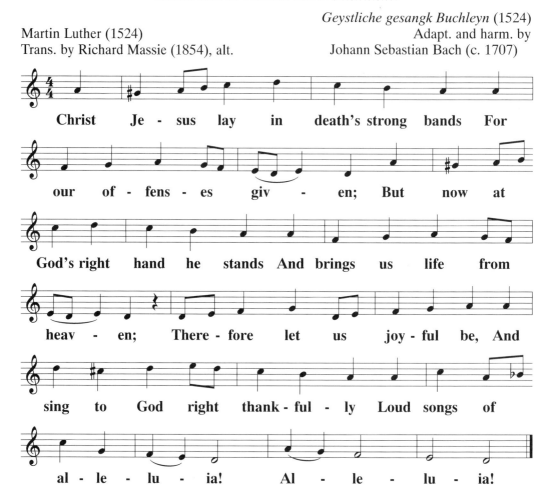

Christ Je - sus lay in death's strong bands For
our of - fens - es giv - en; But now at
God's right hand he stands And brings us life from
heav - en; There - fore let us joy - ful be, And
sing to God right thank - ful - ly Loud songs of
al - le - lu - ia! Al - le - lu - ia!

It was a strange and dreadful strife
When life and death contended;
The victory remained with life,
The reign of death was ended;
Stripped of pow'r, no more he reigns,
An empty form alone remains;
His sting is lost for ever!
Alleluia!

So let us keep the festival
To which the Lord invites us;
Christ is himself the joy of all,
The sun that warms and lights us;
By his grace he doth impart
Eternal sunshine to the heart;
The night of sin is ended!
Alleluia!

Then let us feast this holy day
On the true bread of heaven;
The word of grace hath purged away
The old and wicked leaven;
Christ alone our souls will feed,
He is our meat and drink indeed;
Faith lives upon no other!
Alleluia!

184   Come, Ye Faithful, Raise the Strain

ST. KEVIN 7.6.7.6 D

John of Damascus (c. 675-749)
Trans. by John Mason Neale (1859), alt.   Arthur Seymour Sullivan (1872)

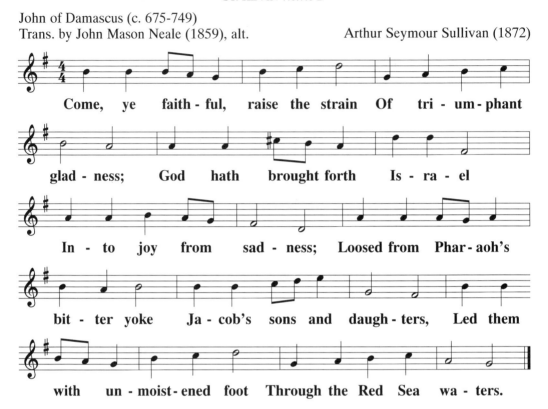

Come, ye faith-ful, raise the strain Of tri-um-phant glad-ness; God hath brought forth Is-ra-el In-to joy from sad-ness; Loosed from Phar-aoh's bit-ter yoke Ja-cob's sons and daugh-ters, Led them with un-moist-ened foot Through the Red Sea wa-ters.

'Tis the spring of souls today; / Christ hath burst his prison,
And from three days' sleep in death / As a sun hath risen;
All the winter of our sins, / Long and dark, is flying
From his light, to whom we give / Laud and praise undying.

Now the queen of seasons, bright / With the day of splendor,
With the royal feast of feasts, / Comes its joy to render;
Comes to glad Jerusalem, / Who with true affection
Welcomes in unwearied strains / Jesus' resurrection.

Neither might the gates of death, / Nor the tomb's dark portal,
Nor the watchers, nor the seal / Hold thee as a mortal;
But today amidst the twelve / Thou didst stand, bestowing
That thy peace which evermore / Passeth human knowing.

"Alleluia!" now we cry / To our King immortal,
Who, triumphant, burst the bars / Of the tomb's dark portal;
"Alleluia!" with the Son, / God the Father praising,
"Alleluia!" yet again / To the Spirit raising.

Christ the Lord Is Risen Today   185

EASTER HYMN 7.7.7.7 with alleluias

Charles Wesley (1739)   *Lyra Davidica* (1708)

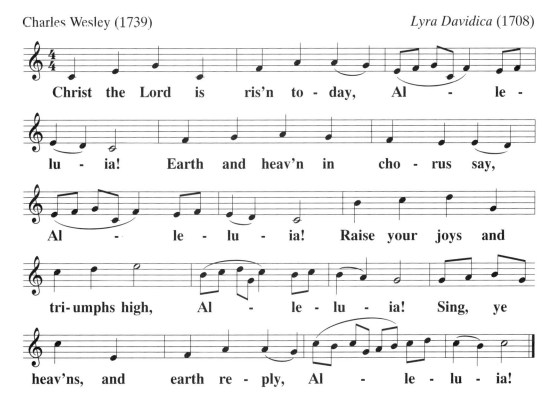

Christ the Lord is ris'n to - day, Al - le - lu - ia! Earth and heav'n in cho - rus say, Al - le - lu - ia! Raise your joys and tri-umphs high, Al - le - lu - ia! Sing, ye heav'ns, and earth re - ply, Al - le - lu - ia!

Love's redeeming work is done, Alleluia!
Fought the fight, the battle won, Alleluia!
Death in vain forbids him rise, Alleluia!
Christ has opened paradise, Alleluia!

Lives again our glorious King, Alleluia!
Where, O death, is now thy sting? Alleluia!
Once he died our souls to save, Alleluia!
Where's thy vict'ry, boasting grave? Alleluia!

Soar we now where Christ has led, Alleluia!
Foll'wing our exalted Head, Alleluia!
Made like him, like him we rise, Alleluia!
Ours the cross, the grave, the skies, Alleluia!

Hail the Lord of earth and heav'n, Alleluia!
Praise to thee by both be giv'n, Alleluia!
Thee we greet triumphant now, Alleluia!
Hail the Resurrection, thou, Alleluia!

186   Alleluia! Sing to Jesus

HYFRYDOL 8.7.8.7 D

Revelation 5:9
William Chatterton Dix (1866)

Rowland H. Prichard (1831)

Al - le - lu - ia! sing to Je - sus! His the scep - ter,
his the throne; Al - le - lu - ia! his the tri - umph,
His the vic - to - ry a - lone; Hark! the
songs of peace - ful Zi - on Thun - der like a
might - y flood; Je - sus out of ev - 'ry
na - tion Has re - deemed us by his blood.

Alleluia! not as orphans
Are we left in sorrow now;
Alleluia! he is near us,
Faith believes, nor questions how:
Though the cloud from sight received him,
When the forty days were o'er,
Shall our hearts forget his promise,
"I am with you evermore"?

Alleluia! Bread of Angels,
Here on earth our food, our stay!
Alleluia! here the sinful
Flee to you from day to day:
Intercessor, friend of sinners,
Earth's redeemer, plead for me,
Where the songs of all the sinless
Sweep across the crystal sea.

Alleluia! King eternal,
You the Lord of lords we own;
Alleluia! born of Mary,
Earth your foot stool, heav'n your throne:
You, within the veil, have entered,
Robed in flesh, our great high priest;
Here on earth both priest and victim
In the eucharistic feast.

187 Crown Him with Many Crowns

DIADEMATA SMD

Revelation 19:12
St. 1, 3, 4, Matthew Bridges (1851)
St. 2, Godfrey Thring (1874)

George J. Elvey (1868)

Crown him with man-y crowns, The Lamb up-on his throne; Hark! how the heav'n-ly an-them drowns All mu-sic but its own. A-wake, my soul, and sing Of him who set us free, And hail him as your heav'n-ly King Through all e-ter-ni-ty.

Crown him the Lord of life,
Who triumphed o'er the grave,
And rose victorious in the strife
For those he came to save.
His glories now we sing,
Who died and rose on high,
Who died, eternal life to bring,
And lives that death may die.

Crown him the Lord of love,
Behold his hands and side,
Rich wounds yet visible above
In beauty glorified.
No angel in the sky
Can fully bear that sight,
But downward bends his burning eye
At mysteries so bright.

Crown him the Lord of peace,
Whose pow'r a scepter sways
From pole to pole, that wars may cease,
Absorbed in prayer and praise.
His reign shall know no end,
And round his piercéd feet
Fair flow'rs of Paradise extend
Their fragrance ever sweet.

Rejoice, the Lord Is King

DARWALL'S 148TH 6.6.6.6.8.8

John Darwall (1770)
Harm. from *The Hymnal 1940*

Charles Wesley (1744)

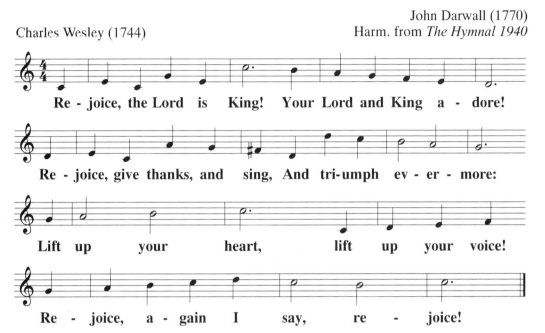

Re - joice, the Lord is King! Your Lord and King a - dore!

Re - joice, give thanks, and sing, And tri-umph ev - er - more:

Lift up your heart, lift up your voice!

Re - joice, a - gain I say, re - joice!

The Lord, our Savior, reigns,
The God of truth and love;
When he had purged our sins,
He took his seat above:
Lift up your heart, lift up your voice!
Rejoice, again I say, rejoice!

His kingdom cannot fail,
He rules o'er earth and heav'n;
The keys of death and hell
Are to our Jesus giv'n:
Lift up your heart, lift up your voice!
Rejoice, again I say, rejoice!

Rejoice in glorious hope!
Our Lord the judge shall come
And take his servants up
To their eternal home:
Lift up your heart, lift up your voice!
Rejoice, again I say, rejoice!

189 Spirit of God, Who Dwells within My Heart
MORECAMBE 10.10.10.10

George Croly (1867), alt.   Frederick C. Atkinson (1870)

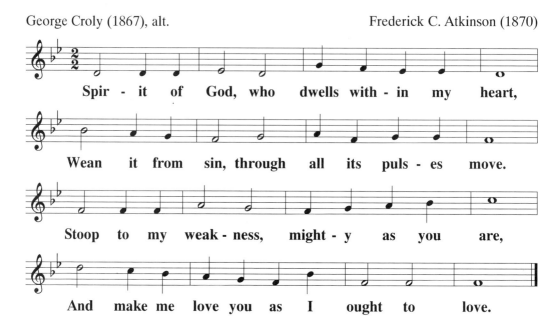

Spir - it of God, who dwells with - in my heart,

Wean it from sin, through all its puls - es move.

Stoop to my weak - ness, might - y as you are,

And make me love you as I ought to love.

I ask no dream, no prophet ecstasies,
No sudden rending of the veil of clay,
No angel visitant, no op'ning skies;
But take the dimness of my soul away.

Did you not bid us love you, God and King,
Love you with all our heart and strength and mind?
I see the cross— there teach my heart to cling.
O let me seek you and O let me find!

Teach me to feel that you are always nigh;
Teach me the struggles of the soul to bear,
To check the rising doubt, the rebel sigh;
Teach me the patience of unceasing prayer.

Teach me to love you as your angels love,
One holy passion filling all my frame:
The fullness of the heav'n-descended Dove;
My heart an altar, and your love the flame.

Holy Ghost, Dispel Our Sadness   190
GENEVA 8.7.8.7 D

Paul Gerhardt (1648)
Trans. by John Christian Jacobi (c. 1725), alt.   George Henry Day (1940)

Ho - ly Ghost, dis - pel our sad - ness; Pierce the
clouds of na - ture's night; Come, O source of joy and
glad - ness, Breathe your life, and spread your light.
From the height which knows no meas - ure, As a gra - cious
show'r de - scend, Bring - ing down the rich - est
treas - ure We can wish, or God can send.

Author of the new creation,
Come, anoint us with your pow'r.
Make our hearts your habitation;
With your grace our spirits show'r.
Hear, O hear our supplication,
Blesséd Spirit, God of peace!
Rest upon this congregation
With the fullness of your grace.

191   For Your Gift of God the Spirit

BLAENWERN 8.7.8.7 D

Margaret Clarkson (1959)   William P. Rowlands (1905)

For your gift of God the Spir - it, Pow'r to make our

lives a - new, Pledge of life and hope of glo - ry,

Sav - ior, we would wor - ship you. Crown - ing gift of

res - ur - rec - tion Sent from your as - cend - ed throne,

Full - ness of the ver - y God - head,

Come to make your life our own.

He who in creation's dawning
Brooded on the lifeless deep,
Still across our nature's darkness
Moves to wake our souls from sleep,
Moves to stir, to draw, to quicken,
Thrusts us through with sense of sin;
Brings to birth and seals and fills us—
Saving Advocate within.

He, himself the living Author,
Wakes to life the sacred Word,
Reads with us its holy pages
And reveals our risen Lord.
He it is who works within us,
Teaching rebel hearts to pray,
He whose holy intercessions
Rise for us both night and day.

He, the mighty God, indwells us;
His to strengthen, help, empow'r;
His to overcome the tempter—
Ours to call in danger's hour.
In his strength we dare to battle
All the raging hosts of sin,
And by him alone we conquer
Foes without and foes within.

Father, grant your Holy Spirit
In our hearts may rule today,
Grieved not, quenched not, but unhindered,
Work in us his sov'reign way.
Fill us with your holy fullness,
God the Father, Spirit, Son;
In us, through us, then, for ever,
Shall your perfect will be done.

192   Breathe on Me, Breath of God
TRENTHAM SM

Edwin Hatch (1878), alt.   Robert Jackson (1894)

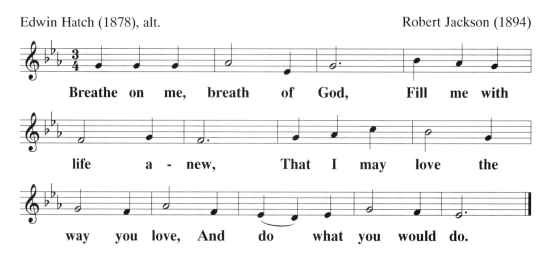

Breathe on me, breath of God, Fill me with life a - new, That I may love the way you love, And do what you would do.

Breathe on me, breath of God,
Until my heart is pure,
Until my will is one with yours,
To do and to endure.

Breathe on me, breath of God,
So shall I never die,
But live with you the perfect life
For all eternity.

I Greet Thee, Who My Sure Redeemer Art 193
TOULON 10.10.10.10

Adapt. from GENEVAN 124
French Psalter, Strassburg (1545)   *Genevan Psalter* (1551)

I greet thee, who my sure Re-deem-er art,

My on-ly trust and Sav-ior of my heart,

Who pain didst un-der-go for my poor sake;

I pray thee from our hearts all cares to take.

Thou art the King of mercy and of grace,
Reigning omnipotent in ev'ry place:
So come, O King, and our whole being sway;
Shine on us with the light of thy pure day.

Thou art the life, by which alone we live,
And all our substance and our strength receive;
Sustain us by thy faith and by thy pow'r,
And give us strength in ev'ry trying hour.

Thou hast the true and perfect gentleness,
No harshness hast thou and no bitterness:
O grant to us the grace we find in thee,
That we may dwell in perfect unity.

Our hope is in no other save in thee;
Our faith is built upon thy promise free;
Lord, give us peace, and make us calm and sure,
That in thy strength we evermore endure.

194   Fairest Lord Jesus

ST. ELIZABETH 5.6.8.5.5.8

Münster Gesangbuch (1677)
Trans. by Joseph August Seiss (1873)

Schlesische Volkslieder (1842)
Arr. by Richard Storrs Willis (1850)

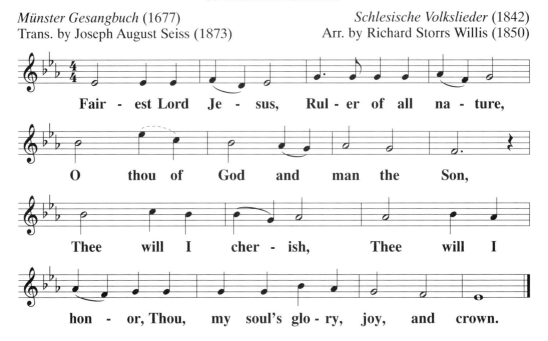

Fair - est Lord Je - sus, Rul - er of all na - ture,

O thou of God and man the Son,

Thee will I cher - ish, Thee will I

hon - or, Thou, my soul's glo - ry, joy, and crown.

Fair are the meadows,	Fair is the sunshine,
Fairer still the woodlands,	Fairer still the moonlight,
Robed in the blooming garb of spring:	And all the twinkling, starry host:
Jesus is fairer,	Jesus shines brighter,
Jesus is purer,	Jesus shines purer,
Who makes the woeful heart to sing.	Than all the angels heav'n can boast.

Beautiful Savior!
Lord of all the nations!
Son of God and Son of Man!
Glory and honor,
Praise, adoration,
Now and for evermore be thine.

Jesus Shall Reign

DUKE STREET LM

Based on Psalm 72
Isaac Watts (1719), alt.

John Hatton (1793)

195

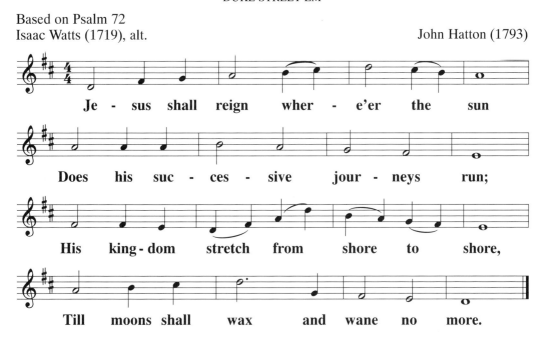

Je - sus shall reign wher - e'er the sun
Does his suc - ces - sive jour - neys run;
His king - dom stretch from shore to shore,
Till moons shall wax and wane no more.

To him shall endless prayer be made,
And praises throng to crown his head;
His Name like sweet perfume shall rise
With ev'ry morning sacrifice.

People and realms of ev'ry tongue
Dwell on his love with sweetest song;
And infant voices shall proclaim
Their early blessings on his Name.

Blessings abound where'er he reigns;
The pris'ner leaps to lose his chains;
The weary find eternal rest,
And all who suffer want are blest.

Let ev'ry creature rise and bring
Blessing and honor to our King;
Angels descend with songs again,
And earth repeat the loud Amen.

196 Christ Is the World's Light

CHRISTE SANCTORUM 10.11.11.6

Fred Pratt Green (1969)   *Paris Antiphoner* (1681)

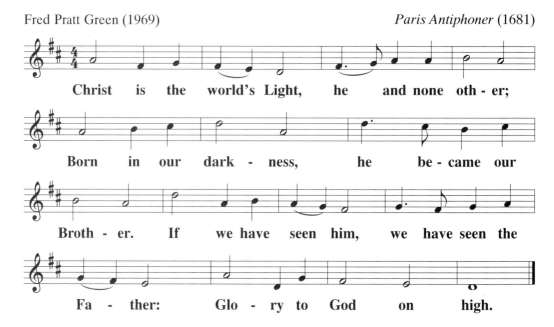

Christ is the world's Light, he and none oth - er;
Born in our dark - ness, he be - came our
Broth - er. If we have seen him, we have seen the
Fa - ther: Glo - ry to God on high.

Christ is the world's Peace, he and none other;
No one can serve him and despise another.
Who else unites us, one in God the Father?
Glory to God on high.

Christ is the world's Life, he and none other;
Sold once for silver, murdered here, our Brother—
He, who redeems us, reigns with God the Father:
Glory to God on high.

Give God the glory, God and none other;
Give God the glory, Spirit, Son and Father;
Give God the glory, God in Man my brother:
Glory to God on high.

There's a Spirit in the Air

197

LAUDS 7.7.7.7

Brian Wren (1979)   John W. Wilson (1967)

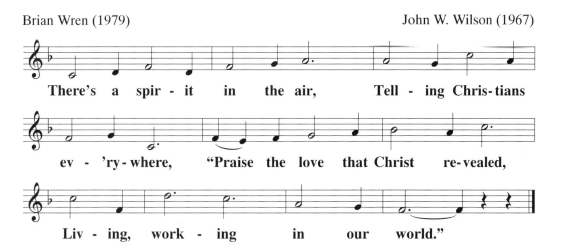

There's a spir - it in the air, Tell - ing Chris - tians
ev - 'ry - where, "Praise the love that Christ re - vealed,
Liv - ing, work - ing in our world."

Lose your shyness, find your tongue;
Tell the world what God has done:
God in Christ has come to stay,
Live tomorrow's life today.

When believers break the bread,
When a hungry child is fed:
Praise the love that Christ revealed,
Living, working in our world.

Still the Spirit gives us light,
Seeing wrong and setting right:
God in Christ has come to stay,
Live tomorrow's life today.

When a stranger's not alone,
Where the homeless find a home,
Praise the love that Christ revealed,
Living, working in our world.

May the Spirit fill our praise,
Guide our thoughts and change our ways.
God in Christ has come to stay,
Live tomorrow's life today.

There's a Spirit in the air,
Calling people ev'rywhere:
Praise the love that Christ revealed:
Living, working in our world.

198 Ask Ye What Great Thing I Know
HENDON 7.7.7.7.7

Johann C. Schwedler (1741)   H. A. César Malan (1827)
Trans. by Benjamin H. Kennedy (1863)   Harm. by Lowell Mason (1841)

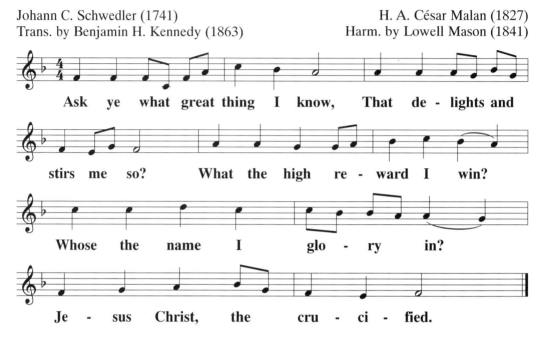

Ask ye what great thing I know, That de - lights and
stirs me so? What the high re - ward I win?
Whose the name I glo - ry in?
Je - sus Christ, the cru - ci - fied.

Who defeats my fiercest foes?   Who is life in life to me?
Who consoles my saddest woes?   Who the death of death will be?
Who revives my fainting heart,   Who will place me on his right,
Healing all its hidden smart?   With the countless hosts of light?
Jesus Christ, the crucified.   Jesus Christ, the crucified.

This is that great thing I know;
This delights and stirs me so:
Faith in him who died to save,
Him who triumphed o'er the grave:
Jesus Christ, the crucified.

To Jesus Christ, Our Sovereign King   199

ICH GLAUB AN GOTT 8.7.8.7 with refrain

Mainz Gesangbuch (1870)

Martin B. Hellrigel, alt.

Harm. by Richard Proulx (1986)

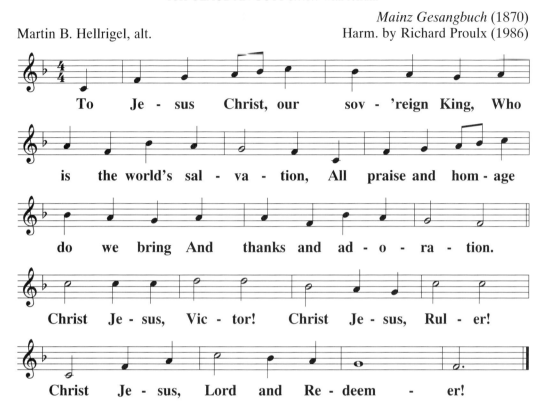

To Je - sus Christ, our sov - 'reign King, Who is the world's sal - va - tion, All praise and hom - age do we bring And thanks and ad - o - ra - tion.

Christ Je - sus, Vic - tor! Christ Je - sus, Rul - er! Christ Je - sus, Lord and Re - deem - er!

Your reign extend, O King benign,
To ev'ry land and nation;
For in your Kingdom, Lord divine,
Alone we find salvation.
  Christ Jesus, Victor!...

To you, and to your church, great King,
We pledge our heart's oblation;
Until before your throne we sing
In endless jubilation.
  Christ Jesus, Victor!...

200   I Love to Tell the Story

HANKEY 7.6.7.6 D with refrain

Katherine Hankey (c. 1868)   William G. Fischer (1869)

I love to tell the sto - ry Of un - seen things a -
bove, Of Je - sus and his glo - ry, Of
Je - sus and his love. I love to tell the sto - ry,
Be - cause I know 'tis true; It sat - is - fies my
long - ings As noth - ing else can do.
I love to tell the sto - ry, 'Twill
be my theme in glo - ry, To tell the old, old
sto - ry Of Je - sus and his love.

I love to tell the story;
More wonderful it seems
Than all the golden fancies
Of all our golden dreams.
I love to tell the story,
It did so much for me;
And that is just the reason
I tell it now to thee.
  I love to tell…

I love to tell the story;
'Tis pleasant to repeat
What seems, each time I tell it,
More wonderfully sweet.
I love to tell the story,
For some have never heard
The message of salvation
From God's own holy Word.
  I love to tell…

I love to tell the story,
For those who know it best
Seem hungering and thirsting
To hear it like the rest.
And when, in scenes of glory,
I sing the new, new song,
'Twill be the old, old story
That I have loved so long.
  I love to tell…

201   All Hail the Power of Jesus' Name
CORONATION CM with repeat

Edward Perronet (1780)
Alt. by John Rippon (1787)   Oliver Holden (1793)

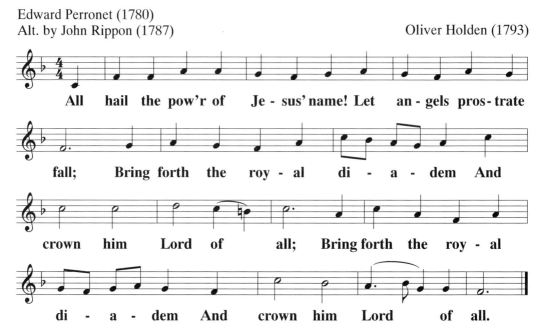

All hail the pow'r of Je-sus' name! Let an-gels pros-trate
fall; Bring forth the roy-al di-a-dem And
crown him Lord of all; Bring forth the roy-al
di-a-dem And crown him Lord of all.

Crown him, ye martyrs of our God,
Who from his altar call;
Extol the stem of Jesse's rod,
And crown him Lord of all;
Extol the stem of Jesse's rod,
And crown him Lord of all.

Ye chosen seed of Israel's race,
A remnant weak and small,
Hail him who saved you by his grace,
And crown him Lord of all;
Hail him who saved you by his grace,
And crown him Lord of all.

O that, with yonder sacred throng,
We at his feet may fall,
Join in the everlasting song,
And crown him Lord of all;
Join in the everlasting song,
And crown him Lord of all.

At the Name of Jesus

KING'S WESTON 6.5.6.5 D

202

Philippians 2:5-7
Caroline M. Noel (1870), alt.   Ralph Vaughan Williams (1925), alt.

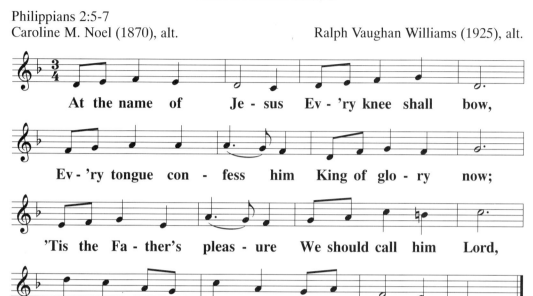

At the name of Je - sus Ev - 'ry knee shall bow,
Ev - 'ry tongue con - fess him King of glo - ry now;
'Tis the Fa - ther's pleas - ure We should call him Lord,
Who from the be - gin - ning Was the might - y Word.

Humbled for a season
To receive a name
From the lips of sinners
Unto whom he came,
Faithfully he bore it,
Spotless to the last,
Brought it back victorious
When through death he passed.

Bore it up triumphant
With its human light,
Through all ranks of creatures,
To the central height,
To the throne of Godhead,
To the Father's breast;
Filled it with the glory
Of that perfect rest.

In your hearts enthrone him;
There let him subdue
All that is not holy,
All that is not true:
Crown him as your Captain
In temptation's hour;
Let his will enfold you
In its light and pow'r.

203   **Jesus, the Very Thought of Thee**

ST. AGNES CM

Attr. to Bernard of Clairvaux (12th C.)
Trans. by Edward Caswall (1849)   John Bacchus Dykes (1866)

Je - sus, the ver - y thought of thee

With sweet - ness fills the breast; But sweet - er far thy

face to see, And in thy pres - ence rest.

O hope of ev'ry contrite heart,   But what to those who find? Ah, this
O joy of all the meek,   Nor tongue nor pen can show;
To those who fall, how kind thou art! The love of Jesus, what it is,
How good to those who seek!   None but his loved ones know.

Jesus, our only joy be thou,
As thou our prize wilt be;
Jesus, be thou our glory now,
And through eternity.

O Christ, the Healer   **204**

ERHALT UNS HERR LM

Fred Pratt Green (1969)

Klug's *Geistliche Lieder* (1543)
Harm. by Johann Sebastian Bach

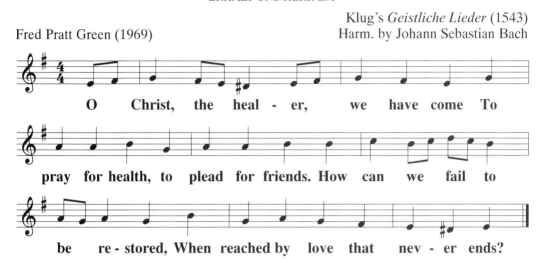

O Christ, the heal - er, we have come To
pray for health, to plead for friends. How can we fail to
be re - stored, When reached by love that nev - er ends?

From ev'ry ailment flesh endures
Our bodies clamor to be freed;
Yet in our hearts we would confess
That wholeness is our deepest need.

How strong, O Lord, are our desires,
How weak our knowledge of ourselves!
Release in us those healing truths
Unconscious pride resists or shelves.

In conflicts that destroy our health
We recognize the world's disease;
Our common life declares our ills:
Is there no cure, O Christ, for these?

Grant that we all, made one in faith,
In your community may find
The wholeness that, enriching us,
Shall reach the whole of humankind.

205 O Love, How Deep

DEO GRACIAS LM

Attr. to Thomas à Kempis (15th C.)
Trans. by Benjamin Webb (1854), alt.

English melody
Harm. from *Hymns Ancient and Modern,
Revised* (1950)

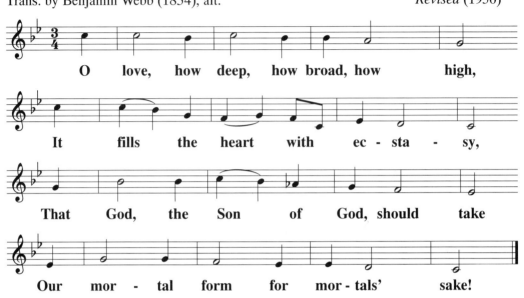

O love, how deep, how broad, how high,

It fills the heart with ec - sta - sy,

That God, the Son of God, should take

Our mor - tal form for mor - tals' sake!

For us baptized, for us he bore
His holy fast and hungered sore,
For us temptation sharp he knew;
For us the tempter overthrew.

For us he prayed; for us he taught;
For us his daily works he wrought;
By words and signs and actions thus
Still seeking not himself, but us.

For us to evil pow'r betrayed,
Scourged, mocked, in purple robe arrayed,
He bore the shameful cross and death,
For us gave up his dying breath.

For us he rose from death again;
For us he went on high to reign;
For us he sent his Spirit here,
To guide, to strengthen, and to cheer.

All glory to our Lord and God
For love so deep, so high, so broad:
The Trinity whom we adore,
For ever and for evermore.

Of the Father's Love Begotten   206

DIVINUM MYSTERIUM 8.7.8.7.8.7.7

Aurelius Clemens Prudentius (4th C.)
Trans. by John Mason Neale (1854)
and Henry Williams Baker (1859)

Plainsong, Mode V
Harm. by Charles Winfred Douglas (1940)

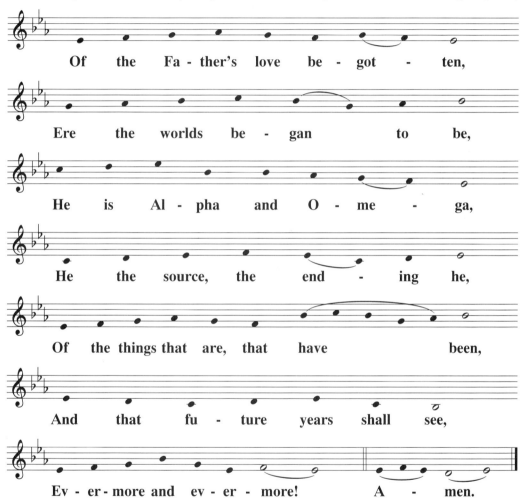

Of the Fa - ther's love be - got - ten,

Ere the worlds be - gan to be,

He is Al - pha and O - me - ga,

He the source, the end - ing he,

Of the things that are, that have been,

And that fu - ture years shall see,

Ev - er - more and ev - er - more! A - men.

O ye heights of heav'n adore him;
Angel hosts, his praises sing;
Pow'rs, dominions, bow before him,
And extol our God and King;
Let no tongue on earth be silent,
Ev'ry voice in concert ring,
Evermore and evermore!

Christ, to thee with God the Father,
And, O Holy Ghost, to thee,
Hymn and chant and high thanksgiving
And unwearied praises be:
Honor, glory and dominion,
And eternal victory,
Evermore and evermore! Amen.

207

I Am the Bread of Life

BREAD OF LIFE Irregular with refrain

John 6
Suzanne Toolan, SM (1966)

Suzanne Toolan, SM (1966)

1._____ I am the Bread of life. You who
2. The bread that_____ I will give is my
3. Un - less_____ you_____ eat of the
4._____ I am the Res - ur - rec - tion,_____
5. Yes, Lord,_____ I be - lieve that_____

come to me shall not hun - ger; and who be -
flesh for the life of the world,_____ and if you
flesh of the Son of Man_____ and_____
I_____ am the life._____ If you be -
you_____ are the Christ,_____ the_____

lieve in me shall not thirst._____ No one can come to
eat_____ of this bread,_____ you shall__ live for
drink_____ of his blood, and drink_____ of his
lieve_____ in_____ me,_____ e - ven__ though you
Son_____ of_____ God,_____ Who_____ has_____

me un - less the__ Fa - ther beck - ons.
ev - er,_____ you shall__ live for ev - er.
blood, you shall not have life with - in you.
die,_____ you shall__ live for ev - er.
come in - to_____ the_____ world.__

And I will raise you up, and I will raise you up, and I will raise you up on the last day.

208 Lift High the Cross

CRUCIFER 10.10 with refrain

1 Corinthians 1:18
George W. Kitchin
and Michael R. Newbolt (1916), alt.

Sidney Hugo Nicholson (1916)

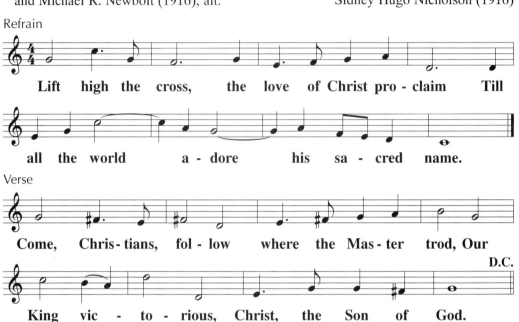

Refrain

Lift high the cross, the love of Christ pro - claim Till
all the world a - dore his sa - cred name.

Verse

Come, Chris - tians, fol - low where the Mas - ter trod, Our
King vic - to - rious, Christ, the Son of God.

D.C.

Led on their way by this triumphant sign,
The hosts of God in conquering ranks combine. *Ref.*

Each newborn foll'wer of the Crucified
Bears on the brow the seal of him who died. *Ref.*

O Lord, once lifted on the glorious tree,
Your death has bought us life eternally. *Ref.*

So shall our song of triumph ever be:
Praise to the Crucified for victory! *Ref.*

Jesus Loves Me   209

JESUS LOVES ME 7.7.7.7 with refrain

St. 1, Anna B. Warner (1860)
Sts. 2-3, David Rutherford McGuire   William B. Bradbury (1862)

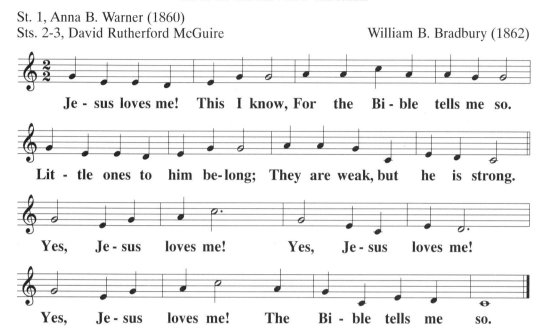

Je - sus loves me! This I know, For the Bi - ble tells me so.

Lit - tle ones to him be - long; They are weak, but he is strong.

Yes, Je - sus loves me! Yes, Je - sus loves me!

Yes, Je - sus loves me! The Bi - ble tells me so.

Jesus loves me! This I know,
As he loved so long ago,
Taking children on his knee,
Saying, "Let them come to me."
  Yes, Jesus…

Jesus loves me still today,
Walking with me on my way,
Wanting as a friend to give
Light and love to all who live.
  Yes, Jesus…

210 The King of Glory

KING OF GLORY 12.12 with refrain

Israeli folk song
Willard F. Jabusch (1966)
Harm. by Richard Proulx (1986)

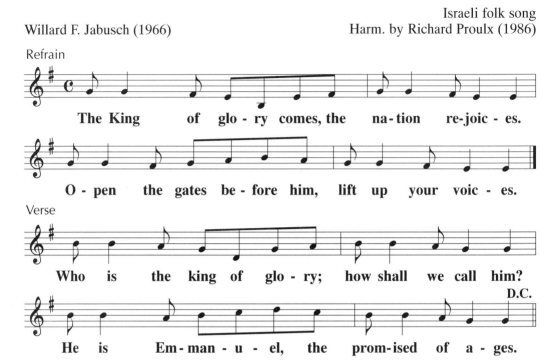

Refrain

The King of glo - ry comes, the na - tion re - joic - es.

O - pen the gates be - fore him, lift up your voic - es.

Verse

Who is the king of glo - ry; how shall we call him?

D.C.

He is Em - man - u - el, the prom - ised of a - ges.

In all of Galilee, in city or village,
He goes among his people curing their illness. *Ref.*

Sing then of David's Son, our Savior and brother;
In all of Galilee was never another. *Ref.*

He gave his life for us, the pledge of salvation,
He took upon himself the sins of the nation. *Ref.*

He conquered sin and death; he truly has risen.
And he will share with us his heavenly vision. *Ref.*

We Come, O Christ, to You

DARWALL'S 148TH 6.6.6.6.4.4.8

211

Margaret Clarkson (1946)   John Darwall (1770)

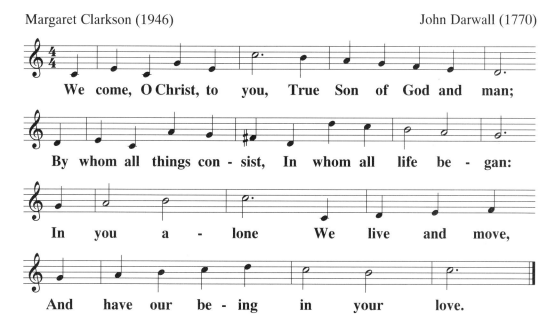

We come, O Christ, to you, True Son of God and man;
By whom all things con - sist, In whom all life be - gan:
In you a - lone We live and move,
And have our be - ing in your love.

You are the way to God, / Your blood our ransom paid;
In you we face our judge / And maker unafraid;
Before the throne / Absolved we stand:
Your love has met your law's demand.

You are the living truth, / All wisdom dwells in you,
The source of ev'ry skill, / The one eternal true!
O great I AM! / In you we rest,
Sure answer to our ev'ry quest.

You only are true life, / To know you is to live
The more abundant life / That earth can never give.
O risen Lord! / We live in you:
In us each day your life renew!

We worship you, Lord Christ, / Our Savior and our King;
To you our youth and strength / Adoringly we bring:
So fill our hearts / That all may view
Your life in us, and turn to you!

212   How Sweet the Name of Jesus
ST. PETER CM

John Newton   Alexander Robert Reinagle (c. 1836)

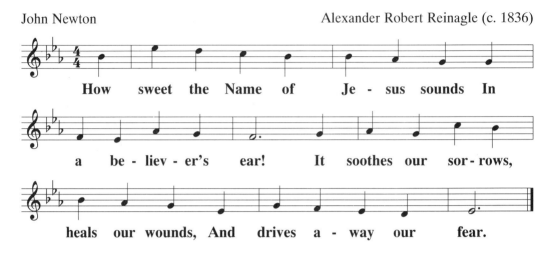

How sweet the Name of Je - sus sounds In
a be - liev - er's ear! It soothes our sor - rows,
heals our wounds, And drives a - way our fear.

It makes the wounded spirit whole,
And calms the troubled breast;
'Tis manna to the hungry soul,
And to the weary, rest.

Dear Name, the rock on which I build,
My shield and hidingplace,
My never-failing treas'ry, filled
With boundless stores of grace!

O Jesus! Shepherd, Guardian, Friend,
O Prophet, Priest, and King,
My Lord, my Life, my Way, my End,
Accept the praise I bring.

Weak is the effort of my heart,
And cold my warmest thought;
But when I see thee as thou art,
I'll praise thee as I ought.

All Praise to Thee, for Thou, O King Divine 213

SINE NOMINE 10.10.10 with alleluias

Philippians 2:5-11
F. Bland Tucker (1938)

Ralph Vaughan Williams (1906)

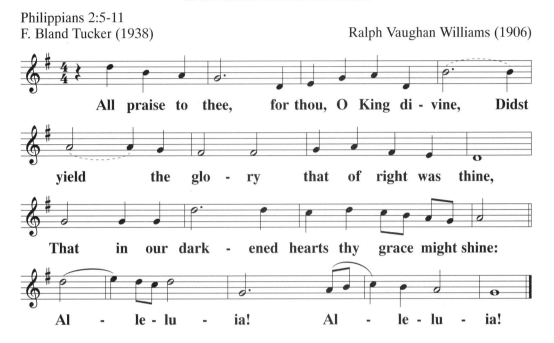

All praise to thee, for thou, O King di - vine, Didst

yield the glo - ry that of right was thine,

That in our dark - ened hearts thy grace might shine:

Al - le - lu - ia! Al - le - lu - ia!

Thou cam'st to us, in lowliness of thought;
By thee the outcast and the poor were sought,
And by thy death was God's salvation wrought:
Alleluia! Alleluia!

Let this mind be in us which was in thee,
Who wast a servant, that we might be free,
Humbling thyself to death on Calvary:
Alleluia! Alleluia!

Wherefore, by God's eternal purpose, thou
Art high exalted o'er all creatures now,
And giv'n the name to which all knees shall bow:
Alleluia! Alleluia!

Let ev'ry tongue confess with one accord
In heav'n and earth that Jesus Christ is Lord;
And God the Father be by all adored:
Alleluia! Alleluia!

214   Sing, My Soul, His Wondrous Love

ST. BEES 7.7.7.7

Anonymous (1800), alt.   John Bacchus Dykes

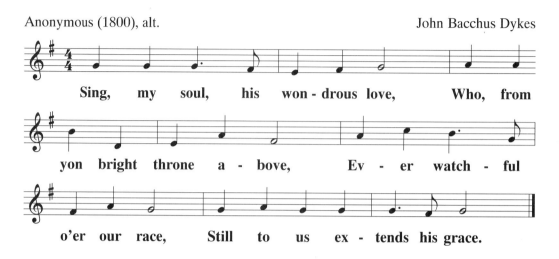

Sing, my soul, his won-drous love, Who, from
yon bright throne a - bove, Ev - er watch - ful
o'er our race, Still to us ex - tends his grace.

Heav'n and earth by him were made;   God, the merciful and good,
All is by his scepter swayed;   Bought us with the Savior's blood,
What are we that he should show   And, to make salvation sure,
So much love to us below?   Guides us by his Spirit pure.

Sing, my soul, adore his name!
Let his glory be thy theme:
Praise him till he calls thee home;
Trust his love for all to come.

Like the Murmur of the Dove's Song   215

BRIDEGROOM 8.7.8.7.6

Carl P. Daw, Jr. (1981)   Peter Cutts (1968)

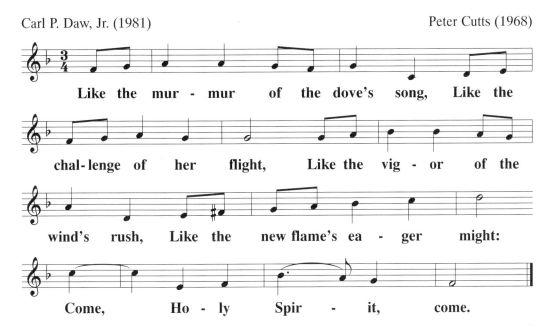

Like the mur - mur of the dove's song, Like the

chal-lenge of her flight, Like the vig - or of the

wind's rush, Like the new flame's ea - ger might:

Come, Ho - ly Spir - it, come.

To the members of Christ's body,
To the branches of the vine,
To the church in faith assembled,
To her midst as gift and sign:
Come, Holy Spirit, come.

With the healing of division,
With the ceaseless voice of prayer,
With the pow'r to love and witness,
With the peace beyond compare:
Come, Holy Spirit, come.

216   Every Time I Feel the Spirit

FEEL THE SPIRIT Irregular

Romans 8:15-17
African-American spiritual

African-American spiritual
Adapt. and arr. by William Farley Smith (1986)

Refrain

Ev - 'ry time I feel the Spir - it Mov-ing

in my heart, I will pray. Yes, ev-'ry time I feel the

Spir - it Mov-ing in my heart, I will pray.

Verse

Up - on the moun - tain, my Lord spoke, Out his

mouth came fire and smoke. All a-round me looks so

D.C.

shine, Ask my Lord if all was mine.

Jordan river runs right cold,
Chills the body, not the soul.
Ain't but one train on this track,
Runs to heaven and right back. *Ref.*

Come, Gracious Spirit, Heavenly Dove   217
MENDON LM

Simon Browne (1720), alt.

Methodist Harmonist (1821)
Adapt. and harm. by Lowell Mason

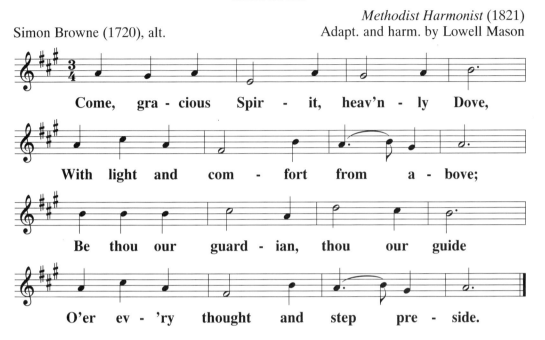

Come, gra - cious Spir - it, heav'n - ly Dove,

With light and com - fort from a - bove;

Be thou our guard - ian, thou our guide

O'er ev - 'ry thought and step pre - side.

The light of truth to us display,
And make us know and choose thy way;
Plant holy fear in ev'ry heart,
That we from thee may ne'er depart.

Lead us to Christ, the living way,
Nor let us from his precepts stray;
Lead us to holiness, the road
That we must take to dwell with God.

Lead us to heav'n, that we may share
Fullness of joy for ever there;
Lead us to God, our final rest,
To be with him for ever blest.

218 Of All the Spirit's Gifts to Me

MEYER 8.8.8.4

Fred Pratt Green (1979)

Meyer's *Seelenfreud* (1692)

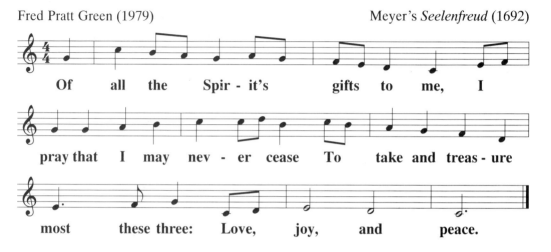

Of all the Spir-it's gifts to me, I pray that I may nev-er cease To take and treas-ure most these three: Love, joy, and peace.

The Spirit shows me love's the root
Of ev'ry gift sent from above,
Of ev'ry flow'r, of ev'ry fruit,
That God is love.

The Spirit shows if I possess
A love no evil can destroy;
However great is my distress,
Then this is joy.

Though what's ahead is mystery,
And life itself is ours on lease,
Each day the Spirit says to me,
"Go forth in peace!"

We go in peace, but made aware
That, in a needy world like this,
Our clearest purpose is to share
Love, joy, and peace.

Come, Holy Ghost, Our Hearts Inspire   219
WINCHESTER OLD CM

Charles Wesley (1740)

Est's *Whole Booke of Psalmes* (1592)
Harm. from *Hymns Ancient and Modern* (1861)

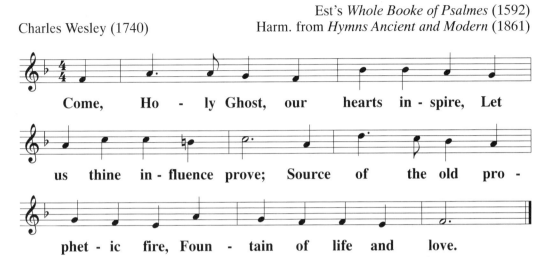

Come, Ho - ly Ghost, our hearts in - spire, Let us thine in - fluence prove; Source of the old pro - phet - ic fire, Foun - tain of life and love.

Come, Holy Ghost (for moved by thee
The prophets wrote and spoke),
Unlock the truth, thyself the key,
Unseal the sacred book.

Expand thy wings, celestial Dove,
Brood o'er our nature's night;
On our disordered spirits move,
And let there now be light.

God, through the Spirit we shall know
If thou within us shine,
And sound, with all thy saints below,
The depths of love divine.

220 O Spirit of the Living God

FOREST GREEN CMD

Acts 2
Henry H. Tweedy (1935)

English folk melody
Arr. by Ralph Vaughan Williams (1906)

O Spir - it of the liv - ing God, Thou
light and fire di - vine, De - scend up - on thy
church once more, And make it tru - ly thine.
Fill it with love and joy and pow'r, With
right - eous - ness and peace; Till Christ shall dwell in
hu - man hearts, And sin and sor - row cease.

Blow, wind of God! With wisdom blow
Until our minds are free
From mists of error, clouds of doubt,
Which blind our eyes to thee.
Burn, wingéd fire! Inspire our lips
With flaming love and zeal,
To preach to all thy great good news,
God's glorious commonweal.

Teach us to utter living words
Of truth which all may hear,
The language all may understand
When love speaks loud and clear;
Till ev'ry age and race and clime
Shall blend their creeds in one,
And earth shall form one family
By whom thy will is done.

So shall we know the pow'r of Christ
Who came this world to save;
So shall we rise with him to life
Which soars beyond the grave;
And earth shall win true holiness,
Which makes thy children whole;
Till, perfected by thee, we reach
Creation's glorious goal!

221   Onward, Christian Soldiers

ST. GERTRUDE 6.5.6.5 with refrain

Sabine Baring-Gould (1864)   Arthur Seymour Sullivan (1871)

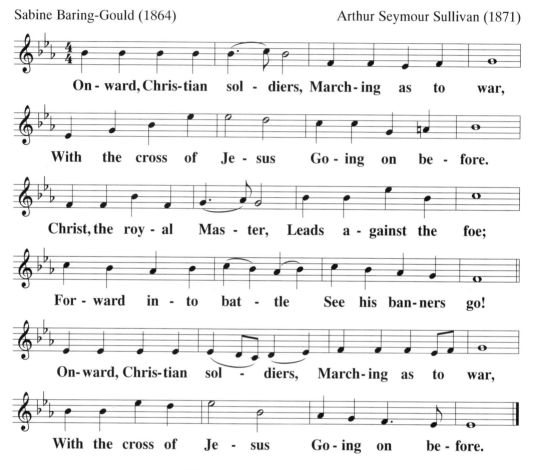

On - ward, Chris-tian sol - diers, March-ing as to war,

With the cross of Je - sus Go - ing on be - fore.

Christ, the roy - al Mas - ter, Leads a - gainst the foe;

For - ward in - to bat - tle See his ban-ners go!

On-ward, Chris-tian sol - diers, March-ing as to war,

With the cross of Je - sus Go - ing on be - fore.

Like a mighty army
Moves the church of God;
Christians, we are treading
Where the saints have trod,
We are not divided;
All one body we—
One in hope and doctrine,
One in charity.
    Onward...

Crowns and thrones may perish,
Kingdoms rise and wane,
But the church of Jesus
Constant will remain,
Gates of hell can never
'Gainst that church prevail.
We have Christ's own promise,
And that cannot fail.
  Onward…

Onward, then, ye people,
Join our happy throng:
Blend with ours your voices
In the triumph song,
Glory, laud, and honor
Unto Christ the King,
We through countless ages
With the angels sing.
  Onward…

222 God of Grace and God of Glory

CWM RHONDDA 8.7.8.7.8.7.7

Harry Emerson Fosdick (1930), alt.   John Hughes (1905)

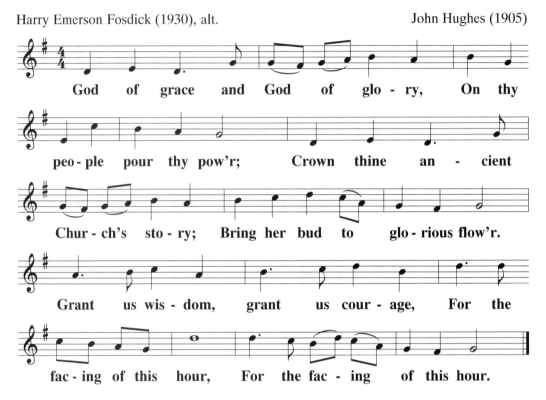

God of grace and God of glo - ry, On thy
peo - ple pour thy pow'r; Crown thine an - cient
Chur - ch's sto - ry; Bring her bud to glo - rious flow'r.
Grant us wis - dom, grant us cour - age, For the
fac - ing of this hour, For the fac - ing of this hour.

Lo! the hosts of evil round us
Scorn thy Christ, assail his ways!
From the fears that long have bound us
Free our hearts to faith and praise:
Grant us wisdom, grant us courage,
For the living of these days,
For the living of these days.

Cure thy children's warring madness,
Bend our pride to thy control;
Shame our wanton, selfish gladness,
Rich in things and poor in soul.
Grant us wisdom, grant us courage,
Lest we miss thy kingdom's goal,
Lest we miss thy kingdom's goal.

Save us from weak resignation
To the evils we deplore;
Let the gift of thy salvation
Be our glory evermore.
Grant us wisdom, grant us courage,
Serving thee whom we adore,
Serving thee whom we adore.

Christ Is Made the Sure Foundation   **223**

WESTMINSTER ABBEY 8.7.8.7.8.7

Angularis fundamentum (11th C.)
Trans. by John Mason Neale (1851), alt.   Adapt. from an anthem of Henry Purcell

Christ is made the sure foun-da-tion, Christ the head and

cor-ner-stone; Cho-sen of the Lord, and pre-cious,

Bind-ing all the Church in one; Ho-ly Zi-on's

help for ev-er, And her con-fi-dence a-lone.

To this temple where we call you,	Grant, we pray, to all your people,
Come, O Lord of hosts, today;	All the grace they ask to gain;
With your wonted loving kindness	What they gain from you for ever
Hear your servants as they pray,	With the blesséd to retain,
And your fullest benediction	And hereafter in your glory
Shed in all its bright array.	Evermore with you to reign.

224 In Christ There Is No East or West

MC KEE CM

Galatians 3:23
John Oxenham (1908)

African-American spiritual
Jubilee Songs (1884)
Adapt. by Harry T. Burleigh (1940)

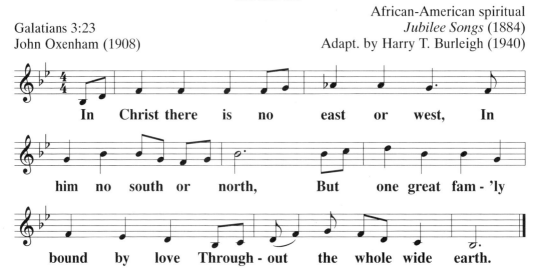

In Christ there is no east or west, In him no south or north, But one great fam-'ly bound by love Through-out the whole wide earth.

In him shall true hearts ev'rywhere
Their high communion find;
His service is the golden cord
Close-binding humankind.

Join hands, disciples in the faith,
Whate'er your race may be!
Who serve each other in Christ's love
Are surely kin to me.

In Christ now meet both east and west,
In him meet south and north,
All Christly souls are one in him,
Throughout the whole wide earth.

Blest Be the Tie That Binds

DENNIS SM

225

Johann Georg Nägeli
Arr. by Lowell Mason (1845)

John Fawcett (1782)

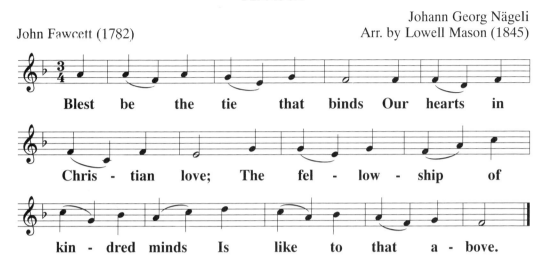

Blest be the tie that binds Our hearts in
Chris - tian love; The fel - low - ship of
kin - dred minds Is like to that a - bove.

Before our Father's throne
We pour our ardent prayers;
Our fears, our hopes, our aims are one,
Our comforts and our cares.

We share each other's woes,
Each other's burdens bear;
And often for each other flows
The sympathizing tear.

From sorrow, toil, and pain,
And sin we shall be free;
And perfect love and joy shall reign
Through all eternity.

226 I Love Thy Kingdom, Lord
ST. THOMAS SM

Aaron Williams (1770)
Harm. by Lowell Mason

Timothy Dwight (1880)

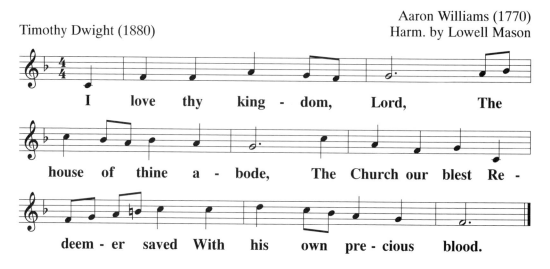

I love thy king - dom, Lord, The

house of thine a - bode, The Church our blest Re -

deem - er saved With his own pre - cious blood.

For her my tears shall fall;
For her my prayers ascend;
To her my cares and toils be giv'n,
Till toils and cares shall end.

Beyond my highest joy
I prize her heav'nly ways,
Her sweet communion, solemn vows,
Her hymns of love and praise.

Jesus, thou friend divine,
Our Savior and our King,
Thy hand from ev'ry snare and foe
Shall great deliv'rance bring.

Sure as thy truth shall last,
To Zion shall be giv'n
The brightest glories earth can yield,
And brighter bliss of heav'n.

The Church's One Foundation

227

AURELIA 7.6.7.6 D

Samuel J. Stone (1866)

Samuel Sebastian Wesley (1864)

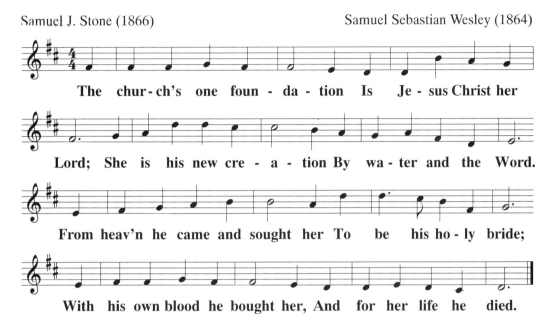

The chur-ch's one foun - da - tion Is Je - sus Christ her
Lord; She is his new cre - a - tion By wa - ter and the Word.
From heav'n he came and sought her To be his ho - ly bride;
With his own blood he bought her, And for her life he died.

Elect from ev'ry nation, / Yet one o'er all the earth;
Her charter of salvation, / One Lord, one faith, one birth;
One holy name she blesses, / Partakes one holy food,
And to one hope she presses, / With ev'ry grace endued.

Though with a scornful wonder / We see her sore oppressed,
By schisms rent asunder, / By heresies distressed
Yet saints their watch are keeping; / Their cry goes up, "How long?"
And soon the night of weeping / Shall be the morn of song.

Mid toil and tribulation, / And tumult of her war,
She waits the consummation / Of peace for evermore;
Till, with the vision glorious, / Her longing eyes are blest,
And the great church victorious / Shall be the church at rest.

Yet she on earth hath union / With God the Three-in-One,
And mystic sweet communion / With those whose rest is won.
O happy ones and holy! / Lord, give us grace that we
Like them, the meek and lowly, / On high may dwell with thee.

228   O Zion, Haste

TIDINGS 11.10.11.10 with refrain

Mary A. Thomson (1894)   James Walch (1875)

O Zi-on, haste, thy mis-sion high ful-fill-ing,
To tell to all the world that God is light,
That he who made all na-tions is not will-ing
One soul should per-ish, lost in shades of night.
Pub-lish glad tid-ings, tid-ings of peace;
Tid-ings of Je-sus, re-demp-tion and re-lease.

Behold how many thousands still are lying
Bound in the darksome prisonhouse of sin,
With none to tell them of the Savior's dying,
Or of the life he died for them to win. *Publish glad tidings...*

Proclaim to ev'ry people, tongue, and nation
That God, in whom they live and move, is love;
Tell how he stooped to save his lost creation,
And died on earth that we might live above. *Publish glad tidings...*

Give of thine own to bear the message glorious;
Give of thy wealth to speed them on their way;
Pour out thy soul for them in prayer victorious;
O Zion, haste to bring the brighter day. *Publish glad tidings...*

Come, Labor On

229

ORA LABORA 4.10.10.10.4

Jane Laurie Borthwick (1859, 1863)   Thomas Tertius Noble (1918)

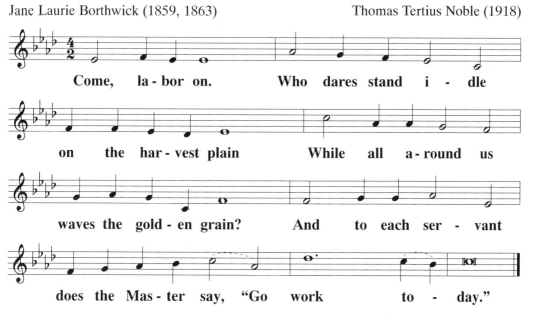

Come, labor on.
Who dares stand idle on the harvest plain
While all around us waves the golden grain?
And to each servant does the Master say, "Go work today."

Come, labor on.
The enemy is watching night and day,
To sow the tares, to snatch the seed away;
While we in sleep our duty have forgot,
He slumbers not.

Come, labor on.
Away with gloomy doubts and faithless fear!
No arm so weak but may do service here:
By feeblest agents may our God fulfill
His righteous will.

Come, labor on.
Claim the high calling angels cannot share:
To young and old the gospel gladness bear.
Redeem the time— its hours so swiftly fly—
The night draws nigh.

Come, labor on.
No time for rest, till glows the western sky,
Till the long shadows o'er our pathway lie
And a glad sound comes with the setting sun:
"Servants, well done."

230   Wonderful Words of Life
WORDS OF LIFE 8.6.8.6.6.6

Philip P. Bliss (1874)   Philip P. Bliss (1874)

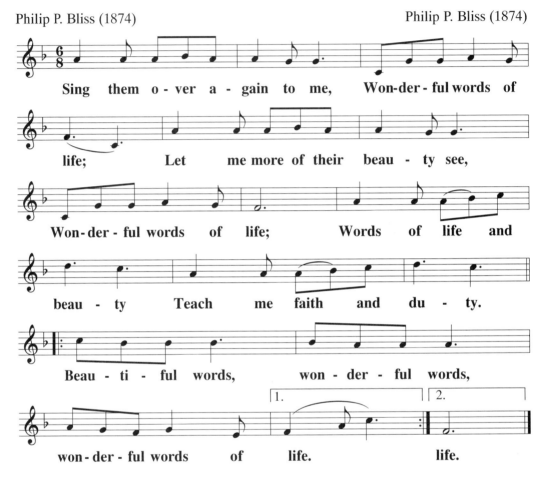

Sing them o-ver a-gain to me, Won-der-ful words of
life; Let me more of their beau-ty see,
Won-der-ful words of life; Words of life and
beau-ty Teach me faith and du-ty.
Beau-ti-ful words, won-der-ful words,

1.
won-der-ful words of life.

2.
life.

Christ, the blesséd one, gives to all
Wonderful words of life;
Sinner, list to the loving call,
Wonderful words of life;
All so freely given,
Wooing us to heaven.
   Beautiful words…

Sweetly echo the gospel call,
Wonderful words of life;
Offer pardon and peace to all,
Wonderful words of life;
Jesus, only Savior,
Sanctify for ever.
   Beautiful words…

O Word of God Incarnate

231

MUNICH 7.6.7.6 D

Neuvermehrtes Meiningisches Gesangbuch (1693)
Harm. by Felix Mendelssohn (1847)

William W. How (1867)

O Word of God in - car - nate, O
Wis - dom from on high, O Truth un - changed, un -
chang - ing, O Light of our dark sky:
We praise you for the ra - diance That
from the hal - lowed page, A lan - tern to our
foot - steps, Shines on from age to age.

The church from you, our Savior, / Received the gift divine,
And still that light is lifted / O'er all the earth to shine.
It is the sacred vessel / Where gems of truth are stored;
It is the heav'n-drawn picture / Of Christ, the living Word.

The Scripture is a banner / Before God's host unfurled;
It is a shining beacon / Above the darkling world.
It is the chart and compass / That o'er life's surging tide,
Mid mists and rocks and quicksands, / To you, O Christ, will guide.

O make your church, dear Savior, / A lamp of purest gold,
To bear before the nations / Your true light as of old.
O teach your wand'ring pilgrims / By this their path to trace,
Till, clouds and darkness ended, / They see you face to face.

232 Break Thou the Bread of Life

BREAD OF LIFE 6.4.6.4 D

Mary Ann Lathbury (1877), alt.   William Fisk Sherwin (1877), alt.

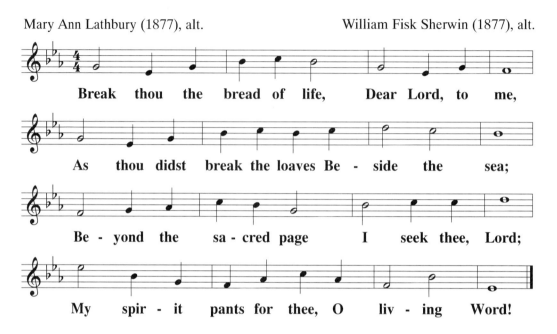

Break thou the bread of life, Dear Lord, to me,

As thou didst break the loaves Be - side the sea;

Be - yond the sa - cred page I seek thee, Lord;

My spir - it pants for thee, O liv - ing Word!

Bless thou the truth, dear Lord,
Now unto me,
As thou didst bless the bread
By Galilee;
Then shall all bondage cease,
All fetters fall;
And I shall find my peace,
My all in all.

Thanks to God Whose Word Was Spoken 233

WYLDE GREEN 8.7.8.7.4.7

R. T. Brooks (1954)　　　　　　　　　　　　　　　　Peter Cutts (1966)

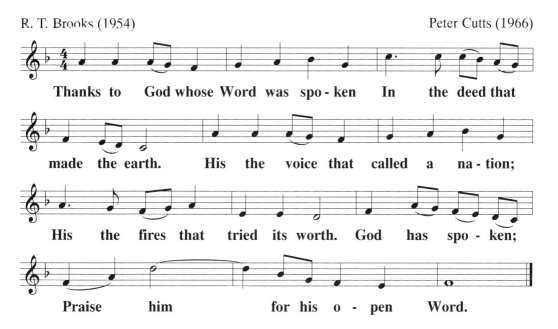

Thanks to God whose Word was spo-ken In the deed that
made the earth. His the voice that called a na-tion;
His the fires that tried its worth. God has spo-ken;
Praise him for his o-pen Word.

Thanks to God whose Word Incarnate,
Our new life in him began.
Deeds and words and death and rising,
Tell the grace in heaven's plan.
God has spoken;
Praise him for his open Word.

Thanks to God whose Word is answered
By the Spirit's voice within.
Here we drink of joy unmeasured,
Life redeemed from death and sin.
God is speaking;
Praise him for his open Word.

234   **One Bread, One Body**

1 Corinthians 10:16, 17, 12:4; Galatians 3:28, The *Didache* 9
John B. Foley, SJ (1978)   John B. Foley, SJ (1978)

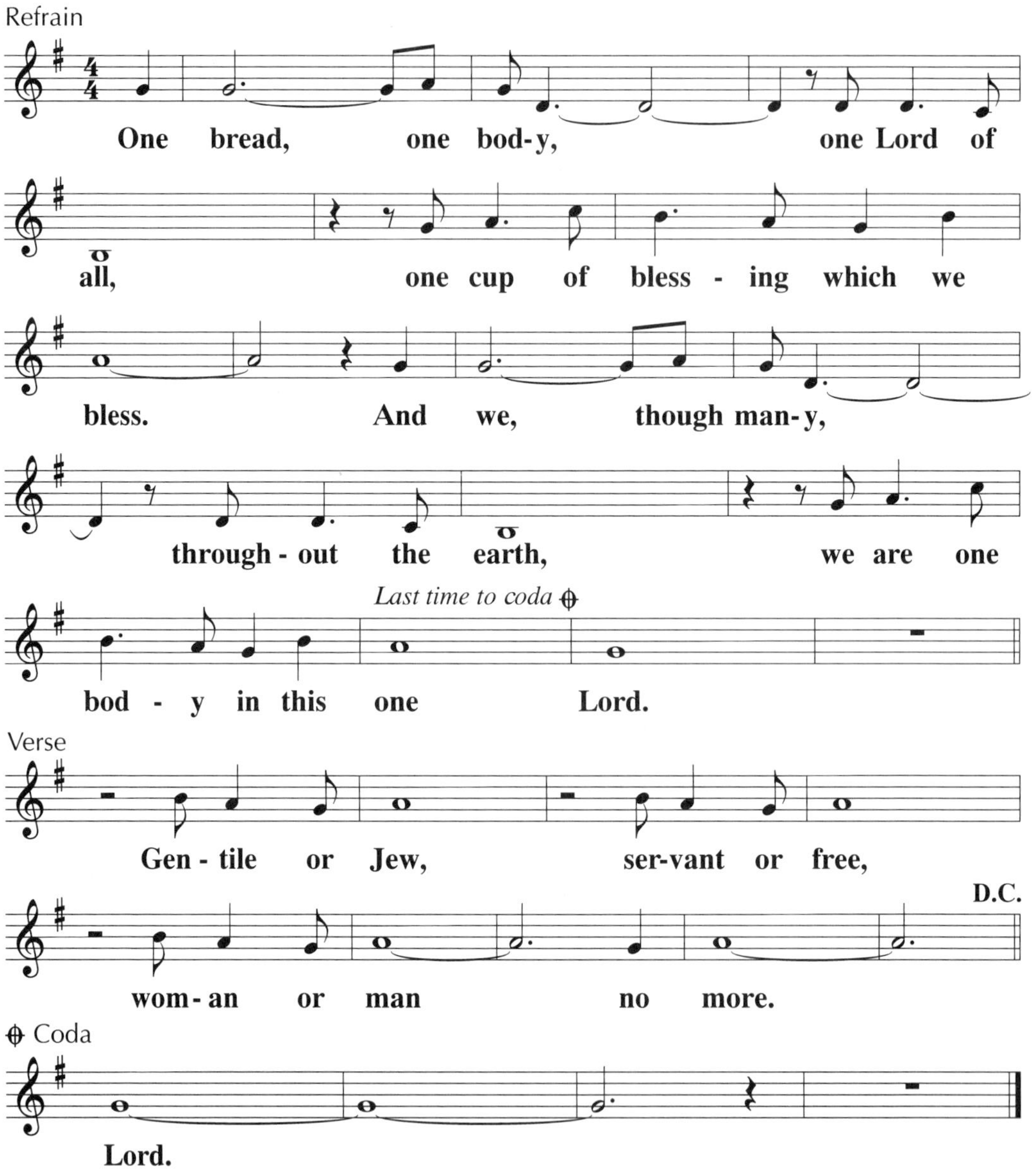

Refrain

One bread, one bod-y, one Lord of all, one cup of bless - ing which we bless. And we, though man-y, through - out the earth, we are one

Last time to coda

bod - y in this one Lord.

Verse

Gen - tile or Jew, ser-vant or free,

D.C.

wom- an or man no more.

Coda

Lord.

Many the gifts,	Grain for the fields,
Many the works,	Scattered and grown,
One in the Lord of all. *Ref.*	Gathered to one for all. *Ref.*

Bread of the World, in Mercy Broken   235
EUCHARISTIC HYMN 9.8.9.8

Reginald Heber (1827)   John S. B. Hodges (1868)

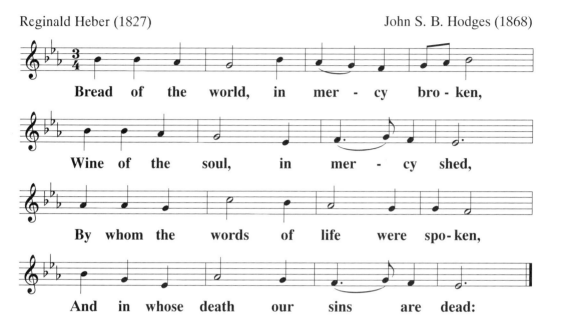

Bread of the world, in mer - cy bro - ken,

Wine of the soul, in mer - cy shed,

By whom the words of life were spo - ken,

And in whose death our sins are dead:

Look on the heart by sorrow broken,
Look on the tears by sinners shed,
And be thy feast to us the token
That by thy grace our souls are fed.

236   # I Come with Joy

LAND OF REST CM

Brian Wren (1969, rev. 1995)

American folk melody
Harm. by Annabel M. Buchanan (1938)

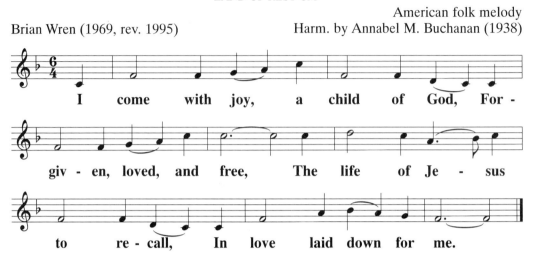

I come with joy, a child of God, Forgiv - en, loved, and free, The life of Je - sus
to re - call, In love laid down for me.

I come with Christians far and near
To find, as all are fed,
The new community of love
In Christ's communion bread.

As Christ breaks bread, and bids us share,
Each proud division ends.
The love that made us, makes us one,
And strangers now are friends.

The Spirit of the risen Christ,
Unseen, but always near,
Is in such friendship better known,
Alive among us here.

Together met, together bound,
By all that God has done,
We'll go with joy, to give the world
The love that makes us one.

Living Word of God Eternal 237

KOMM, O KOMM, DU GEIST DES LEBENS 8.7.8.7.8.7

Jeffery Rowthorn (1983)   *Neuvermehrtes Meiningisches Gesangbuch (1693)*

Liv-ing word of God e-ter-nal, Lay-ing claim to ev-'ry age, Je-sus, speak through all our speak-ing, Bring to life the Bi-ble's page; Let your gos-pel, heard and heed-ed, Set our course of pil-grim-age.

Loving Savior, whose embraces
Our true selves alone unmask,
In this fellowship's small compass
Train us for our common task:
By our love to grow more like you
And to dare what you will ask.

Living bread come down from heaven,
Broken, shared, distributed,
Feed us, gathered at this table,
With your grace unlimited,
And as servants then employ us
Till this hungry world is fed.

Loving Spirit, praying in us,
Giving voice to all our sighs,
Show the wideness of your mercy
To deaf ears and blinded eyes;
Free our tongues to come before you
With our neighbors' joys and cries.

May your word among us spoken,
May the loving which we dare,
May your bread among us broken,
May the prayers in which we share
Daily make us faithful people,
Living signs, Lord, of your care.

238 Let Us Break Bread Together

LET US BREAK BREAD 10.10.6.8.7

American folk hymn
Harm. by David Hurd (1968)

American folk hymn

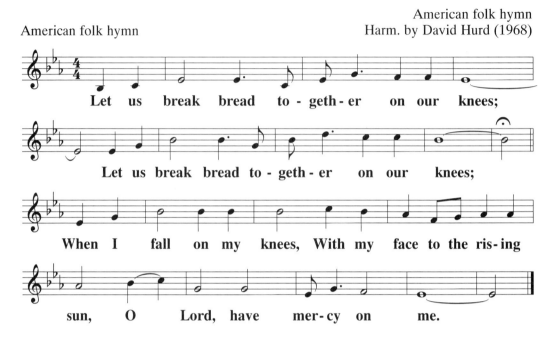

Let us break bread to-geth-er on our knees;

Let us break bread to-geth-er on our knees;

When I fall on my knees, With my face to the ris-ing

sun, O Lord, have mer-cy on me.

Let us drink wine together on our knees;
Let us drink wine together on our knees;
When I fall…

Let us praise God together on our knees;
Let us praise God together on our knees;
When I fall…

Jesus, Thou Joy of Loving Hearts   239

QUEBEC LM

Attr. to Bernard of Clairvaux (12th C.)
Trans. by Ray Palmer (1858)

Henry Baker (1854)

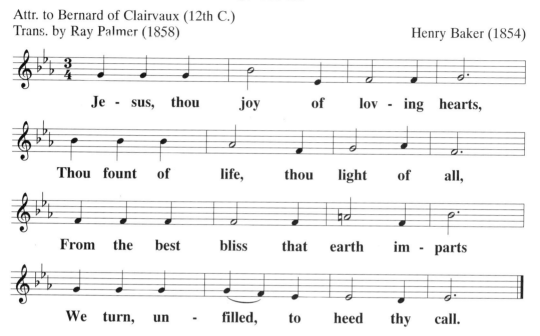

Je - sus, thou joy of lov - ing hearts,

Thou fount of life, thou light of all,

From the best bliss that earth im - parts

We turn, un - filled, to heed thy call.

Thy truth unchanged hath ever stood;
Thou savest those that on thee call;
To them that seek thee thou art good,
To them that find thee, all in all.

We taste thee, O thou living bread,
And long to feast upon thee still;
We drink of thee, the fountainhead,
And thirst our souls from thee to fill.

Our restless spirits yearn for thee,
Where'er our changeful lot is cast,
Glad when thy gracious smile we see,
Blest when our faith can hold thee fast.

O Jesus, ever with us stay,
Make all our moments calm and bright;
O chase the night of sin away,
Shed o'er the world thy holy light.

240

Gather Us In

GATHER US IN Irregular

Marty Haugen (1982)

Marty Haugen (1982)

1. Here in this place new light is stream-ing,
2. We are the young— our lives are a mys-t'ry,
3. Here we will take the wine and the wa-ter,
4. Not in the dark of build-ings con-fin-ing,

Now is the dark-ness van-ished a-way,
We are the old— who yearn for your face,
Here we will take the bread of new birth,
Not in some heav-en, light-years a-way,   But

See in this space our fears and our dream-ings,
We have been sung through-out all of his-t'ry,
Here you shall call your sons and your daugh-ters,
here in this place the new light is shin-ing,

Brought here to you in the light of this
Called to be light to the whole hu-man
Call us a-new to be salt for the
Now is the King-dom, now is the

day.   Gath-er us in— the lost and for-sak-en,
race.   Gath-er us in— the rich and the haugh-ty,
earth.   Give us to drink the wine of com-pas-sion,
day.   Gath-er us in and hold us for ev-er,

Gath - er us in— the blind and the lame;
Gath - er us in— the proud and the strong;
Give us to eat the bread that is you;
Gath - er us in and make us your own;

Call to us now, and we shall a - wak - en,
Give us a heart so meek and so low - ly,
Nour - ish us well, and teach us to fash - ion
Gath - er us in— all peo - ples to - geth - er,

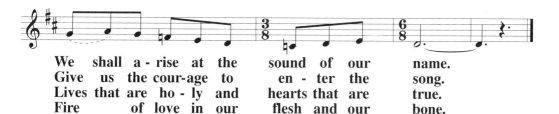

We shall a - rise at the sound of our name.
Give us the cour-age to en - ter the song.
Lives that are ho - ly and hearts that are true.
Fire of love in our flesh and our bone.

241   Deck Thyself, My Soul, with Gladness

SCHMUCKE DICH LMD

John 6:35-58; Johann Franck (1649)
Trans. by Catherine Winkworth (1863), alt.   Johann Crüger (1653)

Deck thy - self, my soul, with glad - ness,

Leave the gloom - y haunts of sad - ness.

Come in - to the day - light's splen - dor;

There with joy thy prais - es ren - der

Un - to Christ, whose grace un - bound - ed

Hath this won - drous ban - quet found - ed.

High o'er all the heav'ns he reign - eth,

Yet to dwell with thee he deign - eth.

Sun, who all my life dost brighten;
Light, who dost my soul enlighten;
Joy, the best that any knoweth;
Fount, whence all my being floweth;
At thy feet I cry, my Maker,
Let me be a fit partaker
Of this blesséd food from heaven,
For our good, thy glory, given.

Jesus, bread of life, I pray thee,
Let me gladly here obey thee;
Never to my hurt invited,
Be thy love with love requited.
From this banquet let me measure,
Lord, how vast and deep its treasure;
Through the gifts thou here dost give me,
As thy guest in heav'n receive me.

242   Gift of Finest Wheat
BICENTENNIAL CM with refrain

John 6:34, 10:1-5; 1 Corinthians 10:16-17
Omer Westendorf (1977)   Robert E. Kreutz (1977)

Refrain

You satisfy the hungry heart With gift of finest wheat. Come, give to us, O saving Lord, The bread of life to eat.

Verse

As when the shepherd calls his sheep, They know and heed his voice, So when you call your fam'ly, Lord, We follow and rejoice.

With joyful lips we sing to you / Our praise and gratitude,
That you should count us worthy, Lord, / To share this heav'nly food. *Ref.*

Is not the cup we bless and share / The blood of Christ outpoured?
Do not one cup, one loaf, declare / Our oneness in the Lord? *Ref.*

The myst'ry of your presence, Lord, / No mortal tongue can tell;
Whom all the world cannot contain / Comes in our hearts to dwell. *Ref.*

You give yourself to us, O Lord; / Then selfless let us be,
To serve each other in your name / In truth and charity. *Ref.*

Here, O My Lord   243

ADORO TE DEVOTE 10.10.10.10

Thomas Aquinas (c. 1225-1274)
Trans. James Russell Woodford (1850)

Benedictine plainsong, Mode V (13th C.)
Harm. from *Hymnal for*
Colleges and Schools (1956)

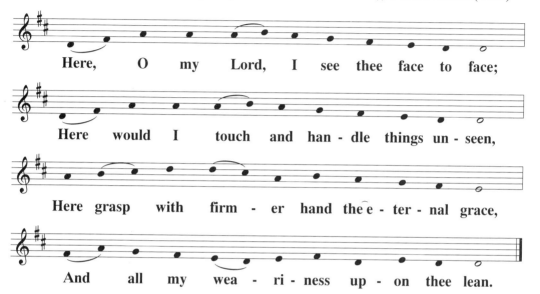

Here, O my Lord, I see thee face to face;
Here would I touch and han-dle things un-seen,
Here grasp with firm-er hand the e-ter-nal grace,
And all my wea-ri-ness up-on thee lean.

Here would I feed upon the bread of God,
Here drink with thee the royal wine of heav'n;
Here would I lay aside each earthly load,
Here taste afresh the calm of sin forgiv'n.

This is the hour of banquet and of song;
This is the heav'nly table spread for me;
Here let me feast, and, feasting, still prolong
The brief, bright hour of fellowship with thee.

Too soon we rise; the symbols disappear;
The feast, though not the love, is past and gone;
The bread and wine remove, but thou art here,
Nearer than ever, still my shield and sun.

I have no help but thine; nor do I need
Another arm save thine to lean upon;
It is enough, my Lord, enough indeed;
My strength is in thy might, thy might alone.

244   Eat This Bread

John 6
Adapt. by Robert J. Batastini and
the Taizé Community (1984)

Jacques Berthier (1984)

Refrain

Eat this bread, drink this cup, come to me and nev-er be hun - gry. Eat this bread, drink this cup, trust in me and you will not thirst.

We Know That Christ Is Raised · 245

ENGELBERG 10.10.10 with alleluia

Romans 6:4, 9
John Brownlow Geyer (1969)   Charles Villiers Stanford (1904)

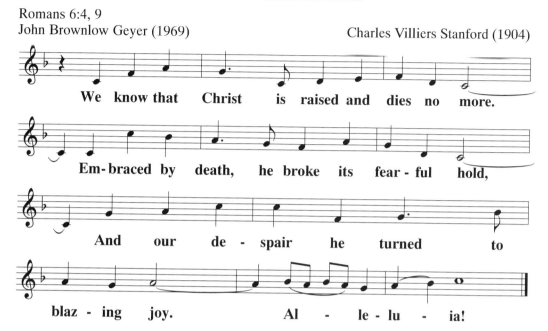

We know that Christ is raised and dies no more.
Em-braced by death, he broke its fear-ful hold,
And our de-spair he turned to
blaz-ing joy. Al - le-lu - ia!

We share by water in his saving death.
Reborn, we share with him an Easter life
As living members of our Savior Christ.
Alleluia!

The Father's splendor clothes the Son with life.
The Spirit's fission shakes the Church of God.
Baptized, we live with God the Three-in-One.
Alleluia!

A new creation comes to life and grows
As Christ's new body takes on flesh and blood.
The universe restored and whole will sing:
Alleluia!

246   May the Grace of Christ Our Savior
STAINER 8.7.8.7

John Newton (1779)   John Stainer (1898)

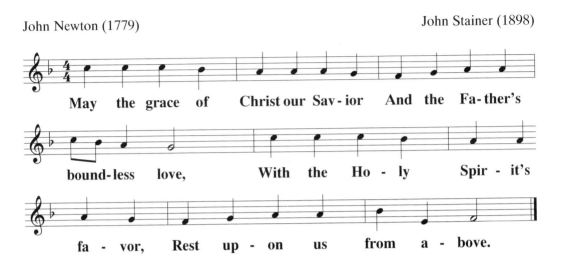

May the grace of Christ our Sav-ior And the Fa-ther's

bound-less love,   With the Ho - ly   Spir - it's

fa - vor,   Rest up - on   us   from   a - bove.

Thus may we abide in union
With each other and the Lord,
And possess, in sweet communion,
Joys which earth cannot afford.

I Need Thee Every Hour

NEED 6.4.6.4 with refrain

247

John 15:5
Annie S. Hawks (1872)

Robert Lowry (1873)

I need thee ev-'ry hour, Most gra - cious Lord;

No ten - der voice like thine Can peace af - ford.

I need thee, O I need thee; Ev - 'ry hour I need thee;

O bless me now, my Sav - ior, I come to thee.

I need thee ev'ry hour;
Stay thou nearby;
Temptations lose their pow'r
When thou art nigh.
  I need thee…

I need thee ev'ry hour,
In joy or pain;
Come quickly and abide,
Or life is vain.
  I need thee…

I need thee ev'ry hour;
Teach me thy will;
And thy rich promises
In me fulfill.
  I need thee…

I need thee ev'ry hour,
Most Holy One;
O make me thine indeed,
Thou blesséd Son.
  I need thee…

248   Just As I Am, without One Plea
WOODWORTH LM

Charlotte Elliott (1835)   William B. Bradbury (1849)

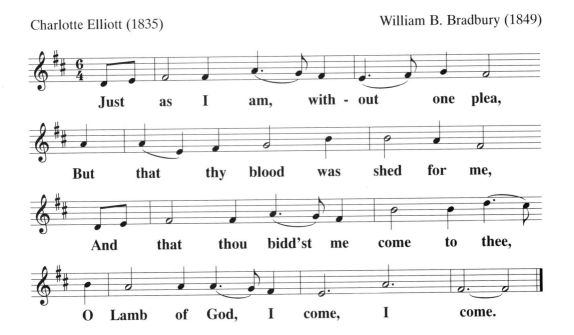

Just as I am, without one plea,

But that thy blood was shed for me,

And that thou bidd'st me come to thee,

O Lamb of God, I come, I come.

Just as I am, though tossed about
With many a conflict, many a doubt;
Fightings and fears within, without,
O Lamb of God, I come, I come.

Just as I am, poor, wretched, blind;
Sight, riches, healing of the mind,
Yea, all I need, in thee to find,
O Lamb of God, I come, I come.

Just as I am, thou wilt receive;
Wilt welcome, pardon, cleanse, relieve,
Because thy promise I believe,
O Lamb of God, I come, I come.

Just as I am, thy love unknown
Has broken ev'ry barrier down;
Now to be thine, yea, thine alone,
O Lamb of God, I come, I come.

Just as I am, of thy great love
The breadth, length, depth, and height to prove,
Here for a season, then above:
O Lamb of God, I come, I come.

I Sought the Lord

FAITH 10.10.10.6

Matthew 14:22-23
Anonymous (c. 1878)

Harold Moyer (1969)

249

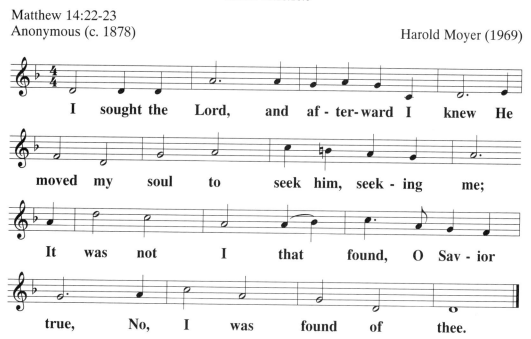

I sought the Lord, and af-ter-ward I knew He
moved my soul to seek him, seek - ing me;
It was not I that found, O Sav - ior
true, No, I was found of thee.

Thou didst reach forth thy hand and mine enfold,
I walked and sank not on the storm-vexed sea;
'Twas not so much that I on thee took hold
As thou, dear Lord, on me.

I find, I walk, I love, but O the whole
Of love is but my answer, Lord, to thee!
For thou wert long beforehand with my soul;
Always thou lovedst me.

250   There Is a Balm in Gilead

BALM IN GILEAD Irregular with refrain

Jeremiah 8:22
African-American spiritual

African-American spiritual
Acc. by Robert J. Batastini (1987)

Refrain

There is a balm in Gil - e - ad To make the wound - ed whole, There is a balm in Gil - e - ad To heal the sin - sick soul.

Verse

Some - times I feel dis - cour - aged And think my work's in vain, But then the Ho - ly Spir - it Re - vives my soul a - gain.

D.C.

If you cannot preach like Peter,
It you cannot pray like Paul,
You can tell the love of Jesus,
And say, "He died for all!" *Ref.*

Don't ever feel discouraged,
For Jesus is your friend;
And if you lack for knowledge
He'll ne'er refuse to lend. *Ref.*

Take My Life

HENDON 7.7.7.7.7

Frances Ridley Havergal (1874)   H. A. César Malan (1827)

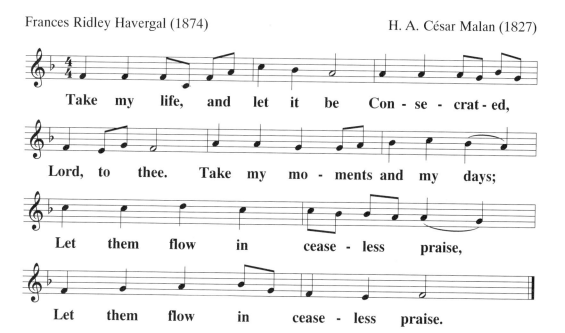

Take my life, and let it be Con - se - crat - ed,
Lord, to thee. Take my mo - ments and my days;
Let them flow in cease - less praise,
Let them flow in cease - less praise.

Take my hands, and let them move
At the impulse of thy love.
Take my feet, and let them be
Swift and beautiful for thee,
Swift and beautiful for thee.

Take my voice, and let me sing,
Always, only, for my King.
Take my lips, and let them be
Filled with messages from thee,
Filled with messages from thee.

Take my silver and my gold,
Not a mite would I withhold;
Take my intellect, and use
Ev'ry pow'r as thou shalt choose,
Ev'ry pow'r as thou shalt choose.

Take my will, and make it thine;
It shall be no longer mine.
Take my heart, it is thine own;
It shall be thy royal throne,
It shall be thy royal throne.

Take my love; my Lord, I pour
At thy feet its treasure store.
Take myself, and I will be
Ever, only, all for thee,
Ever, only, all for thee.

252 It Is Well with My Soul

VILLE DU HAVRE 11.8.11.9 with refrain

Horatio G. Spafford (1873)   Philip P. Bliss (1876)

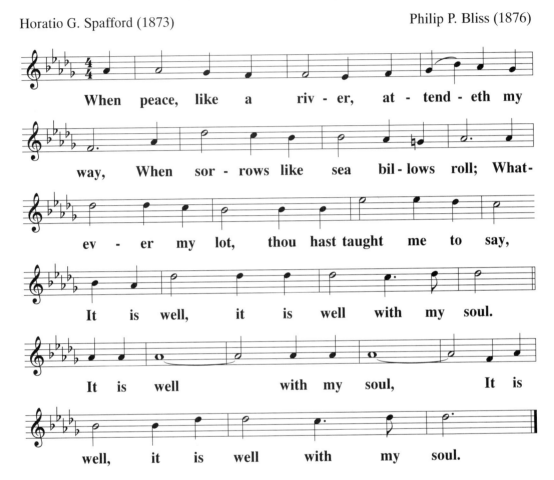

When peace, like a riv-er, at-tend-eth my way, When sor-rows like sea bil-lows roll; What-ev-er my lot, thou hast taught me to say, It is well, it is well with my soul.

It is well with my soul, It is well, it is well with my soul.

Though Satan should buffet, though trials should come,
Let this blest assurance control,
That Christ has regarded my helpless estate,
And hath shed his own blood for my soul. *It is well...*

My sin, oh, the bliss of this glorious thought!
My sin, not in part but the whole,
Is nailed to the cross, and I bear it no more,
Praise the Lord, praise the Lord, O my soul! *It is well...*

And, Lord, haste the day when my faith shall be sight,
The clouds be rolled back as a scroll;
The trump shall resound, and the Lord shall descend,
Even so, it is well with my soul. *It is well...*

We Remember

253

Marty Haugen (1980)   Marty Haugen (1980)

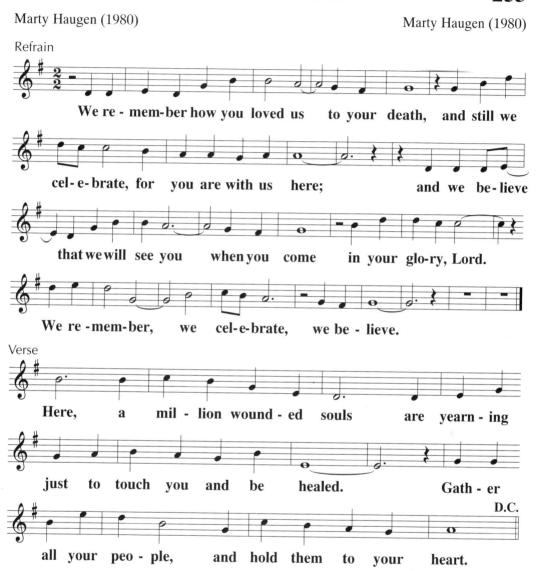

Refrain

We re-mem-ber how you loved us to your death, and still we cel-e-brate, for you are with us here; and we be-lieve that we will see you when you come in your glo-ry, Lord. We re-mem-ber, we cel-e-brate, we be-lieve.

Verse

Here, a mil-lion wound-ed souls are yearn-ing just to touch you and be healed. Gath-er all your peo-ple, and hold them to your heart.

D.C.

Now we recreate your love, we bring the bread and wine to share a meal.
Sign of grace and mercy, the presence of the Lord. *Ref.*

Christ, the Father's great "Amen" to all the hopes and dreams of ev'ry heart,
Peace beyond all telling, and freedom from all fear. *Ref.*

See the face of Christ revealed in ev'ry person standing by your side,
Gift to one another, and temples of your love. *Ref.*

254   Take Time to Be Holy

HOLINESS 6.5.6.5 D

1 Peter 1:16
William D. Longstaff (c. 1882)   George C. Stebbins (1890)

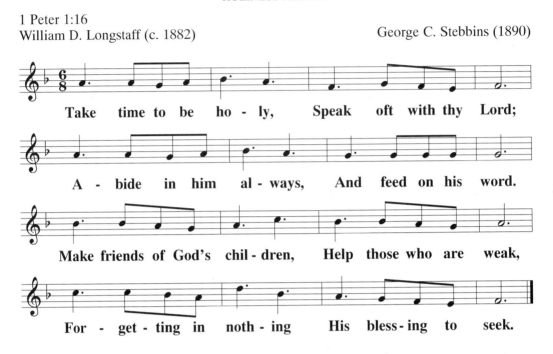

Take time to be ho - ly, Speak oft with thy Lord;

A - bide in him al - ways, And feed on his word.

Make friends of God's chil - dren, Help those who are weak,

For - get - ting in noth - ing His bless - ing to seek.

Take time to be holy,
The world rushes on;
Spend much time in secret
With Jesus alone.
By looking to Jesus,
Like him thou shalt be;
Thy friends in thy conduct
His likeness shall see.

Take time to be holy,
Let him be thy guide,
And run not before him,
Whatever betide.
In joy or in sorrow,
Still follow the Lord,
And, looking to Jesus,
Still trust in his word.

Take time to be holy,
Be calm in thy soul,
Each thought and each motive
Beneath his control.
Thus led by his spirit
To fountains of love,
Thou soon shalt be fitted
For service above.

Come to the Water

255

Isaiah 55:1, 2; Matthew 11:28-30
John B. Foley, SJ (1978)   John B. Foley, SJ (1978)

O let all who thirst, let them come to the water. And let all who have noth-ing, let them come to the Lord: With-out mon-ey, with-out price. Why should you pay the price, ex - cept for the Lord?

And let all who seek, let them come to the water.
And let all who have nothing, let them come to the Lord:
Without money, without strife.
Why should you spend your life, except for the Lord?

And let all who toil, let them come to the water.
And let all who are weary, let them come to the Lord:
All who labor, without rest.
How can your soul find rest, except for the Lord?

And let all the poor, let them come to the water.
Bring the ones who are laden, bring them all to the Lord:
Bring the children without might.
Easy the load and light: come to the Lord.

256 Savior, Like a Shepherd Lead Us

BRADBURY 8.7.8.7 D

John 10:1-29
Attr. to Dorothy A. Thrupp (1836)

William B. Bradbury (1859)

Sav - ior, like a shep-herd lead us,

Much we need thy ten - der care;

In thy pleas - ant pas-tures feed us,

For our use thy folds pre - pare.

Bless - ed Je - sus, bless - ed Je - sus! Thou hast

bought us, thine we are. Bless - ed Je - sus, bless - ed

Je - sus! Thou hast bought us, thine we are.

We are thine, thou dost befriend us,
Be the guardian of our way;
Keep thy flock, from sin defend us,
Seek us when we go astray.
Blessèd Jesus, blessèd Jesus!
Hear, O hear us when we pray.
Blessèd Jesus, blessèd Jesus!
Hear, O hear us when we pray.

Thou hast promised to receive us,
Poor and sinful though we be;
Thou hast mercy to relieve us,
Grace to cleanse and pow'r to free.
Blesséd Jesus, blesséd Jesus!
We will early turn to thee.
Blesséd Jesus, blesséd Jesus!
We will early turn to thee.

Early let us seek thy favor,
Early let us do thy will;
Blesséd Lord and only Savior,
With thy love our bosoms fill.
Blesséd Jesus, blesséd Jesus!
Thou hast loved us, love us still.
Blesséd Jesus, blesséd Jesus!
Thou hast loved us, love us still.

257   I Am Thine, O Lord

I AM THINE 10.7.10.7 with refrain

Fanny J. Crosby (1875)   William H. Doane (1875)

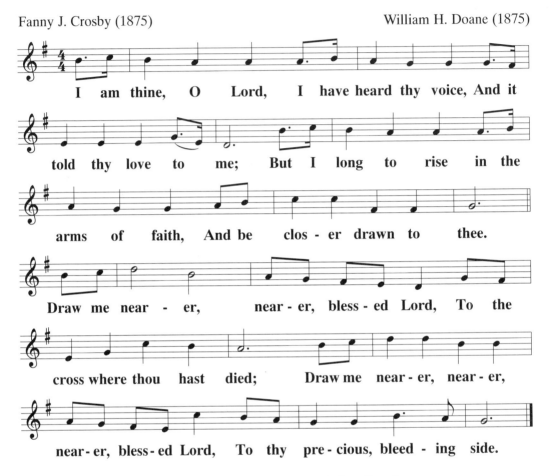

I am thine, O Lord, I have heard thy voice, And it
told thy love to me; But I long to rise in the
arms of faith, And be clos - er drawn to thee.

Draw me near - er, near - er, bless - ed Lord, To the
cross where thou hast died; Draw me near - er, near - er,
near - er, bless - ed Lord, To thy pre - cious, bleed - ing side.

Consecrate me now to thy service, Lord,
By the pow'r of grace divine;
Let my soul look up with a steadfast hope,
And my will be lost in thine. *Draw me nearer...*

O, the pure delight of a single hour
That before thy throne I spend,
When I kneel in prayer, and with thee, my God,
I commune as friend with friend! *Draw me nearer...*

There are depths of love that I cannot know
Till I cross the narrow sea;
There are heights of joy that I may not reach
Till I rest in peace with thee. *Draw me nearer...*

Blessed Assurance: Jesus Is Mine   258

ASSURANCE 9.10.9.9 with refrain

St. 1&3, Fanny J. Crosby (1873)
St. 2, Marie J. Post (1985)

Phoebe P. Knapp (1873)

Bless - ed as - sur - ance: Je - sus is mine! Oh, what a

fore - taste of glo - ry di - vine! Heir of sal -

va - tion, pur - chase of God, Born of his

Spir - it, washed in his blood.

This is my sto - ry, this is my song, Prais-ing my

Sav - ior all the day long; This is my sto - ry, this is my

song, Prais-ing my Sav - ior all the day long.

Joyful confession: I am his own!
Following Jesus, I'm never alone.
Born of his Spirit, I am restored,
Challenged to serve my Savior and Lord. *This is my story...*

Perfect submission: all is at rest,
I in my Savior am happy and blest;
Watching and waiting, looking above,
Filled with his goodness, kept in his love. *This is my story...*

259   O Happy Day, That Fixed My Choice

HAPPY DAY LM with refrain

2 Chronicles 15:15
Philip Doddridge (1755)   Anonymous
Refrain from *Wesleyan Sacred Harp* (1854)   Refrain attr. to Edward F. Rimbault (1854)

O hap-py day, that fixed my choice On thee, my
Sav-ior and my God! Well may this glow-ing heart rejoice, And tell its rap-tures all a-broad.
Hap-py day, hap-py day, When Je-sus washed my sins a-
way! He taught me how to watch and pray, And live re-
joic-ing ev-'ry day. Hap-py day, hap-py
day, When Je-sus washed my sins a-way!

O happy bond, that seals my vows
To him who merits all my love!
Let cheerful anthems fill his house,
While to that sacred shrine I move.
Happy day...

It's done: the great transaction's done!
I am the Lord's and he is mine;
He drew me and I followed on,
Charmed to confess the voice divine.
  Happy day…

Now rest, my long-divided heart,
Fixed on this blissful center, rest.
Here have I found a nobler part;
Here heav'nly pleasures fill my breast.
  Happy day…

High heav'n, that heard the solemn vow,
That vow renewed shall daily hear,
Till in life's latest hour I bow
And bless in death a bond so dear.
  Happy day…

260   In the Cross of Christ I Glory

RATHBUN 8.7.8.7

John Bowring (1825)   Ithamar Conkey (1849)

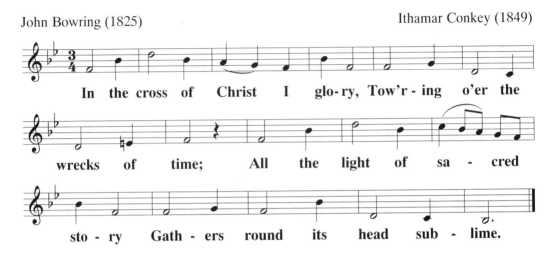

In the cross of Christ I glo-ry, Tow'r-ing o'er the
wrecks of time; All the light of sa - cred
sto - ry Gath - ers round its head sub - lime.

When the woes of life o'ertake me,
Hopes deceive, and fears annoy,
Never shall the cross forsake me:
Lo! it glows with peace and joy.

When the sun of bliss is beaming
Light and love upon my way,
From the cross the radiance streaming
Adds more luster to the day.

Bane and blessing, pain and pleasure,
By the cross are sanctified;
Peace is there that knows no measure,
Joys that through all time abide.

Amazing Grace
NEW BRITAIN CM

St. 1-4, John Newton (1779)
St. 5, ascr. to John Rees

Virginia Harmony (1831)
Harm. by John Barnard (1982)

261

A - maz - ing grace! how sweet the sound, That saved a wretch like me! I once was lost, but now am found, Was blind, but now I see.

’Twas grace that taught my heart to fear,
And grace my fears relieved;
How precious did that grace appear
The hour I first believed!

The Lord has promised good to me,
His word my hope secures;
He will my shield and portion be
As long as life endures.

Through many dangers, toils, and snares,
I have already come;
’Tis grace has brought me safe thus far,
And grace will lead me home.

When we’ve been there ten thousand years,
Bright shining as the sun,
We’ve no less days to sing God’s praise
Than when we’d first begun.

262   Be Thou My Vision

SLANE 10.10.9.10

Irish poem; trans. by Mary E. Byrne (1905)
Vrs. by Eleanor Hull (1912), alt.

Irish ballad
Harm. by David Evans (1927)

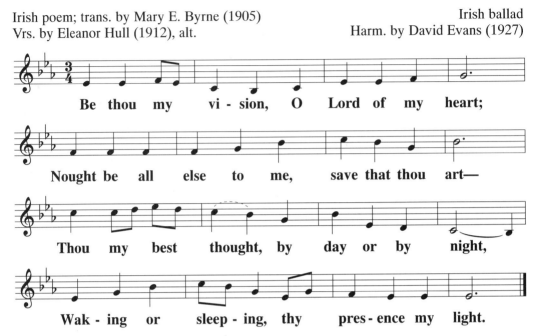

Be thou my vi - sion, O Lord of my heart;

Nought be all else to me, save that thou art—

Thou my best thought, by day or by night,

Wak - ing or sleep - ing, thy pres - ence my light.

Riches I heed not, nor vain, empty praise,
Thou mine inheritance, now and always:
Thou and thou only, first in my heart,
Great God of heaven, my treasure thou art.

Be thou my wisdom, and thou my true word;
I ever with thee and thou with me, Lord;
Heart of my own heart, whatever befall,
Still be my vision, O Ruler of all.

Jesus Calls Us

GALILEE 8.7.8.7

263

Matthew 4:18-22
Cecil Frances Alexander (1852)

William H. Jude (1874)

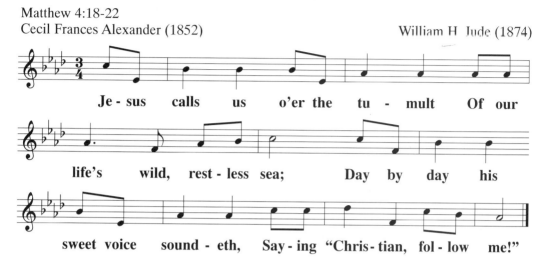

Je - sus calls us o'er the tu - mult Of our
life's wild, rest - less sea; Day by day his
sweet voice sound - eth, Say - ing "Chris - tian, fol - low me!"

As of old the apostles heard it
By the Galilean lake,
Turned from home and toil and kindred,
Leaving all for Jesus' sake.

Jesus calls us from the worship
Of the vain world's golden store,
From each idol that would keep us,
Saying, "Christian, love me more!"

In our joys and in our sorrows,
Days of toil and hours of ease,
Still he calls, in cares and pleasures,
"Christian, love me more than these!"

Jesus calls us! By thy mercies,
Savior, may we hear thy call,
Give our hearts to thine obedience,
Serve and love thee best of all.

264 Nobody Knows the Trouble I See

DUBOIS Irregular with refrain

African-American spiritual

African-American spiritual
Adapt. and arr. by William Farley Smith (1986)

Refrain

No-bod-y knows the troub-le I see, No-bod-y knows but Je-sus; Oh, no-bod-y knows the troub-le I see, Glo-ry hal-le-lu-jah!

Verse

Some-times I'm up, some-times I'm down, Oh, yes, Lord! Some-times I'm al-most to the ground, Oh, yes, Lord! Oh,

Although you see me going long so,
Oh, yes, Lord!
I have my troubles here below,
Oh, yes, Lord! Oh, *Ref.*

What makes old Satan hate me so?
Oh, yes, Lord!
'Cause he got me once and let me go,
Oh, yes, Lord! Oh, *Ref.*

Dear Lord and Father of Mankind   265

REST 8.6.8.8.6

John Greenleaf Whittier (1872)   Frederick C. Maker (1887)

Dear Lord and Fa - ther of man - kind, For -
give our fool - ish ways; Re - clothe us in our
right - ful mind, In pur - er lives thy
serv - ice find, In deep - er rev - 'rence, praise.

In simple trust like theirs who heard,
Beside the Syrian sea,
The gracious calling of the Lord,
Let us, like them, without a word,
Rise up and follow thee.

O sabbath rest by Galilee,
O calm of hills above,
Where Jesus knelt to share with thee
The silence of eternity,
Interpreted by love!

Drop thy still dews of quietness,
Till all our strivings cease;
Take from our souls the strain and stress,
And let our ordered lives confess
The beauty of thy peace.

Breathe through the heats of our desire
Thy coolness and thy balm;
Let sense be dumb, let flesh retire;
Speak through the earthquake, wind, and fire,
O still, small voice of calm.

266   Be Not Afraid

Isaiah 43:2-3; Luke 6:20ff
Bob Dufford, SJ (1975)

Bob Dufford, SJ (1975)
Acc. by Sr. Theophane Hytrek, OSF

Verse 1

1. You shall cross the bar-ren des-ert, but you

shall not die of thirst. You shall wan-der far in

safe-ty though you do not know the way. You shall

speak your words in for-eign lands and all will un-der-

stand. You shall see the face of God and live.

Refrain

Be not a-fraid. I go be-fore you al-ways. Come, fol-low

me, and I will give you rest.

Verse 2

2. If you pass through rag-ing wa-ters in the

sea, you shall not drown. If you walk a-mid the burn-ing flames,

you shall not be harmed. If you stand be-fore the

pow'r of hell and death is at your side, know that I am

D.S.

with you through it all.

Verse 3

3. Bless-ed are your poor, for the king-dom shall be theirs.

Blest are you that weep and mourn, for one day you shall

laugh. And if wick-ed tongues in-sult and hate you

all be-cause of me, bless-ed,

D.S.

bless - ed are you!

267 O God of Bethel, by Whose Hand

DUNDEE CM

Philip Doddridge (1736) and
  John Logan (1781), alt.

*Scottish Psalte*r (1615)

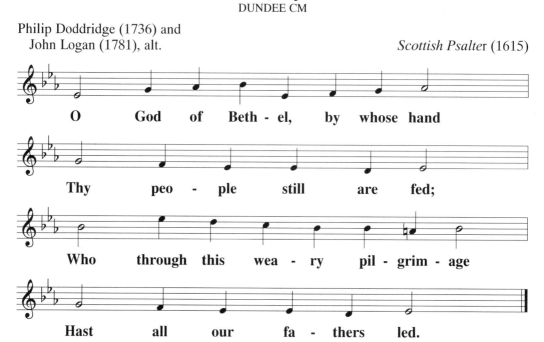

O God of Beth - el, by whose hand

Thy peo - ple still are fed;

Who through this wea - ry pil - grim - age

Hast all our fa - thers led.

Our vows, our prayers, we now present
Before thy throne of grace;
God of our fathers, be the God
Of their succeeding race.

Through each perplexing path of life
Our wand'ring footsteps guide;
Give us each day our daily bread,
And raiment fit provide.

O spread thy cov'ring wings around
Till all our wand'rings cease,
And at our Father's loved abode
Our souls arrive in peace.

Day By Day

SUMNER Irregular

268

Attr. to Richard of Chichester

Arthur Henry Biggs

Day by day, dear Lord, of thee three things I pray: To

see thee more clear - ly, Love thee more dear - ly,

Fol - low thee more near - ly, day by day.

269   I Want to Walk as a Child of the Light

HOUSTON 10.7.10.8.9.9.10.7

Ephesians 5:8-10; Revelation 21:23;
  John 12:46; 1 John 1:5; Hebrews 12:1
Kathleen Thomerson (1970)   Kathleen Thomerson (1970)

I want to walk as a child of the light.

I want to fol - low Je - sus.

God set the stars to give light to the world. The

star of my life is Je - sus.

In him there is no dark - ness at all. The

night and the day are both a - like. The

Lamb is the light of the cit - y of God.

Shine in my heart, Lord Je - sus.

I want to see the brightness of God.
I want to look at Jesus.
Clear sun of righteousness shine on my path,
And show me the way to the Father.
   In him…

I'm looking for the coming of Christ.
I want to be with Jesus.
When we have run with patience the race,
We shall know the joy of Jesus.
   In him…

270 Stand Up, Stand Up for Jesus

WEBB 7.6.7.6 D

Ephesians 6:10-17
George Duffield, Jr. (1858)

George J. Webb (1830)

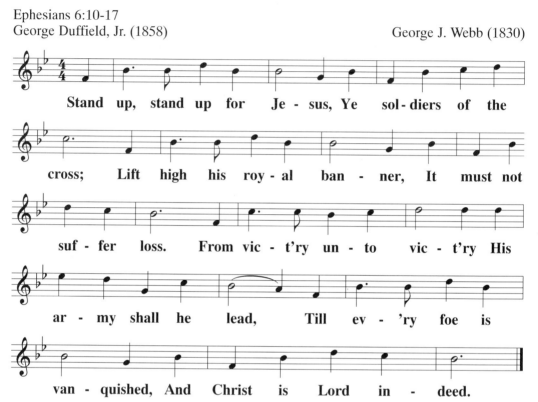

Stand up, stand up for Je - sus, Ye sol - diers of the cross; Lift high his roy - al ban - ner, It must not suf - fer loss. From vic - t'ry un - to vic - t'ry His ar - my shall he lead, Till ev - 'ry foe is van - quished, And Christ is Lord in - deed.

Stand up, stand up for Jesus,
The trumpet call obey;
Forth to the mighty conflict,
In this his glorious day.
Ye that are brave now serve him
Against unnumbered foes;
Let courage rise with danger,
And strength to strength oppose.

Stand up, stand up for Jesus,
Stand in his strength alone;
The arm of flesh will fail you,
Ye dare not trust your own.
Put on the gospel armor,
Each piece put on with prayer;
Where duty calls or danger,
Be never wanting there.

Stand up, stand up for Jesus,
The strife will not be long;
This day the noise of battle,
The next the victor's song.
To those who vanquish evil
A crown of life shall be;
They with the King of Glory
Shall reign eternally.

Love Divine, All Loves Excelling   271

HYFRYDOL 8.7.8.7 D

Charles Wesley (1747), alt.   Rowland H. Prichard (c. 1830)

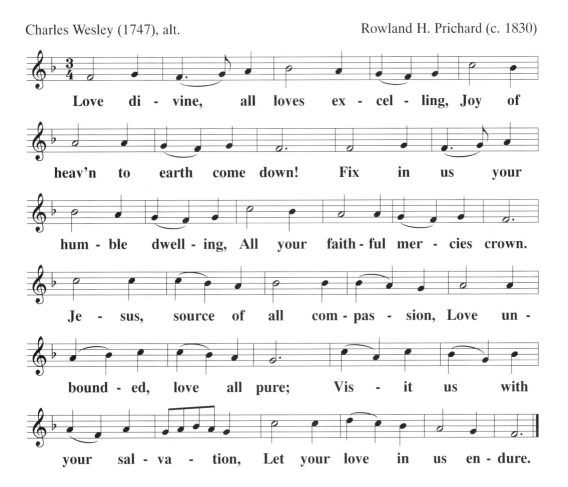

Love di - vine, all loves ex - cel - ling, Joy of
heav'n to earth come down! Fix in us your
hum - ble dwell - ing, All your faith - ful mer - cies crown.
Je - sus, source of all com - pas - sion, Love un -
bound - ed, love all pure; Vis - it us with
your sal - va - tion, Let your love in us en - dure.

Come, almighty to deliver,
Let us all your life receive;
Suddenly return and never,
Never more your temples leave.
Lord, we would be always blessing,
Serve you as your hosts above,
Pray, and praise you without ceasing,
Glory in your precious love.

Finish then your new creation,
Pure and spotless, gracious Lord,
Let us see your great salvation
Perfectly in you restored.
Changed from glory into glory,
Till in heav'n we take our place,
Till we sing before the almighty
Lost in wonder, love and praise.

272   Come, Thou Fount of Every Blessing

NETTLETON 8.7.8.7 D

Robert Robinson (1758)   Wyeth's *Repository of Sacred Music* (1813)

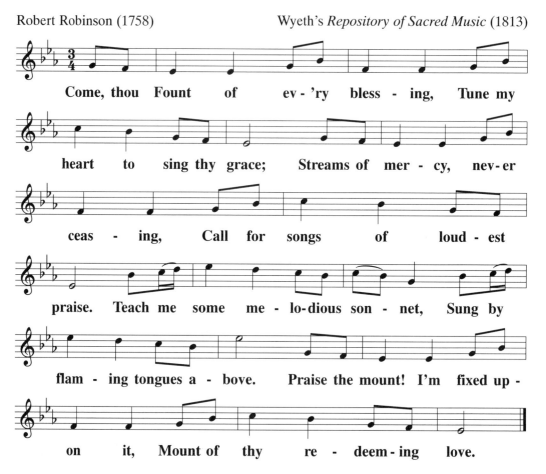

Come, thou Fount of ev-'ry bless-ing, Tune my
heart to sing thy grace; Streams of mer-cy, nev-er
ceas-ing, Call for songs of loud-est
praise. Teach me some me-lo-dious son-net, Sung by
flam-ing tongues a-bove. Praise the mount! I'm fixed upon it, Mount of thy re-deem-ing love.

Here I raise mine Ebenezer;	O to grace how great a debtor
Hither by thy help I'm come;	Daily I'm constrained to be!
And I hope, by thy good pleasure,	Let thy goodness, like a fetter,
Safely to arrive at home.	Bind my wand'ring heart to thee.
Jesus sought me when a stranger,	Prone to wander, Lord, I feel it,
Wand'ring from the fold of God;	Prone to leave the God I love;
He, to rescue me from danger,	Here's my heart, O take and seal it,
Interposed his precious blood.	Seal it for thy courts above.

'Tis the Gift to Be Simple

273

SIMPLE GIFTS Irregular with refrain

Shaker melody
Arr. by Margaret W. Mealy

Shaker song (18th C.)

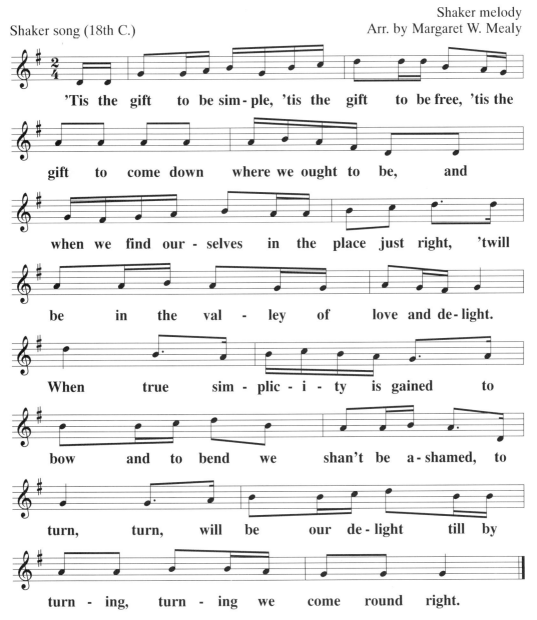

'Tis the gift to be sim-ple, 'tis the gift to be free, 'tis the

gift to come down where we ought to be, and

when we find our-selves in the place just right, 'twill

be in the val-ley of love and de-light.

When true sim-plic-i-ty is gained to

bow and to bend we shan't be a-shamed, to

turn, turn, will be our de-light till by

turn-ing, turn-ing we come round right.

274   God Be in My Head

LYTLINGTON Irregular

Sarum Primer (1514)   Sydney Hugo Nicholson

God be in my head, and in my un-der-stand-ing;

God be in mine eyes, and in my look-ing;

God be in my mouth, and in my speak-ing;

God be in my heart, and in my think-ing;

God be at mine end, and at my de-part-ing.

O Savior, in This Quiet Place

ST. STEPHEN CM

275

Fred Pratt Green (1974)   William Jones (1789)

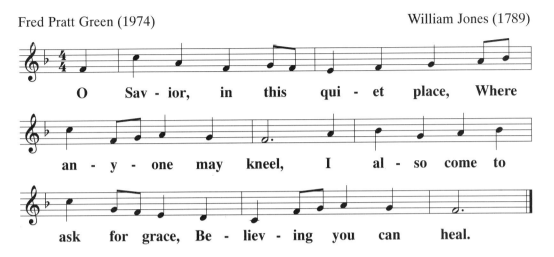

O Sav - ior, in this qui - et place, Where
an - y - one may kneel, I al - so come to
ask for grace, Be - liev - ing you can heal.

If pain of body, stress of mind,
Destroys my inward peace,
In prayer for others may I find
The secret of release.

If self upon its sickness feeds
And turns my life to gall,
Let me not brood upon my needs,
But simply tell you all.

You never said, "You ask too much,"
To any troubled soul.
I long to feel your healing touch;
Will you not make me whole?

But if the thing I most desire
Is not your way for me,
May faith, when tested in the fire,
Prove its integrity.

Of all my prayers, may this be chief:
Till faith is fully grown,
Lord, disbelieve my unbelief,
And claim me as your own.

276 How Firm a Foundation

FOUNDATION 11.11.11.11

2 Timothy 2:19; Isaiah 41:10; Isaiah 43:2;
Isaiah 46:4; Hebrews 13:5
Rippon's *A Selection of Hymns* (1787)

Funk's *Compilation of
Genuine Church Music* (1832)
Harm. by Richard Proulx (1975)

How firm a foun - da - tion, ye saints of the
Lord, Is laid for your faith in his ex - cel - lent
Word! What more can he say than to you he hath
said, To you who for ref - uge to Je - sus have fled?

"Fear not, I am with thee, O be not dismayed,
For I am thy God and will still give thee aid;
I'll strengthen and help thee, and cause thee to stand,
Upheld by my righteous, omnipotent hand."

"When through the deep waters I call thee to go,
The rivers of woe shall not thee overflow;
For I will be with thee, thy troubles to bless,
And sanctify to thee thy deepest distress."

"When through fiery trials thy pathways shall lie,
My grace, all sufficient, shall be thy supply;
The flame shall not hurt thee; I only design
Thy dross to consume, and thy gold to refine."

"E'en down to old age all my people shall prove
My sov'reign, eternal, unchangeable love;
And when hoary hairs shall their temples adorn,
Like lambs they shall still in my bosom be borne."

"The soul that on Jesus still leans for repose,
I will not, I will not desert to its foes;
That soul, though all hell should endeavor to shake,
I'll never, no, never, no, never forsake."

277 Tell Me the Stories of Jesus

STORIES OF JESUS 8.4.8.4.5.4.5.4

Matthew 16:13-15, 21:8-9;
  Mark 10:13-16, 11:8-10; John 12:13
William H. Parker (1885)

Frederick A. Challinor (1903)

Tell me the sto-ries of Je - sus I love to hear;

Things I would ask him to tell me If he were here:

Scenes by the way - side, Tales of the sea,

Sto - ries of Je - sus, Tell them to me.

First let me hear how the children
Stood 'round his knee,
And I shall fancy his blessing
Resting on me;
Words full of kindness,
Deeds full of grace,
All in the lovelight
Of Jesus' face.

Into the city I'd follow
The children's band,
Waving a branch of the palm tree
High in my hand;
One of his heralds,
Yes, I would sing
Loudest hosannas,
"Jesus is King!"

Jesus, Lover of My Soul   278

ABERYSTWYTH 7.7.7.7 D

Charles Wesley (1740), alt.   Joseph Parry (1879)

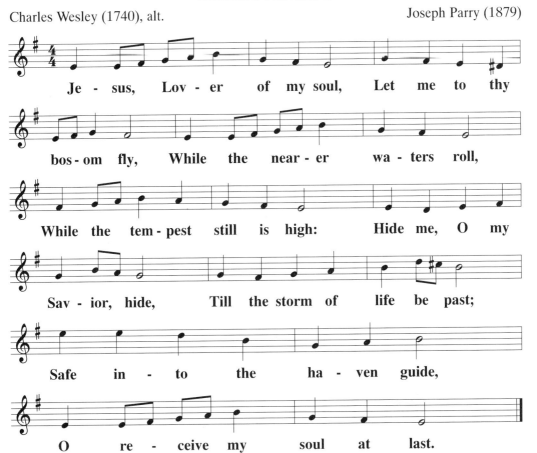

Je - sus, Lov - er of my soul, Let me to thy

bos - om fly, While the near - er wa - ters roll,

While the tem - pest still is high: Hide me, O my

Sav - ior, hide, Till the storm of life be past;

Safe in - to the ha - ven guide,

O re - ceive my soul at last.

Other refuge have I none,	Plenteous grace with thee is found,
Hangs my helpless soul on thee;	Grace to cleanse from ev'ry sin;
Leave, ah! leave me not alone,	Let the healing streams abound,
Still support and comfort me!	Make and keep me pure within.
All my trust on thee is stayed;	Thou of life the fountain art,
All my help from thee I bring;	Freely let me take of thee:
Cover my defenseless head	Spring thou up within my heart,
With the shadow of thy wing.	Rise to all eternity.

279   Jesus, Priceless Treasure

JESU, MEINE FREUDE 6.6.5.6.6.5.7.8.6

Johann Franck (1653)
Trans. by Catherine Winkworth (1863)

Praxis Pietatis Melica (1656)
Harm. by Johann Sebastian Bach (1723)

Je - sus, price - less treas - ure, Source of pur - est
pleas - ure, Tru - est friend to me,
Long my heart hath pant - ed, Till it well - nigh
faint - ed, Thirst - ing af - ter thee.
Thine I am, O spot - less Lamb, I will suf - fer
naught to hide thee, Ask for naught be - side thee.

In thine arms I rest me;
Foes who would molest me
Cannot reach me here.
Though the earth be shaking,
Ev'ry heart be quaking,
Jesus calms our fear;
Sin and hell in conflict fell
With their heaviest storms assail us;
Jesus will not fail us.

Hence, all thoughts of sadness!
For the Lord of gladness,
Jesus, enters in.
Those who love the Father,
Though the storms may gather,
Still have peace within;
Yea, whate'er we here must bear,
Still in thee lies purest pleasure,
Jesus, priceless treasure!

God Will Take Care of You   280

MARTIN CM with refrain

Civilla D. Martin (1904)   W. Stillman Martin (1905)

Be not dis - mayed what - e'er be - tide, God will take care of you; Be-neath his wings of love a - bide, God will take care of you.

God will take care of you, Through ev - 'ry day, o'er all the way; He will take care of you, God will take care of you.

Through days of toil when heart doth fail,
God will take care of you;
When dangers fierce your path assail,
God will take care of you.
   God will take care...

All you may need he will provide,
God will take care of you;
Nothing you ask will be denied,
God will take care of you.
   God will take care...

No matter what may be the test,
God will take care of you;
Lean, weary one, upon his breast,
God will take care of you.
   God will take care...

281   O Master, Let Me Walk with Thee

MARYTON LM

Washington Gladden (1879)   H. Percy Smith (1874)

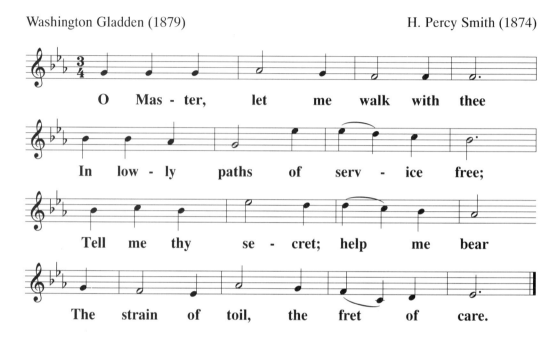

O Mas - ter, let me walk with thee

In low - ly paths of serv - ice free;

Tell me thy se - cret; help me bear

The strain of toil, the fret of care.

Help me the slow of heart to move
By some clear, winning word of love;
Teach me the wayward feet to stay,
And guide them in the homeward way.

Teach me thy patience; still with thee
In closer, dearer company,
In work that keeps faith sweet and strong,
In trust that triumphs over wrong;

In hope that sends a shining ray
Far down the future's broad'ning way,
In peace that only thou canst give,
With thee, O Master, let me live.

May the Mind of Christ, My Savior   282

ST. LEONARDS 8.7.8.5

Kate B. Wilkinson (1925)   A. Cyril Barham-Gould (1925)

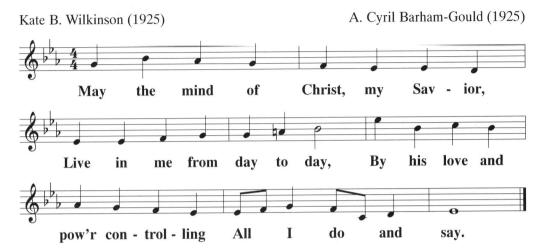

May the mind of Christ, my Sav - ior,

Live in me from day to day, By his love and

pow'r con - trol - ling All I do and say.

May the word of God dwell richly
In my heart from hour to hour,
So that all may see I triumph
Only through his pow'r.

May the peace of God, my Father,
Rule my life in ev'rything,
That I may be calm to comfort
Sick and sorrowing.

May the love of Jesus fill me
As the waters fill the sea.
Him exalting, self abasing:
This is victory.

May we run the race before us,
Strong and brave to face the foe,
Looking only unto Jesus
As we onward go.

283 Seek the Lord

GENEVA 8.7.8.7 D

Isaiah 55:6-11
Fred Pratt Green (1986)

George Henry Day (1940)

Seek the Lord who now is pres-ent,
Pray to One who is at hand. Let the wick-ed
cease from sin-ning, E-vil-do-ers change their mind.
On the sin-ful God has pit-y;
Those re-turn-ing God for-gives. This is what the
Lord is say-ing To a world that dis-be-lieves:

"Judge me not by human standards!
As the vault of heaven soars
High above the earth, so higher
Are my thoughts and ways than yours.
See how rain and snow from heaven
Make earth blossom and bear fruit,
Giving you, before returning,
Seed for sowing, bread to eat:

"So my word returns not fruitless;
Does not from its labors cease
Till it has achieved my purpose
In a world of joy and peace."
God is love! How close the prophet
To that vital gospel word!
In Isaiah's inspiration
It is Jesus we have heard!

My Shepherd Will Supply My Need   **284**
RESIGNATION CMD

Psalm 23   Funk's *Compilation of Genuine Church Music* (1832)
Isaac Watts (1719), alt.   Harm. by Richard Proulx (1975)

My Shep-herd will sup-ply my need; The
God of love su-preme; In pas-tures green you
make me feed, Be-side the liv-ing stream. You
bring my wan-d'ring spir-it back, When I forsake your ways; And lead me for your
mer-cy's sake, In paths of truth and grace.

When I walk through the shades of death,
Your presence is my stay;
One word of your supporting breath
Drives all my fears away.
Your hand, in sight of all my foes,
Does still my table spread;
My cup with blessings overflows,
Your oil anoints my head.

The sure provisions of my God
Attend me all my days;
O may your house be my abode,
And all my work be praise!
There would I find a settled rest,
While others go and come,
No more a stranger nor a guest;
But like a child at home.

285 What a Friend We Have in Jesus
CONVERSE 8.7.8.7 D

Joseph M. Scriven (c. 1855)

Charles C. Converse (1868)

What a friend we have in Je - sus,

All our sins and griefs to bear!

What a priv - i - lege to car - ry

Ev - 'ry-thing to God in prayer!

O what peace we of - ten for - feit,

O what need - less pain we bear,

All be - cause we do not car - ry

Ev - 'ry-thing to God in prayer!

Have we trials and temptations?
Is there trouble anywhere?
We should never be discouraged—
Take it to the Lord in prayer.
Can we find a friend so faithful
Who will all our sorrows share?
Jesus knows our ev'ry weakness—
Take it to the Lord in prayer.

Are we weak and heavy-laden,
Cumbered with a load of care?
Precious Savior, still our refuge—
Take it to the Lord in prayer.
Do thy friends despise, forsake thee?
Take it to the Lord in prayer!
In his arms he'll take and shield thee—
Thou wilt find a solace there.

286   Near to the Heart of God

McAFEE CM with refrain

Cleland B. McAfee (1903)   Cleland B. McAfee (1903)

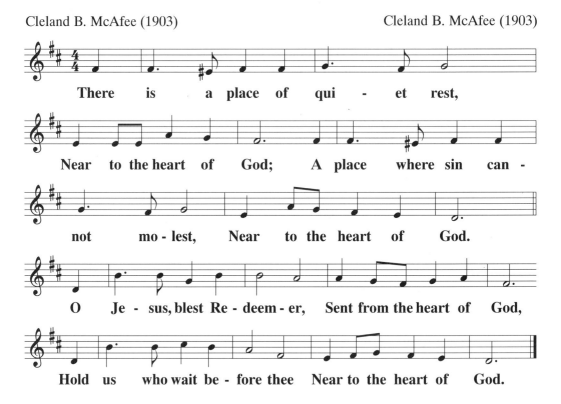

There is a place of qui - et rest,

Near to the heart of God; A place where sin can -

not mo - lest, Near to the heart of God.

O Je - sus, blest Re - deem - er, Sent from the heart of God,

Hold us who wait be - fore thee Near to the heart of God.

There is a place of comfort sweet,	There is a place of full release,
Near to the heart of God;	Near to the heart of God;
A place where we our Savior meet,	A place where all is joy and peace,
Near to the heart of God.	Near to the heart of God.
O Jesus...	*O Jesus...*

Lord of All Hopefulness

SLANE 10.11.11.12

287

Irish ballad
Adapt. from *The Church Hymnary* (1927)

Jan Struther (1931)

Harm. from *The Hymnal 1982*

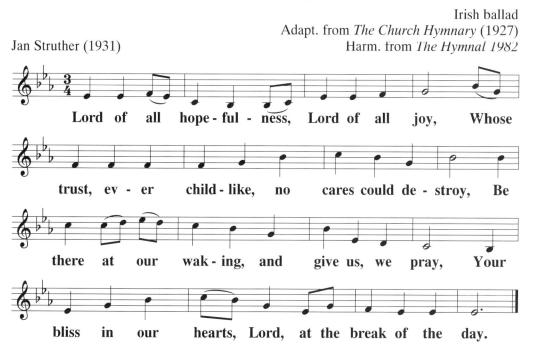

Lord of all hope-ful-ness, Lord of all joy, Whose
trust, ev-er child-like, no cares could de-stroy, Be
there at our wak-ing, and give us, we pray, Your
bliss in our hearts, Lord, at the break of the day.

Lord of all eagerness, Lord of all faith,
Whose strong hands were skilled at the plane and the lathe,
Be there at our labors, and give us, we pray,
Your strength in our hearts, Lord, at the noon of the day.

Lord of all kindliness, Lord of all grace,
Your hands swift to welcome, your arms to embrace,
Be there at our homing, and give us, we pray,
Your love in our hearts, Lord, at the eve of the day.

Lord of all gentleness, Lord of all calm,
Whose voice is contentment, whose presence is balm,
Be there at our sleeping, and give us, we pray,
Your peace in our hearts, Lord, at the end of the day.

288 Jesu, Jesu, Fill Us with Your Love

CHEREPONI Irregular with refrain

John 13:3-5
Tom Colvin (1963)

Ghanaian folk song
Adapt. by Tom Colvin (1963)
Arr. by Jane M. Marshall (1982)

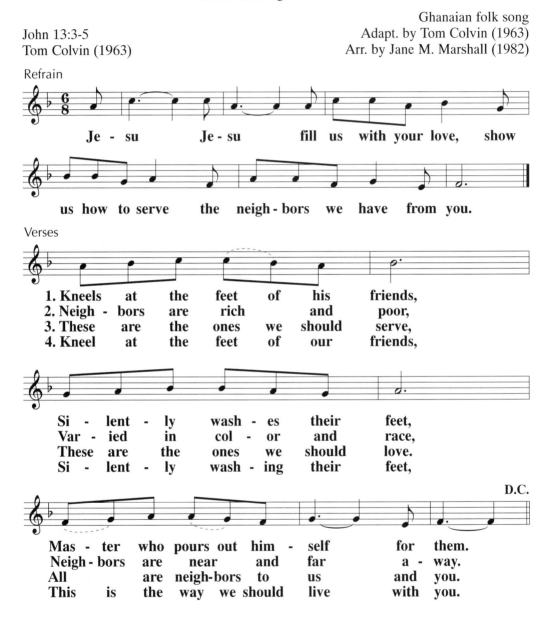

Refrain

Je - su   Je - su   fill us   with your love,   show

us how to serve   the neigh - bors   we   have   from you.

Verses

1. Kneels   at   the   feet   of   his   friends,
2. Neigh - bors   are   rich   and   poor,
3. These   are   the   ones   we   should   serve,
4. Kneel   at   the   feet   of   our   friends,

Si - lent - ly   wash - es   their   feet,
Var - ied   in   col - or   and   race,
These   are   the   ones   we   should   love.
Si - lent - ly   wash - ing   their   feet,

D.C.

Mas - ter   who pours out him - self   for   them.
Neigh - bors   are   near   and   far   a - way.
All   are   neigh-bors   to   us   and   you.
This   is   the   way   we should   live   with   you.

O Jesus Christ, May Grateful Hymns Be Rising 289
CHARTERHOUSE 11.10.11.10

Bradford G. Webster (1954)   David Evans (1927)

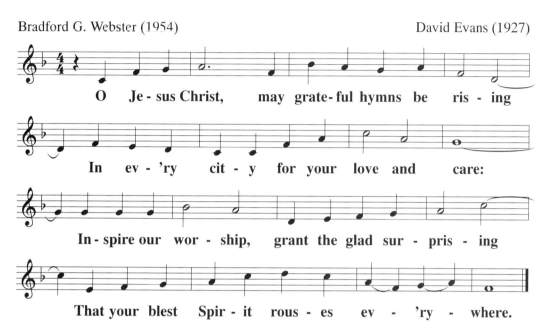

O Je - sus Christ, may grate- ful hymns be ris - ing

In ev - 'ry cit - y for your love and care:

In - spire our wor - ship, grant the glad sur - pris - ing

That your blest Spir - it rous - es ev - 'ry - where.

Grant us new courage, sacrificial, humble,
Strong in your strength to venture and to dare,
To lift the fallen, guide the feet that stumble,
Seek out the lonely, and God's mercy share.

Show us your Spirit, brooding o'er each city
As you once wept above Jerusalem,
Seeking to gather all in love and pity,
And healing those who touch your garment's hem.

290 Lord, You Give the Great Commission

ABBOT'S LEIGH 8.7.8.7 D

Jeffery Rowthorn (1978)

Cyril V. Taylor (1942)

Lord, you give the great com - mis - sion:

"Heal the sick and preach the word."

Lest the Church ne - glect its mis - sion,

And the Gos - pel go un - heard,

Help us wit - ness to your pur - pose

With re - newed in - teg - ri - ty;

With the Spir - it's gifts em - pow'r us

For the work of min - is - try.

Lord, you call us to your service:
"In my name baptize and teach."
That the world may trust your promise,
Life abundant meant for each,
Give us all new fervor, draw us
Closer in community;
With the Spirit's gifts empow'r us
For the work of ministry.

Lord you make the common holy:
"This my body, this my blood."
Let us all, for earth's true glory,
Daily lift life heavenward,
Asking that the world around us
Share your children's liberty;
With the Spirit's gifts empow'r us
For the work of ministry.

Lord, you show us love's true measure:
"Father, what they do, forgive."
Yet we hoard as private treasure
All that you so freely give.
May your care and mercy lead us
To a just society;
With the Spirit's gifts empow'r us
For the work of ministry.

Lord, you bless with words assuring:
"I am with you to the end."
Faith and hope and love restoring,
May we serve as you intend,
And, amid the cares that claim us,
Hold in mind eternity;
With the Spirit's gifts empow'r us
For the work of ministry.

291 Not for Tongues of Heaven's Angels
BRIDEGROOM 8.7.8.7.6

1 Corinthians 13
Timothy Dudley-Smith (1985)   Peter Cutts (1969)

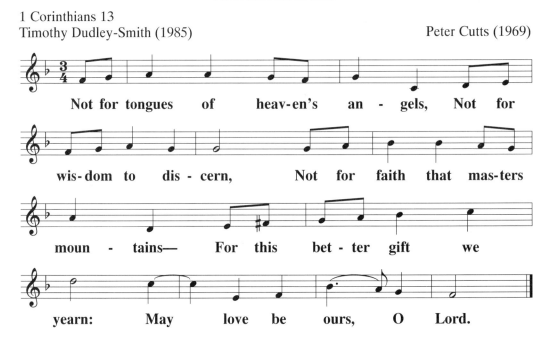

Not for tongues of heav-en's an - gels, Not for
wis-dom to dis - cern, Not for faith that mas-ters
moun - tains— For this bet-ter gift we
yearn: May love be ours, O Lord.

Love is humble, love is gentle,
Love is tender, true and kind;
Love is gracious, ever-patient,
Generous of heart and mind—
May love be ours, O Lord.

Never jealous, never selfish,
Love will not rejoice in wrong;
Never boastful nor resentful,
Love believes and suffers long—
May love be ours, O Lord.

In the day this world is fading,
Faith and hope will play their part;
But when Christ is seen in glory,
Love shall reign in ev'ry heart:
May love be ours, O Lord.

Christ for the World We Sing   292

MOSCOW 6.6.4.6.6.6.4

Felice de Giardini (1769)

Samuel Wolcott (1869)

Harm. from *The New Hymnal* (1916)

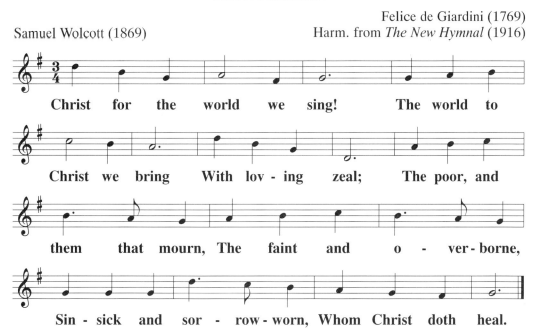

Christ for the world we sing! The world to
Christ we bring With lov-ing zeal; The poor, and
them that mourn, The faint and o-ver-borne,
Sin-sick and sor-row-worn, Whom Christ doth heal.

Christ for the world we sing!
The world to Christ we bring
With fervent prayer;
The wayward and the lost,
By restless passions tossed,
Redeemed at countless cost
From dark despair.

Christ for the world we sing!
The world to Christ we bring
With one accord;
With us the work to share,
With us reproach to dare,
With us the cross to bear,
For Christ our Lord.

Christ for the world we sing!
The world to Christ we bring
With joyful song;
The newborn souls, whose days,
Reclaimed from error's ways,
Inspired with hope and praise,
To Christ belong.

293 Here I Am, Lord

Isaiah 6
Dan Schutte (1981)

Dan Schutte (1981)
Arr. by Michael Pope, SJ and John Weissrock

I, the Lord of sea and sky, I have heard my

peo - ple cry. All who dwell in dark and sin

My hand will save. I who made the stars of night,

I will make their dark-ness bright. Who will bear my

light to them? Whom shall I send?

Here I am, Lord. Is it I, Lord?

I have heard you call - ing in the night.

I will go, Lord, if you lead me.

I will hold your peo - ple in my

heart.　　　　　　　　　　　　　　　　　　　　heart.

I, the Lord of snow and rain,
I have borne my people's pain.
I have wept for love of them.
They turn away.
I will break their hearts of stone,
Give them hearts for love alone.
I will speak my word to them.
Whom shall I send?
　Here I am…

I, the Lord of wind and flame,
I will tend the poor and lame.
I will set a feast for them.
My hand will save.
Finest bread I will provide.
Till their hearts be satisfied.
I will give my life to them.
Whom shall I send?
　Here I am…

294   Fight the Good Fight

PENTECOST LM

John Samuel Bewley Monsell (1863), alt.   William Boyd (1864)

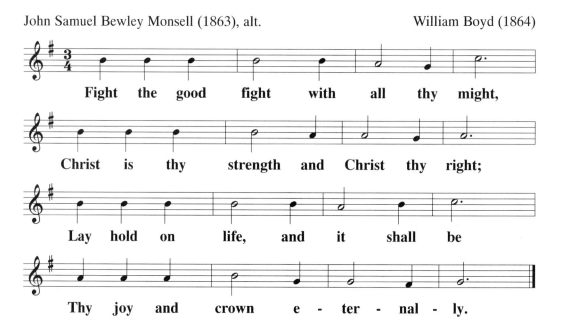

Fight the good fight with all thy might,
Christ is thy strength and Christ thy right;
Lay hold on life, and it shall be
Thy joy and crown e-ter-nal-ly.

Run the straight race through God's good grace,
Lift up thine eyes and seek his face;
Life with its way before us lies,
Christ is the path and Christ the prize.

Cast care aside, lean on thy Guide;
His boundless mercy will provide;
Trust, and thy trusting soul shall prove
Christ is its life and Christ its love.

Faint not nor fear, his arms are near;
He changeth not, and thou art dear;
Only believe, and thou shalt see
That Christ is all in all to thee.

O Day of God, Draw Nigh   295

ST. MICHAEL SM

Robert B. Y. Scott (1937)

Genevan Psalter (1551)
Arr. by William Crotch (1836)

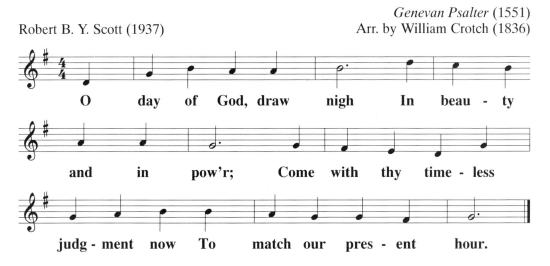

O day of God, draw nigh In beau - ty

and in pow'r; Come with thy time - less

judg - ment now To match our pres - ent hour.

Bring to our troubled minds,
Uncertain and afraid,
The quiet of a steadfast faith,
Calm of a call obeyed.

Bring justice to our land,
That all may dwell secure,
And finely build for days to come
Foundations that endure.

Bring to our world of strife
Thy sov'reign word of peace,
That war may haunt the earth no more,
And desolation cease.

O day of God, draw nigh
As at creation's birth;
Let there be light again, and set
Thy judgments on the earth.

296   Make Me a Channel of Your Peace

Prayer of St. Francis
Adapt. by Sebastian Temple (1967)

Sebastian Temple (1967)
Acc. by Robert J. Batastini (1996)

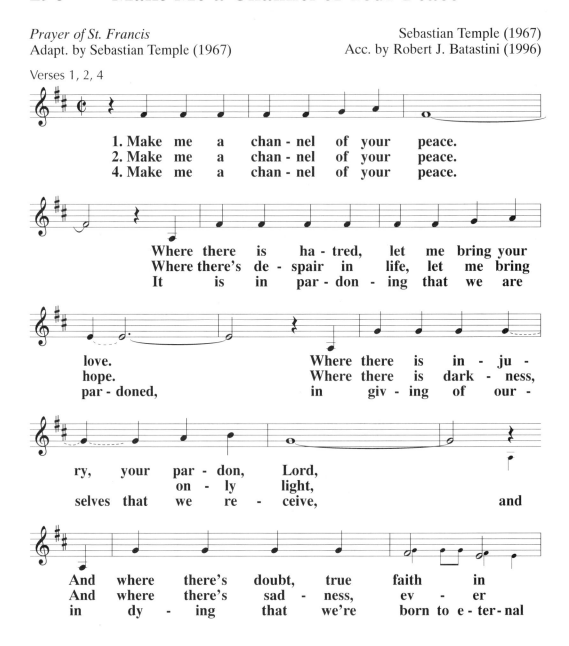

Verses 1, 2, 4

1. Make me a chan-nel of your peace.
2. Make me a chan-nel of your peace.
4. Make me a chan-nel of your peace.

Where there is ha-tred, let me bring your
Where there's de-spair in life, let me bring
It is in par-don-ing that we are

love. Where there is in-ju-
hope. Where there is dark-ness,
par-doned, in giv-ing of our-

ry, your par-don, Lord,
on-ly light,
selves that we re-ceive, and

And where there's doubt, true faith in
And where there's sad-ness, ev-er
in dy-ing that we're born to e-ter-nal

you.
joy.
life.

Verse 3

3. Oh, Mas - ter, grant that I may nev - er

seek   So much to be con - soled as   to con -

sole.   To be   un - der - stood

as   to   un - der - stand.   To be

loved   as   to   love with all   my   soul.

297 O God of Every Nation

LLANGLOFFAN 7.6.7.6 D

Welsh hymn melody
William Watkins Reid, Jr. (1958), alt.   Evans' *Hymnau a Thonau* (1865)

O God of ev-'ry nation, Of ev-'ry race and land, Re-deem the whole cre-a-tion With your al-might-y hand; Where hate and fear di-vide us And bit-ter threats are hurled, In love and mer-cy guide us And heal our strife-torn world.

From search for wealth and power
And scorn of truth and right,
From trust in bombs that shower
Destruction through the night,
From pride of race and nation
And blindness to your way,
Deliver ev'ry nation,
Eternal God, we pray!

Lord, strengthen all who labor
That we may find release
From fear of rattling saber,
From dread of war's increase;
When hope and courage falter,
Your still small voice be heard;
With faith that none can alter,
Your servants undergird.

Keep bright in us the vision
Of days when war shall cease,
When hatred and division
Give way to love and peace,
Till dawns the morning glorious
When truth and justice reign
And Christ shall rule victorious
O'er all the world's domain.

298 God the Omnipotent

RUSSIA 11.10.11.9

Sts. 1-2, Henry Fothergill Chorley, alt.
Sts. 3-4, John Ellerton, alt.

Alexis Lvov (1833)

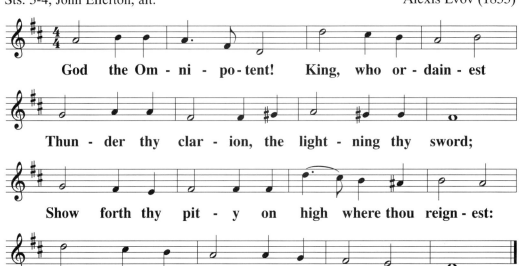

God the Om - ni - po - tent! King, who or - dain - est

Thun - der thy clar - ion, the light - ning thy sword;

Show forth thy pit - y on high where thou reign - est:

Give to us peace in our time, O Lord.

God the All-merciful! earth hath forsaken
Thy ways all holy, and slighted thy word;
Bid not thy wrath in its terrors awaken:
Give to us peace in our time, O Lord.

God the All-righteous One! earth hath defied thee;
Yet to eternity standeth thy word,
Falsehood and wrong shall not tarry beside thee:
Give to us peace in our time, O Lord.

God the All-provident! earth by thy chast'ning
Yet shall to freedom and truth be restored;
Through the thick darkness thy kingdom is hast'ning:
Thou wilt give peace in thy time, O Lord.

Hope of the World

DONNE SECOURS 11.10.11.10

Genevan Psalter (1551)

Georgia Harkness (1954), alt.

Harm. by Claude Goudimel

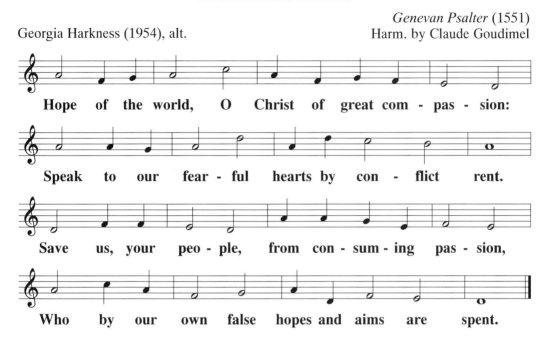

Hope of the world, O Christ of great com - pas - sion:

Speak to our fear - ful hearts by con - flict rent.

Save us, your peo - ple, from con - sum - ing pas - sion,

Who by our own false hopes and aims are spent.

Hope of the world, God's gift from highest heaven,
Bringing to hungry souls the bread of life:
Still let your Spirit unto us be given
To heal earth's wounds and end our bitter strife.

Hope of the world, afoot on dusty highways,
Showing to wand'ring souls the path of light:
Walk now beside us lest the tempting byways
Lure us away from you to endless night.

Hope of the world, who by your cross did save us
From death and dark despair, from sin and guilt:
We render back the love your mercy gave us;
Take now our lives and use them as you will.

Hope of the world, O Christ, o'er death victorious,
Who by this sign did conquer grief and pain:
We would be faithful to your gospel glorious;
You are our Lord! And you for ever reign!

300 God the Spirit, Guide and Guardian
HOLY MANNA 8.7.8.7 D

Carl P. Daw, Jr. (1987)   William Moore (1825)

God the Spir - it, guide and guard - ian,

Wind - sped flame and hov - 'ring dove,

Breath of life and voice of proph - ets,

Sign of bless - ing, pow'r of love: Give to those who

lead your peo - ple Fresh a - noint - ing of your grace;

Send them forth as bold a - pos - tles

To your church in ev - 'ry place.

Christ our Savior, sov'reign, shepherd,
Word made flesh, love crucified,
Teacher, healer, suff'ring servant,
Friend of sinners, foe of pride:
In your tending may your servants
Learn and live a shepherd's care;
Grant them courage and compassion
Shown through word and deed and prayer.

Great Creator, life-bestower,
Truth beyond all thought's recall,
Fount of wisdom, womb of mercy,
Giving and forgiving all:
As you know our strength and weakness,
So may those the church exalts
Oversee her life steadfastly,
Yet not overlook her faults.

Triune God, mysterious being,
Undivided and diverse,
Deeper than our minds can fathom,
Greater than our creeds rehearse:
Help us in our varied callings
Your full image to proclaim,
That our ministries uniting
May give glory to your name.

301   Let There Be Peace on Earth

Sy Miller, Jill Jackson (1955)
Acc. by Diana Kodner (1993)

Sy Miller, Jill Jackson (1955)

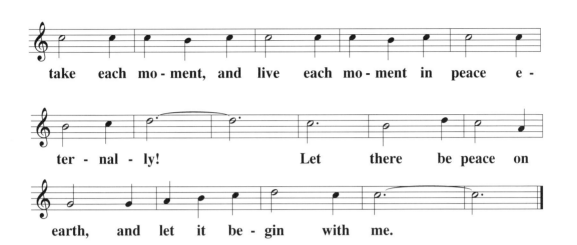

take each mo - ment, and live each mo - ment in peace e -

ter - nal - ly! Let there be peace on

earth, and let it be - gin with me.

302   How Clear Is Our Vocation, Lord

REPTON 8.6.8.8.6.6

Fred Pratt Green (1981)   Charles Hubert Hastings Parry (1888)

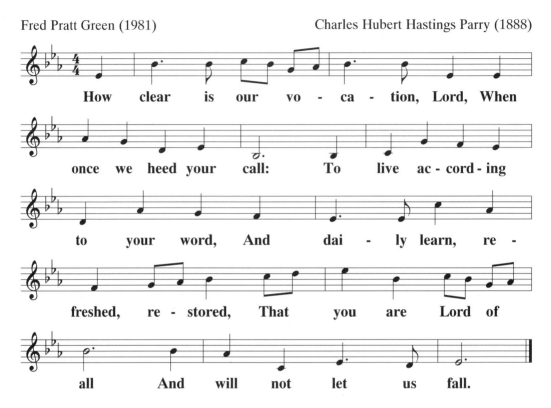

How clear is our vo - ca - tion, Lord, When
once we heed your call: To live ac - cord - ing
to your word, And dai - ly learn, re -
freshed, re - stored, That you are Lord of
all And will not let us fall.

But if, forgetful, we should find
Your yoke is hard to bear,
If worldly pressures fray the mind
And love itself cannot unwind
Its tangled skein of care:
Our inward life repair.

We mark your saints, how they become
In hindrances more sure,
Whose joyful virtues put to shame
The casual way we wear your name,
And by our faults obscure
Your pow'r to cleanse and cure.

In what you give us, Lord, to do,
Together or alone,
In old routines or ventures new,
May we not cease to look to you—
The cross you hung upon—
All you endeavored done.

Lead on, O King Eternal
LANCASHIRE 7.6.7.6 D

303

Ernest Warburton Shurtleff (1887)   Henry Thomas Smart (1835)

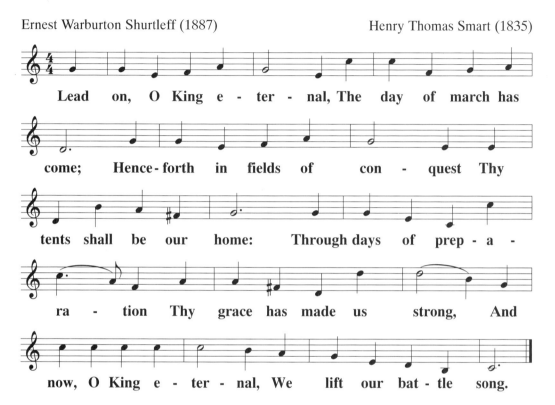

Lead on, O King e-ter-nal, The day of march has come; Hence-forth in fields of con-quest Thy tents shall be our home: Through days of prep-a-ra-tion Thy grace has made us strong, And now, O King e-ter-nal, We lift our bat-tle song.

Lead on, O King eternal,
Till sin's fierce war shall cease,
And holiness shall whisper
The sweet amen of peace;
For not with swords loud clashing,
Nor roll of stirring drums,
But deeds of love and mercy,
The heav'nly kingdom comes.

Lead on, O King eternal:
We follow, not with fears;
For gladness breaks like morning
Where'er thy face appears.
Thy cross is lifted o'er us;
We journey in its light:
The crown awaits the conquest;
Lead on, O God of might!

304   Whatsoever You Do

WHATSOEVER YOU DO 10.10.11 with refrain

Matthew 5:3-12

Willard F. Jabusch (1966)

Willard F. Jabusch (1966)

Harm. by Robert J. Batastini (1975)

Refrain

What-so-ev-er you do to the least of my

peo-ple, that you do un-to me.

Verse

When I was hun-gry, you gave me to eat;

When I was thirst-y, you gave me to drink.

D.C.

Now en-ter in-to the home of my Fa - ther.

When I was homeless, you opened your door;
When I was naked, you gave me your coat.
Now enter into the home of my Father. *Ref.*

When I was weary, you helped me find rest;
When I was anxious, you calmed all my fears.
Now enter into the home of my Father. *Ref.*

When I was little, you taught me to read;
When I was lonely, you gave me your love.
Now enter into the home of my Father. *Ref.*

When in a prison you came to my cell;
When on a sickbed, you cared for my needs.
Now enter into the home of my Father. *Ref.*

In a strange country, you made me at home;
Seeking employment, you found me a job.
Now enter into the home of my Father. *Ref.*

Hurt in a battle, you bound up my wounds;
Searching for kindness, you held out your hand.
Now enter into the home of my Father. *Ref.*

When I was Black, or Latino, or white;
Mocked and insulted, you carried my cross.
Now enter into the home of my Father. *Ref.*

When I was agéd, you bothered to smile;
When I was restless, you listened and cared.
Now enter into the home of my Father. *Ref.*

You saw me covered with spittle and blood;
You knew my features, though grimy with sweat.
Now enter into the home of my Father. *Ref.*

When I was laughed at, you stood by my side;
When I was happy, you shared in my joy.
Now enter into the home of my Father. *Ref.*

305   O God of Love, O King of Peace

TALLIS' CANON LM

Henry Williams Baker (1860)   Thomas Tallis (c. 1567)

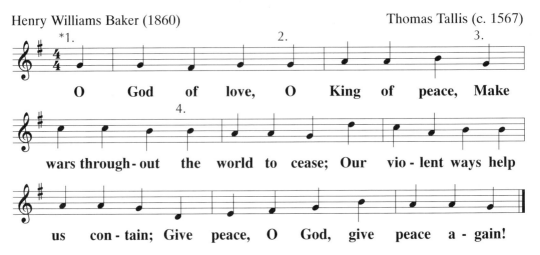

O God of love, O King of peace, Make
wars through-out the world to cease; Our vio-lent ways help
us con-tain; Give peace, O God, give peace a-gain!

May be sung as a two or four-voice canon.

Whom shall we trust but you, O Lord?
Where rest but on your faithful word?
None ever called on you in vain;
Give peace, O God, give peace again!

Where saints and angels dwell above,
All hearts are joined in holy love;
O bind us in that heav'nly chain;
Give peace, O God, give peace again!

Where Cross the Crowded Ways of Life   306
GERMANY LM

Matthew 22:9
Frank Mason North (1903)   Gardiner's *Sacred Melodies* (1815)

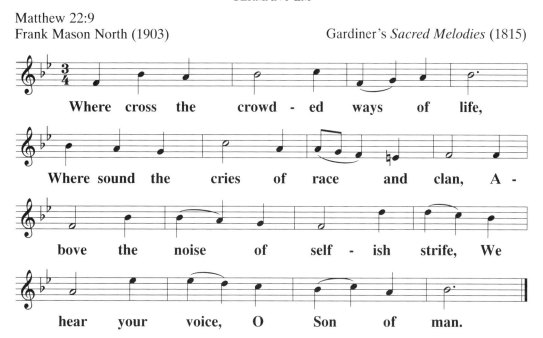

Where cross the crowd - ed ways of life,

Where sound the cries of race and clan, A -

bove the noise of self - ish strife, We

hear your voice, O Son of man.

In haunts of wretchedness and need,
On shadowed thresholds dark with fears,
From paths where hide the lures of greed,
We catch the vision of your tears.

From tender childhood's helplessness,
From woman's grief, man's burdened toil,
From famished souls, from sorrow's stress,
Your heart has never known recoil.

The cup of water giv'n for you
Still holds the freshness of your grace;
Yet long these multitudes to view
The sweet compassion of your face.

O Master, from the mountainside
Make haste to heal these hearts of pain;
Among these restless throngs abide;
O tread the city's streets again,

Till all the world shall learn your love
And follow where your feet have trod,
Till, glorious from your heav'n above,
Shall come the city of our God!

307 Lord Christ, When First You Came to Earth
MIT FREUDEN ZART 8.7.8.7.8.8.7

Walter Russell Bowie (1928), alt.   Bohemian Brethren's *Kirchengesange* (1566)

Lord Christ, when first you came to earth, Upon a cross they bound you. And
mocked your sav - ing king - ship's worth By
thorns with which they crowned you. And
still our wrongs may fash - ion now New
thorns to pierce that stead - y brow, And
robe of sor - row round you.

O awesome Love, which finds no room
In life where sin denies you.
And, doomed to death, shall bring to doom
The pow'r which crucifies you,
Till not a stone be left on stone,
And then the nations' pride, o'erthrown,
Will nevermore defy you!

New advent of the love of Christ,
Will we again refuse you.
Till in the night of hate and war
We perish as we lose you?
From ancient doubts our minds release
To seek the kingdom of your peace,
By which alone we choose you.

O wounded hands of Jesus, build
In us your new creation:
Our pride is dust, our boasting stilled:
We wait your revelation.
O Love that triumphs over loss,
We bring our hearts before your cross
To finish your salvation.

308 Lord, Whose Love in Humble Service

IN BABILONE 8.7.8.7 D

Albert F. Bayly (1961)

Traditional Dutch melody
Arr. by Julius Röntgen (1906)

Lord, whose love in hum - ble serv - ice

Bore the weight of hu - man need,

Who did on the Cross for - sak - en,

Show us mer - cy's per - fect deed;

We, your ser - vants, bring the wor - ship

Not of voice a - lone, but heart:

Con - se - crat - ing to your pur - pose

Ev - 'ry gift which you im - part.

Still your children wander homeless;
Still the hungry cry for bread;
Still the captives long for freedom;
Still in grief we mourn our dead.
As, O Lord, your deep compassion
Healed the sick and freed the soul,
Use the love your Spirit kindles
Still to save and make us whole.

As we worship, grant us vision,
Till your love's revealing light,
Till the height and depth and greatness
Dawns upon our human sight:
Making known the needs and burdens
Your compassion bids us bear,
Stirring us to faithful service,
Your abundant life to share.

Called from worship into service
Forth in your great name we go,
To the child, the youth, the aged,
Love in living deeds to show;
Hope and health, goodwill and comfort,
Counsel, aid, and peace we give
That your children, Lord, in freedom,
May your mercy know and live.

309

O Jesus, I Have Promised

ANGEL'S STORY 7.6.7.6 D

Luke 9:57
John Ernest Bode (c. 1866)

Arthur Henry Mann (1881)

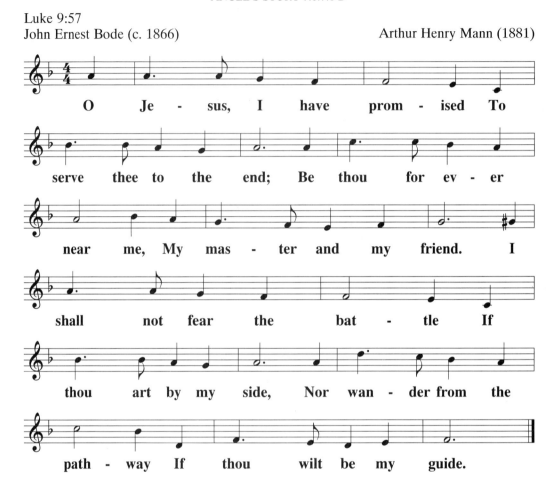

O Je - sus, I have prom - ised To

serve thee to the end; Be thou for ev - er

near me, My mas - ter and my friend. I

shall not fear the bat - tle If

thou art by my side, Nor wan - der from the

path - way If thou wilt be my guide.

O let me feel thee near me!
The world is ever near;
I see the sights that dazzle,
The tempting sounds I hear;
My foes are ever near me,
Around me and within;
But Jesus, draw thou nearer,
And shield my soul from sin.

O let me hear thee speaking
In accents clear and still,
Above the storms of passion,
The murmurs of self-will.
O speak to reassure me,
To hasten or control;
O speak, and make me listen,
Thou guardian of my soul.

O Jesus, thou hast promised
To all who follow thee
That where thou art in glory
There shall thy servant be.
And Jesus, I have promised
To serve thee to the end;
O give me grace to follow,
My master and my friend.

310   O God of Earth and Altar

LLANGLOFFAN 7.6.7.6 D

Gilbert K. Chesterton (1906)

Welsh hymn melody
Evans' *Hymnau a Thonau* (1865)

O God of earth and al - tar, Bow down and hear our

cry; Our earth - ly rul - ers fal - ter, Our

peo - ple drift and die; The walls of gold en -

tomb us, The swords of scorn di - vide; Take

not thy thun - der from us, But take a - way our pride.

From all that terror teaches,
From lies of tongue and pen;
From all the easy speeches
That comfort cruel men;
From sale and profanation
Of honor and the sword;
From sleep and from damnation,
Deliver us, good Lord!

Tie in a living tether
The prince and priest and thrall;
Bind all our lives together,
Smite us and save us all;
In ire and exultation
Aflame with faith, and free,
Lift up a living nation,
A single sword to thee.

Nearer, My God, to Thee

311

BETHANY 6.4.6.4.6.6.6.4

Genesis 28:10-22
Sarah F. Adams (1841)   Lowell Mason (1856)

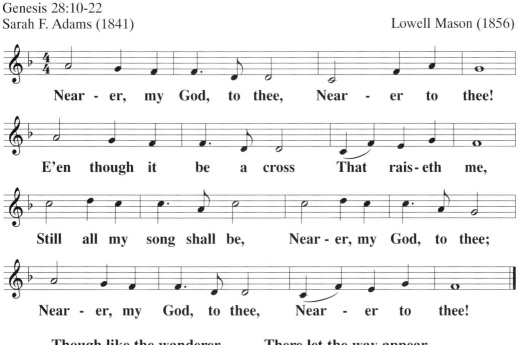

Near - er, my God, to thee, Near - er to thee!

E'en though it be a cross That rais - eth me,

Still all my song shall be, Near - er, my God, to thee;

Near - er, my God, to thee, Near - er to thee!

Though like the wanderer,
The sun gone down,
Darkness be over me,
My rest a stone;
Yet in my dreams I'd be
  Nearer...

There let the way appear,
Steps unto heav'n;
All that thou sendest me,
In mercy giv'n;
Angels to beckon me
  Nearer...

Then, with my waking thoughts
Bright with thy praise,
Out of my stony griefs
Bethel I'll raise;
So by my woes to be
  Nearer...

Or if, on joyful wing
Cleaving the sky,
Sun, moon, and stars forgot,
Upward I fly,
Still all my song shall be,
  Nearer...

312   You Are Near

Psalm 139   Dan Schutte (1971)
Dan Schutte (1971)   Acc. by Sr. Theophane Hytrek, OSF

Refrain

Yah-weh, I know you are near,

stand-ing al - ways at my side.

You guard me from the foe, and you

lead me in ways ev-er-last-ing.

Verses

1. Lord, you have searched my heart, and you
2. Where can I run from your love? If I
3. You know my heart and its ways, you who
4. Mar-vel-ous to me are your works; how pro -

know when I sit and when I stand. Your
climb to the heav-ens you are there; if I
formed me be - fore I was born in the
found are your thoughts, my Lord. E - ven

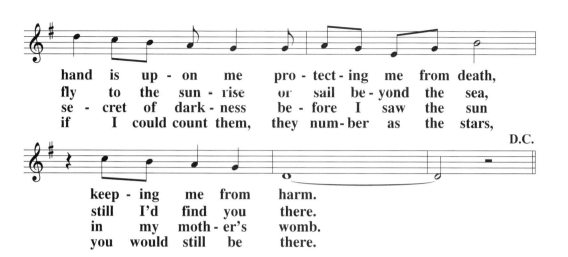

hand   is   up - on   me   pro - tect - ing   me   from   death,
fly   to   the   sun - rise   or   sail   be - yond   the   sea,
se - cret   of   dark - ness   be - fore   I   saw   the   sun
if   I   could count them,   they   num - ber   as   the   stars,

D.C.

keep - ing   me   from   harm.
still   I'd   find   you   there.
in   my   moth - er's   womb.
you   would   still   be   there.

313   O Day of Peace

JERUSALEM LMD

Isaiah 11:6-7   Charles Hubert Hastings Parry (1916)
Carl P. Daw, Jr. (1982)   Arr. by Janet Wyatt (1977)

1. O day of peace that dim - ly shines Through all our
2. Then shall the wolf dwell with the lamb, Nor shall the

hopes and prayers and dreams, Guide us to jus - tice, truth, and
fierce de - vour the small; As beasts and cat - tle calm - ly

love, De - liv - ered from our self - ish schemes. May swords of
graze, A lit - tle child shall lead them all. Then en - e -

hate fall from our hands, Our hearts from en - vy find re -
mies shall learn to love, All crea - tures find their true ac -

lease, Till by God's grace our war - ring world Shall see Christ's
cord; The hope of peace shall be ful - filled, For all the

1.

prom - ised reign of peace.
earth shall know the

2.

Lord.

O God, Our Help in Ages Past   **314**

ST. ANNE CM

Psalm 90
Isaac Watts (1719)   Attr. to William Croft (1708)

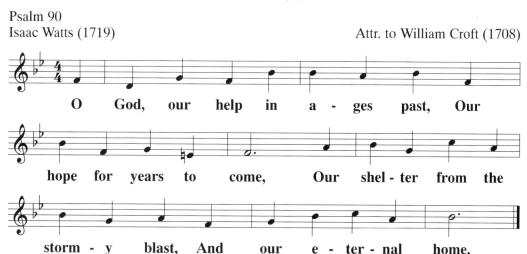

O God, our help in a - ges past, Our
hope for years to come, Our shel - ter from the
storm - y blast, And our e - ter - nal home.

Under the shadow of your throne
Your saints have dwelt secure;
Sufficient is your arm alone,
And our defense is sure.

Before the hills in order stood,
Or earth received its frame,
From everlasting you are God,
To endless years the same.

A thousand ages in your sight
Are like an evening gone,
Short as the watch that ends the night
Before the rising sun.

Time like an ever-rolling stream,
Soon bears us all away;
We fly forgotten, as a dream
Dies at the op'ning day.

O God, our help in ages past,
Our hope for years to come,
Still be our guard while troubles last,
And our eternal home.

315   God of Day and God of Darkness

BEACH SPRING 8.7.8.7 D

The Sacred Harp (1844)
Harm. by Marty Haugen (1985)

Marty Haugen (1985)

God of day and God of dark - ness, Now we

stand be - fore the night; As the shad - ows stretch and

deep - en, Come and make our dark - ness bright. All cre -

a - tion still is groan - ing For the dawn - ing of your

might, When the Sun of peace and jus - tice

Fills the earth with ra - diant light.

Still the nations curse the darkness,
Still the rich oppress the poor;
Still the earth is bruised and broken
By the ones who still want more.
Come and wake us from our sleeping,
So our hearts cannot ignore
All your people lost and broken,
All your children at our door.

Show us Christ in one another,
Make us servants strong and true;
Give us all your love of justice
So we do what you would do.
Let us call all people holy,
Let us pledge our lives anew,
Make us one with all the lowly,
Let us all be one in you.

You shall be the path that guides us,
You the light that in us burns;
Shining deep within all people,
Yours the love that we must learn,
For our hearts shall wander restless
'Til they safe to you return;
Finding you in one another,
We shall all your face discern.

Praise to you in day and darkness,
You our source and you our end;
Praise to you who love and nurture us
As a father, mother, friend.
Grant us all a peaceful resting,
Let each mind and body mend,
So we rise refreshed tomorrow,
Hearts renewed to Kingdom tend.

316 Give to the Winds Thy Fears

FESTAL SONG SM

Psalm 37:5; Paul Gerhardt (1653)
Trans. by John Wesley (1739)

William H. Walter (1894)

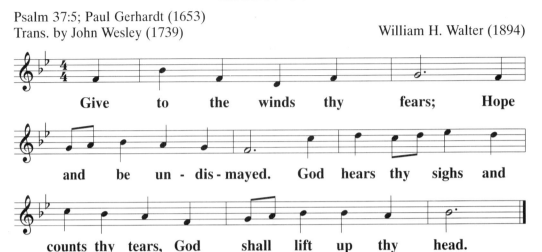

Give to the winds thy fears; Hope
and be un-dis-mayed. God hears thy sighs and
counts thy tears, God shall lift up thy head.

Through waves and clouds and storms,
God gently clears thy way;
Wait thou God's time; so shall this night
Soon end in joyous day.

Leave to God's sov'reign sway
To choose and to command;
So shalt thou, wond'ring, own that way,
How wise, how strong this hand.

Let us in life, in death,
Thy steadfast truth declare,
And publish with our latest breath
Thy love and guardian care.

Kum Ba Yah

DESMOND Irregular

317

African-American spiritual

African-American spiritual
Harm. by Carlton R. Young (1988)

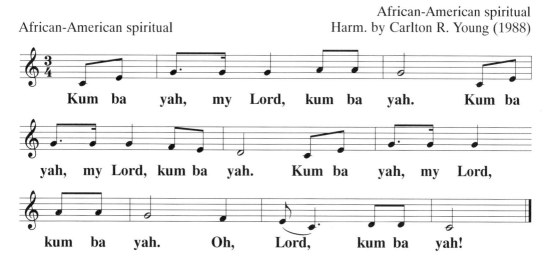

Kum ba yah, my Lord, kum ba yah. Kum ba

yah, my Lord, kum ba yah. Kum ba yah, my Lord,

kum ba yah. Oh, Lord, kum ba yah!

Someone's praying, Lord...

Someone's crying, Lord...

Someone needs you, Lord...

Someone's singing, Lord...

Let us praise the Lord...

318   Almighty Father, Strong to Save

MELITA 8.8.8.8.8.8

St. 1&4, William Whiting (1860)
St. 2-3, Robert Nelson Spencer, alt.

John Bacchus Dykes (1861)

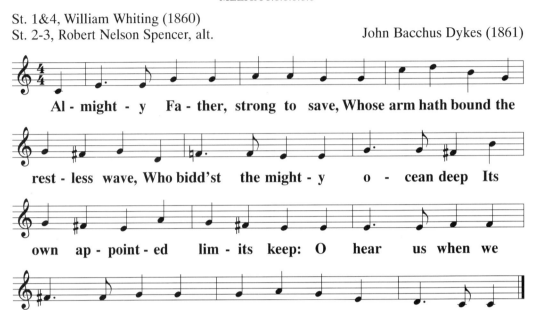

Al - might - y Fa - ther, strong to save, Whose arm hath bound the

rest - less wave, Who bidd'st the might - y o - cean deep Its

own ap - point - ed lim - its keep: O hear us when we

cry to thee For those in per - il on the sea.

O Christ, the Lord of hill and plain
O'er which our traffic runs amain
By mountain pass or valley low;
Wherever, Lord, thy people go,
Protect them by thy guarding hand
From ev'ry peril on the land.

O Spirit, whom the Father sent
To spread abroad the firmament;
O Wind of heaven, by thy might
Save all who dare the eagle's flight,
And keep them by thy watchful care
From ev'ry peril in the air.

O Trinity of love and pow'r,
Our people shield in danger's hour;
From rock and tempest, fire and foe,
Protect them wheresoe'er they go;
Thus evermore shall rise to thee
Glad praise from space, air, land, and sea.

Rock of Ages, Cleft for Me

TOPLADY 7.7.7.7.7.7

319

Augustus M. Toplady (1776)   Thomas Hastings (1830)

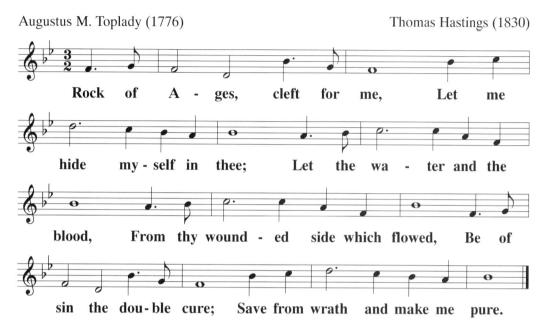

Rock of A - ges, cleft for me, Let me
hide my - self in thee; Let the wa - ter and the
blood, From thy wound - ed side which flowed, Be of
sin the dou - ble cure; Save from wrath and make me pure.

Not the labors of my hands
Can fulfill thy law's demands;
Could my zeal no respite know,
Could my tears for ever flow,
All for sin could not atone;
Thou must save, and thou alone.

Nothing in my hand I bring,
Simply to the cross I cling;
Naked, come to thee for dress;
Helpless, look to thee for grace;
Foul, I to the fountain fly;
Wash me, Savior, or I die.

While I draw this fleeting breath,
When mine eyes shall close in death,
When I soar to worlds unknown,
See thee on thy judgment throne,
Rock of Ages, cleft for me,
Let me hide myself in thee.

320   God Is Working His Purpose Out
PURPOSE Irregular

Habakkuk 1:14
Arthur C. Ainger (1894), alt.

Martin Shaw (1931)

1. God is work - ing his pur - pose out As
2. From ut - most east to ut - most west, Wher -
3. March we forth in the strength of God, With the
4. All we can do is worth - less toil Un -

year suc - ceeds to year:
ev - er foot has trod,
ban - ner of Christ un - furled,
less God bless - es the deed;

By the
That the

God is work - ing his pur - pose out, And the
mouth of man - y mes - sen - gers Goes
light of the glo - rious gos - pel of truth May
Vain - ly we hope for the har - vest - tide Till

time is draw - ing near;
forth the voice of God;
shine through - out the world:
God gives life to the seed;

Yet

Near - er and near - er draws the time, The
Give ear to me, you con - ti - nents, You
Fight we the fight with sor - row and sin To
near - er and near - er draws the time, The

time   that shall sure - ly   be,   When the
isles,   give   ear   to   me,   That the
set   their   cap - tives   free,   That the
time   that shall sure - ly   be,   When the

earth   shall be filled   with the   glo - ry   of God   As the
earth   may   be filled   with the   glo - ry   of God   As the
earth   may   be filled   with the   glo - ry   of God   As the
earth   shall be filled   with the   glo - ry   of God   As the

1.- 3.   4.

wa - ters   cov-er the   sea.
wa - ters   cov-er the   sea.
wa - ters   cov-er the   sea.
wa - ters   cov-er the   sea.

321 More Love to Thee, O Christ

MORE LOVE TO THEE 6.4.6.4.6.6.4.4

Elizabeth P. Prentiss (1869)

William H. Doane (1870)

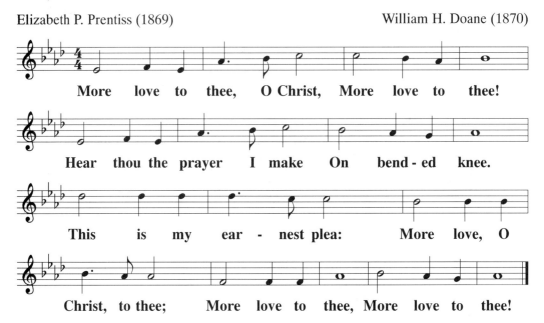

More love to thee, O Christ, More love to thee!

Hear thou the prayer I make On bend-ed knee.

This is my ear - nest plea: More love, O

Christ, to thee; More love to thee, More love to thee!

Once earthly joy I craved,
Sought peace and rest;
Now thee alone I seek,
Give what is best.
This all my prayer shall be:
More love, O Christ, to thee;
More love to thee,
More love to thee!

Let sorrow do its work,
Come grief and pain;
Sweet are thy messengers,
Sweet their refrain,
When they can sing with me:
More love, O Christ, to thee;
More love to thee,
More love to thee!

Then shall my latest breath
Whisper thy praise;
This be the parting cry
My heart shall raise;
This still its prayer shall be:
More love, O Christ, to thee;
More love to thee,
More love to thee!

Jesus, Remember Me   322

Luke 23:42
Taizé Community (1981)

Jacques Berthier (1981)

Ostinato Refrain

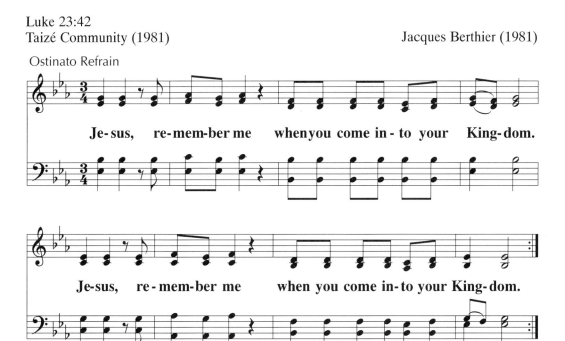

323   O Love That Wilt Not Let Me Go

ST. MARGARET 8.8.8.8.6

George Matheson (1882)   Albert L. Peace (1884)

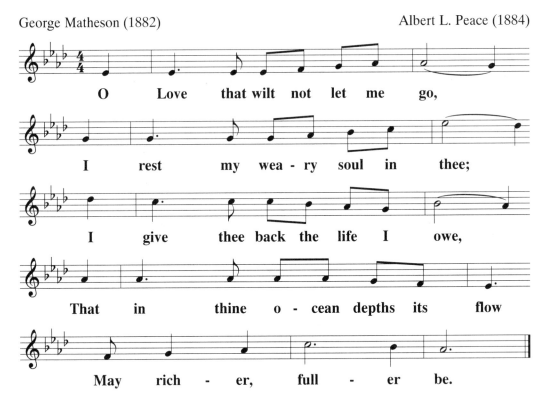

O Love that wilt not let me go,
I rest my wea-ry soul in thee;
I give thee back the life I owe,
That in thine o-cean depths its flow
May rich - er, full - er be.

O Light that followest all my way,
I yield my flick'ring torch to thee;
My heart restores its borrowed ray,
That in thy sunshine's blaze its day
May brighter, fairer be.

O Joy that seekest me through pain,
I cannot close my heart to thee;
I trace the rainbow thru the rain,
And feel the promise is not vain,
That morn shall tearless be.

O Cross that liftest up my head,
I dare not ask to fly from thee;
I lay in dust life's glory dead,
And from the ground there blossoms red
Life that shall endless be.

Be Still, My Soul

324

FINLANDIA 10.10.10.10.10.10

Katharina von Schlegel (1752)   Jean Sibelius (1899)
Trans. by Jane Laurie Borthwick (1855)   Arr. from *The Hymnal* (1933)

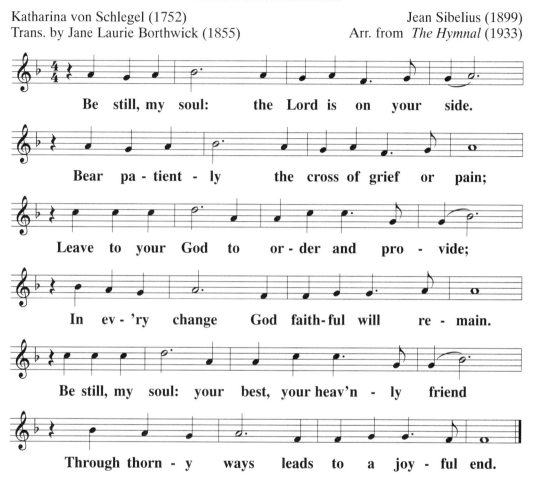

Be still, my soul: the Lord is on your side.

Bear pa - tient - ly the cross of grief or pain;

Leave to your God to or - der and pro - vide;

In ev - 'ry change God faith-ful will re - main.

Be still, my soul: your best, your heav'n - ly friend

Through thorn - y ways leads to a joy - ful end.

Be still, my soul: your God will undertake
To guide the future, as in ages past.
Your hope, your confidence let nothing shake;
All now mysterious shall be bright at last.
Be still, my soul: the waves and winds still know
The Christ who ruled them while he dwelt below.

Be still, my soul: the hour is hast'ning on
When we shall be for ever with the Lord,
When disappointment, grief, and fear are gone,
Sorrow forgot, love's purest joys restored.
Be still, my soul: when change and tears are past,
All safe and blessèd we shall meet at last.

325   Sweet Hour of Prayer

SWEET HOUR LMD

William Walford (1845)   William B. Bradbury (1861)

Sweet hour of prayer! sweet hour of prayer! That
calls me from a world of care, And
bids me at my Fa - ther's throne Make
all my wants and wish - es known.
In sea - sons of dis - tress and grief, My
soul has of - ten found re - lief, And
oft es - caped the tempt - er's snare By
thy re - turn, sweet hour of prayer!

Sweet hour of prayer! sweet hour of prayer!
The joys I feel, the bliss I share
Of those whose anxious spirits burn
With strong desires for thy return!
With such I hasten to the place
Where God my Savior shows his face,
And gladly take my station there,
And wait for thee, sweet hour of prayer!

Sweet hour of prayer! sweet hour of prayer!
Thy wings shall my petition bear
To him whose truth and faithfulness
Engage the waiting soul to bless.
And since he bids me seek his face,
Believe his word, and trust his grace,
I'll cast on him my ev'ry care,
And wait for thee, sweet hour of prayer!

326   Open My Eyes, That I May See

OPEN MY EYES 8.8.9.8 with refrain

Clara H. Scott (1895)   Clara H. Scott (1895)

O - pen my eyes, that I may see

Glimps - es of truth thou hast for me;

Place in my hands the won - der - ful key

That shall un - clasp and set me free.

Si - lent - ly now I wait for thee,

Read - y, my God, thy will to see. O - pen my eyes,

il - lu - mine me, Spir - it di - vine!

Open my ears, that I may hear	Open my mouth, and let me bear
Voices of truth thou sendest clear;	Gladly the warm truth ev'rywhere;
And while the wavenotes fall on my ear,	Open my heart and let me prepare
Ev'rything false will disappear.	Love with thy children thus to share.
Silently now …	*Silently now …*

I Heard the Voice of Jesus Say   327

KINGSFOLD CMD

English folk melody
Horatius Bonar (1846)
Harm. by Ralph Vaughan Williams (1906)

I heard the voice of Je - sus say, "Come un - to me and rest; Lay down, O wea - ry one, lay down Your head up - on my breast." I came to Je - sus as I was, So wea - ry, worn, and sad; I found in him a rest - ing place, And he has made me glad.

I heard the voice of Jesus say,
"Behold, I freely give
The living water; thirsty one,
Stoop down, and drink, and live."
I came to Jesus, and I drank
Of that life-giving stream;
My thirst was quenched, my soul revived,
And now I live in him.

I heard the voice of Jesus say,
"I am this dark world's light;
Look unto me, your morn shall rise,
And all your day be bright."
I looked to Jesus, and I found
In him my star, my sun;
And in that light of life I'll walk
Till trav'ling days are done.

328 My Hope Is Built

THE SOLID ROCK LM with refrain

Edward Mote (1834)   William B. Bradbury (1863)

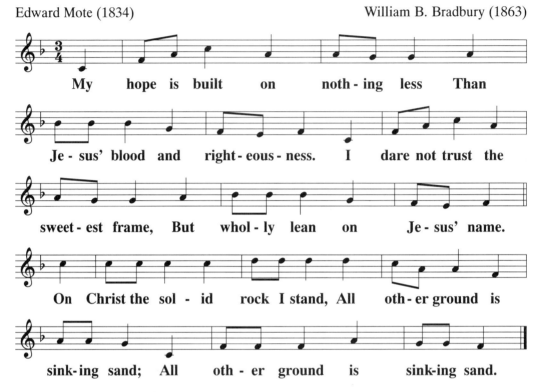

My hope is built on noth-ing less Than
Je-sus' blood and right-eous-ness. I dare not trust the
sweet-est frame, But whol-ly lean on Je-sus' name.
On Christ the sol-id rock I stand, All oth-er ground is
sink-ing sand; All oth-er ground is sink-ing sand.

When darkness veils his lovely face,
I rest on his unchanging grace.
In ev'ry high and stormy gale,
My anchor holds within the veil.
 On Christ…

His oath, his covenant, his blood
Support me in the whelming flood.
When all around my soul gives way,
He then is all my hope and stay.
 On Christ…

When he shall come with trumpet sound,
O may I then in him be found!
Dressed in his righteousness alone,
Faultless to stand before the throne!
 On Christ…

Come Down, O Love Divine

DOWN AMPNEY 6.6.11 D

329

Bianco da Siena
Trans. by Richard F. Littledale (1867)

Ralph Vaughan Williams (1906)

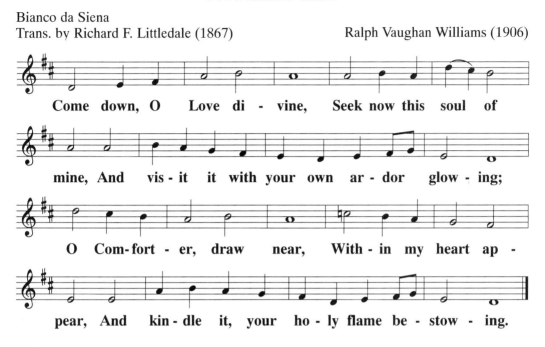

Come down, O Love di-vine, Seek now this soul of mine, And vis-it it with your own ar-dor glow-ing; O Com-fort-er, draw near, With-in my heart ap-pear, And kin-dle it, your ho-ly flame be-stow-ing.

O let it freely burn,
Till earthly passions turn
To dust and ashes in its heat consuming;
And let your glorious light
Shine ever on my sight,
And clothe me round, the while my path illuming.

And so the yearning strong,
With which the soul will long,
Shall far outpass the pow'r of human telling;
For none can guess its grace,
Till love creates the place
Wherein the Holy Spirit makes its dwelling.

330   A Mighty Fortress Is Our God

EIN' FESTE BURG 8.7.8.7.6.6.6.6.7

Martin Luther (1529)
Trans. Frederick Henry Hedge (1852)

Martin Luther (1529)
Harm. by Johann Sebastian Bach

A might-y for-tress is our God, A
bul-wark nev-er fail-ing; Our help-er he a-
mid the flood Of mor-tal ills pre-
vail-ing: For still our an-cient foe Doth
seek to work us woe; His craft and pow'r are great, And,
armed with cru-el hate, On earth is not his e-qual.

Did we in our own strength confide,
Our striving would be losing;
Were not the right man on our side,
The man of God's own choosing:
Dost ask who that may be?
Christ Jesus, it is he;
Lord Sabaoth his Name,
From age to age the same,
And he must win the battle.

And though this world, with devils filled,
Should threaten to undo us;
We will not fear, for God hath willed
His truth to triumph through us;
The prince of darkness grim,
We tremble not for him;
His rage we can endure,
For lo! his doom is sure,
One little word shall fell him.

That word above all earthly pow'rs,
No thanks to them, abideth;
The Spirit and the gifts are ours
Through him who with us sideth:
Let goods and kindred go,
This mortal life also;
The body they may kill:
God's truth abideth still,
His kingdom is for ever.

331   God Is Here! As We His People

ABBOT'S LEIGH 8.7.8.7 D

Fred Pratt Green (1979)   Cyril V. Taylor (1942)

God is here! As we his peo - ple,

Meet to of - fer praise and prayer,

May we find in ful - ler meas - ure

What it is in Christ we share:

Here, as in the world a - round us,

All our var - ied skills and arts

Wait the com - ing of his Spir - it

In - to o - pen minds and hearts.

Here are symbols to remind us
Of our lifelong need of grace;
Here are table, font and pulpit,
Here the cross has central place:
Here in honesty of preaching,
Here in silence as in speech,
Here in newness and renewal
God the Spirit comes to each.

Here our children find a welcome
In the Shepherd's flock and fold;
Here, as bread and wine are taken,
Christ sustains us as of old:
Here the servants of the Servant
Seek in worship to explore
What it means in daily living
To believe and to adore.

Lord of all, of church and kingdom,
In an age of change and doubt,
Keep us faithful to the gospel,
Help us work your purpose out:
Here, in this day's dedication,
All we have to give, receive;
We who cannot live without you,
We adore you! We believe!

332   God Himself Is with Us
ARNSBERG 6.6.8.6.6.8.6.6.6

Gerhardt Tersteegen (1729)   Joachim Neander (1680)

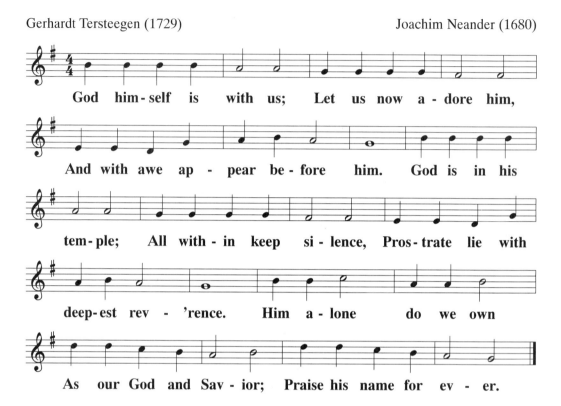

God him-self is with us; Let us now a-dore him,

And with awe ap-pear be-fore him. God is in his

tem-ple; All with-in keep si-lence, Pros-trate lie with

deep-est rev-'rence. Him a-lone do we own

As our God and Sav-ior; Praise his name for ev-er.

God himself is with us;
Hear the harps resounding!
See the crowds the throne surrounding!
"Holy, holy, holy,"
Hear the hymn ascending,
Angels, saints, their voices blending!
Bow your ear to us here;
Hear, O Christ, the praises
That your church now raises.

Fount of ev'ry blessing,
Purify my spirit,
Trusting only in your merit.
Like the holy angels
Who behold your glory,
May I ceaselessly adore you,
And in all, great and small,
Seek to do most nearly
What you love so dearly.

O Day of Rest and Gladness 333

MENDEBRAS 7.6.7.6 D

Old German melody
Arr. by Lowell Mason (1839)

Christopher Wordsworth (1862)

O day of rest and glad-ness, O day of
joy and light, O balm of care and sad - ness,
Most beau - ti - ful, most bright; On thee the high and
low - ly, Through a - ges joined in tune, Sing ho - ly,
ho - ly, ho - ly, To the great God Tri - une.

On thee, at the Creation,
The light first had its birth;
On thee, for our salvation,
Christ rose from depths of earth;
On thee our Lord, victorious,
The Spirit sent from heav'n;
And thus on thee, most glorious,
A triple light was giv'n.

New graces ever gaining
From this our day of rest,
We reach the rest remaining
To spirits of the blest.
To Holy Ghost be praises,
To Father, and to Son;
The Church her voice upraises
To thee, blest Three-in-One.

334   We Gather Together
KREMSER 12.11.12.11

Netherlands folk hymn (1625)
Trans. by Theodore Baker (1894)

Neder-landtsch Gedenckclanck (1626)
Harm. by Edward Kremser (1877)

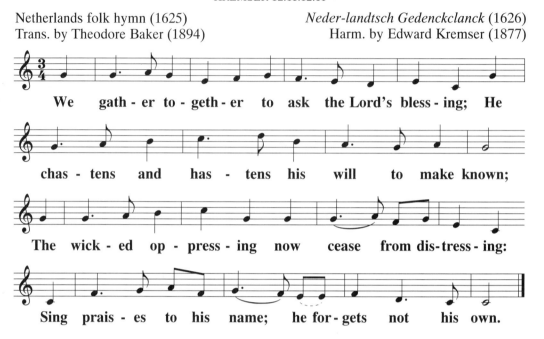

We gath-er to-geth-er to ask the Lord's bless-ing; He
chas-tens and has-tens his will to make known;
The wick-ed op-press-ing now cease from dis-tress-ing:
Sing prais-es to his name; he for-gets not his own.

Beside us to guide us, our God with us joining,
Whose kingdom calls all to the love which endures.
So from the beginning the fight we were winning:
You, Lord, were at our side; all glory be yours!

We all do extol you our leader triumphant,
And pray that you still our defender will be.
Let your congregation escape tribulation:
Your name be ever praised! O Lord, make us free!

Lord, Dismiss Us with Thy Blessing   335

SICILIAN MARINERS 8.7.8.7.8.7

The European Magazine and Review (1792)
Harm. from the *Methodist Hymn
and Tune Book* (1889), alt.

Attr. to John Fawcett (1773)

Lord, dis - miss us with thy bless-ing; Fill our hearts with

joy and peace; Let us each, thy love pos - sess-ing,

Tri-umph in re - deem-ing grace. O re - fresh us,

O re - fresh us, Trav- 'ling through this wil - der - ness.

Thanks we give and adoration
For thy Gospel's joyful sound.
May the fruits of thy salvation
In our hearts and lives abound;
Ever faithful, ever faithful
To the truth may we be found.

336   God Be with You Till We Meet Again

RANDOLPH 9.8.8.9

Jeremiah E. Rankin (1880)   Ralph Vaughan Williams (1906)

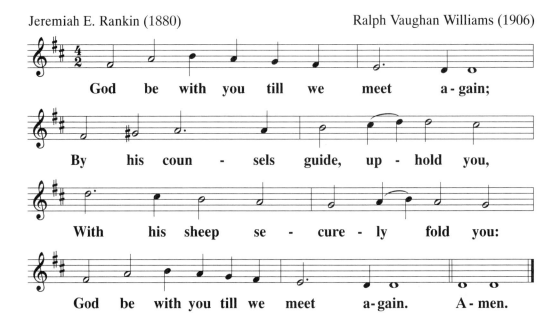

God be with you till we meet a-gain;

By his coun - sels guide, up-hold you,

With his sheep se - cure-ly fold you:

God be with you till we meet a-gain. A-men.

God be with you till we meet again;
'Neath his wings protecting hide you,
Daily manna still provide you:
God be with you till we meet again.

God be with you till we meet again;
When life's perils thick confound you,
Put his arms unfailing round you:
God be with you till we meet again.

God be with you till we meet again;
Keep love's banner floating o'er you,
Smite death's threat'ning wave before you:
God be with you till we meet again. Amen.

God Be with You Till We Meet Again   337
GOD BE WITH YOU 9.8.8.9

Jeremiah E. Rankin (1880)   William G. Tomer (1880)

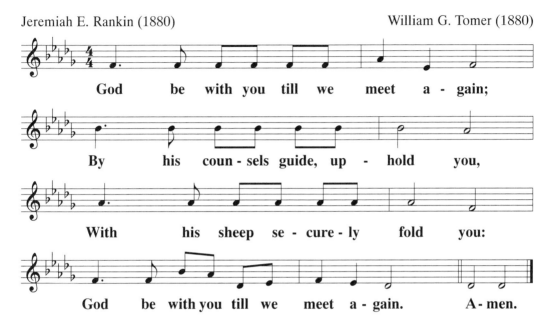

God be with you till we meet again;
'Neath his wings protecting hide you,
Daily manna still provide you:
God be with you till we meet again.

God be with you till we meet again;
When life's perils thick confound you,
Put his arms unfailing round you:
God be with you till we meet again.

God be with you till we meet again;
Keep love's banner floating o'er you,
Smite death's threat'ning wave before you:
God be with you till we meet again. Amen.

338 Savior, Again to Thy Dear Name

ELLERS 10.10.10.10

John Ellerton (1866), alt.

Edward J. Hopkins (1869)

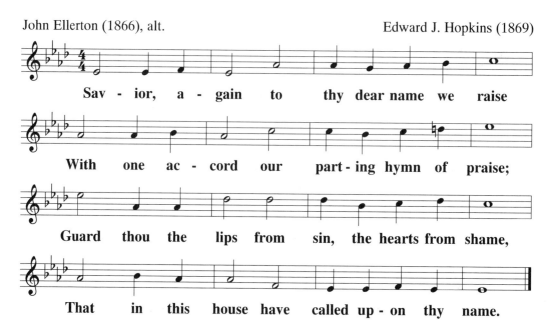

Sav - ior, a - gain to thy dear name we raise

With one ac - cord our part - ing hymn of praise;

Guard thou the lips from sin, the hearts from shame,

That in this house have called up - on thy name.

Grant us thy peace upon our homeward way;
With thee began, with thee shall end the day.
From harm and danger keep thy children free,
For dark and light are both alike to thee.

Grant us thy peace throughout our earthly life;
Peace to thy church from error and from strife;
Peace to our land, the fruit of truth and love;
Peace in each heart, thy Spirit from above;

Thy peace in life, the balm of ev'ry pain;
Thy peace in death, the hope to rise again;
Then, when thy voice shall bid our conflict cease,
Call us, O Lord, to thine eternal peace.

Father, We Praise You

339

CHRISTE SANCTORUM 11.11.11.5

Attr. to St. Gregory the Great
Trans. by Percy Dearmer (1906), alt.

La Feillees *Methode du plain-chant* (1782)

Fa - ther, we praise you, now the night is o - ver,

Ac - tive and watch - ful, stand we all be -

fore you; Sing - ing we of - fer prayer and med - i -

ta - tion: Thus we a - dore you.

Maker of all things, fit us for your mansions;
Banish our weakness, health and wholeness sending;
Bring us to heaven, where your saints united
Joy without ending.

All-holy Father, Son and equal Spirit,
Trinity blesséd, send us your salvation;
Yours is the glory, gleaming and resounding
Through all creation.

340 When Morning Gilds the Skies

LAUDES DOMINI 6.6.6 D

Katholisches Gesangbuch (1828)
Trans. by Edward Caswall (1854)

Joseph Barnby (1868)

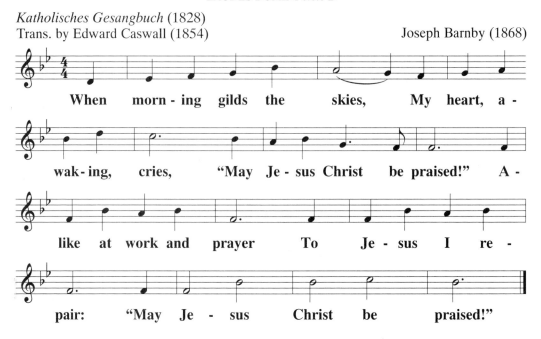

When morn-ing gilds the skies, My heart, a-
wak-ing, cries, "May Je-sus Christ be praised!" A-
like at work and prayer To Je-sus I repair: "May Je-sus Christ be praised!"

To God, the Word, on high
The hosts of angels cry:
"May Jesus Christ be praised!"
Let mortals, too, upraise
Their voice in hymns of praise:
"May Jesus Christ be praised!"

Let earth's wide circle round
In joyful notes resound:
"May Jesus Christ be praised!"
Let air, and sea, and sky,
From depth to height, reply:
"May Jesus Christ be praised!"

Be this while life is mine
My canticle divine:
"May Jesus Christ be praised!"
Be this the eternal song,
Through all the ages long:
"May Jesus Christ be praised!"

Christ, Whose Glory Fills the Skies   341
RATISBON 7.7.7.7.7.7

J. G. Werner's *Choralbuch* (1815)
Harm. by William Henry Havergal (1861)

Charles Wesley (1740)

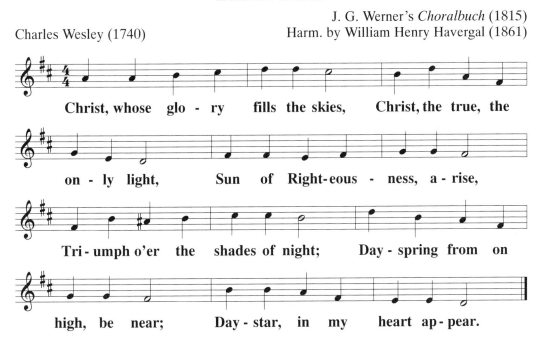

Christ, whose glo - ry fills the skies, Christ, the true, the
on - ly light, Sun of Right-eous - ness, a - rise,
Tri - umph o'er the shades of night; Day - spring from on
high, be near; Day - star, in my heart ap - pear.

Dark and cheerless is the morn
Unaccompanied by thee;
Joyless is the day's return,
Till thy mercy's beams I see;
Till they inward light impart,
Cheer my eyes and warm my heart.

Visit then this soul of mine;
Pierce the gloom of sin and grief;
Fill me, Radiancy divine,
Scatter all my unbelief;
More and more thyself display,
Shining to the perfect day.

342   Awake, My Soul, and with the Sun

OLD HUNDREDTH LM

Thomas Ken (1674), alt.   Attr. to Louis Bourgeois (1551)

A - wake, my soul, and with the sun Thy
dai - ly stage of du - ty run; Shake off dull sloth, and
joy - ful rise To pay thy morn - ing sac - ri - fice:

Lord, I my vows to thee renew;
Disperse my sins as morning dew;
Guard my first springs of thought and will,
And with thyself my spirit fill.

Direct, control, suggest, this day,
All I design, or do, or say;
That all my pow'rs, with all their might,
In thy sole glory may unite.

Praise God, from whom all blessings flow;
Praise him, all creatures here below;
Praise him above, ye heav'nly host:
Praise Father, Son, and Holy Ghost.

Morning Has Broken

BUNESSAN 5.5.5.4 D

343

Gaelic melody
Harm. by David Evans (1927)

Eleanor Farjeon (1931)

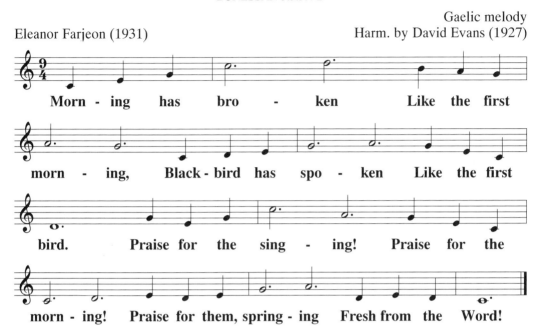

Morn - ing has bro - ken Like the first morn - ing, Black - bird has spo - ken Like the first bird. Praise for the sing - ing! Praise for the morn - ing! Praise for them, spring - ing Fresh from the Word!

Sweet the rain's new fall
Sunlit from heaven,
Like the first dewfall
On the first grass.
Praise for the sweetness
Of the wet garden,
Sprung in completeness
Where his feet pass.

Mine is the sunlight!
Mine is the morning
Born of the one light
Eden saw play!
Praise with elation,
Praise ev'ry morning,
God's recreation
Of the new day!

344 Day Is Dying in the West

CHAUTAUQUA 7.7.7.7.4 with refrain

Isaiah 6:3
Mary A. Lathbury (1878)

William F. Sherwin (1877)

Day is dy - ing in the west;

Heav'n is touch - ing earth with rest;

Wait and wor - ship while the night Sets the eve - ning

lamps a - light Through all the sky.

Ho - ly, ho - ly, ho - ly, Lord God of Hosts!

Heav'n and earth are full of thee! Heav'n and earth are

prais - ing thee, O Lord most high!

Lord of life, beneath the dome
Of the universe, thy home,
Gather us who seek thy face
To the fold of thy embrace,
For thou art nigh. *Holy...*

While the deep'ning shadows fall,
Heart of love enfolding all,
Through the glory and the grace
Of the stars that veil thy face,
Our hearts ascend. *Holy...*

When for ever from our sight
Pass the stars, the day, the night,
Lord of angels, on our eyes
Let eternal morning rise
And shadows end. *Holy...*

345 Abide with Me
EVENTIDE 10.10.10.10

Henry Francis Lyte (1847) William Henry Monk (1861)

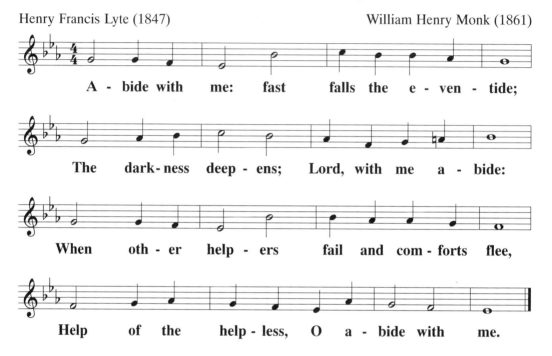

A - bide with me: fast falls the e - ven - tide;

The dark- ness deep - ens; Lord, with me a - bide:

When oth - er help - ers fail and com - forts flee,

Help of the help - less, O a - bide with me.

I need thy presence every passing hour;
What but thy grace can foil the tempter's pow'r?
Who, like thyself, my guide and stay can be?
Through cloud and sunshine, Lord, abide with me.

I fear no foe, with thee at hand to bless;
Ills have no weight, and tears no bitterness.
Where is death's sting? Where, grave, thy victory?
I triumph still, if thou abide with me.

Hold thou thy cross before my closing eyes;
Shine through the gloom, and point me to the skies;
Heav'n's morning breaks, and earth's vain shadows flee;
In life, in death, O Lord, abide with me.

O Gladsome Light   346

NUNC DIMITTIS 6.6.7.6.6.7

Ancient Greek hymn
Trans. by Robert S. Bridges (1899)

Louis Bourgeois (1547)
Harm. by Claude Goudimel (1551)

O glad-some light, O grace Of our Cre - a - tor's face,

The e - ter - nal splen-dor wear - ing: Ce - les - tial, ho - ly blest,

Our Sav - ior Je - sus Christ, Joy - ful in your ap-pear - ing!

As fades the day's last light
We see the lamps of night,
Our common hymn outpouring,
O God of might unknown,
You, the incarnate Son,
And Spirit blest adoring.

To you of right belongs
All praise of holy songs,
O Son of God, Lifegiver;
You, therefore, O Most High,
The world does glorify
And shall exalt for ever.

347 Now the Day Is Over

MERRIAL 6.5.6.5

Sabine Baring-Gould (1865), alt.   Joseph Barnby (1868)

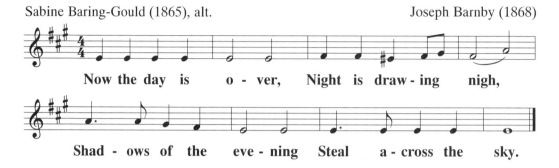

Now the day is o - ver, Night is draw - ing nigh,

Shad - ows of the eve - ning Steal a - cross the sky.

Jesus, give the weary
Calm and sweet repose;
With thy tend'rest blessing
May mine eyelids close.

Comfort those who suffer,
Watching late in pain;
Those who plan some evil
From their sin restrain.

When the morning wakens,
Then may I arise
Pure, and fresh, and sinless
In thy holy eyes.

The Day You Gave Us, Lord, Is Ended   348
ST. CLEMENT 9.8.9.8

John Ellerton (1870), alt.   Clement C. Scholefield (1874)

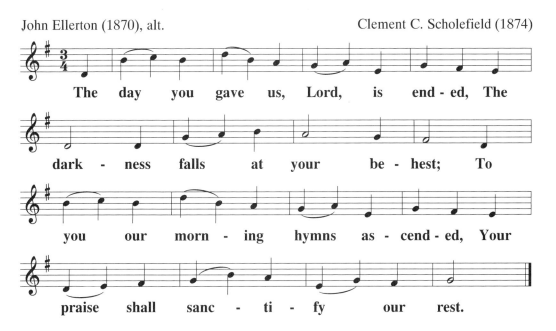

The day you gave us, Lord, is end-ed, The
dark - ness falls at your be - hest; To
you our morn - ing hymns as - cend-ed, Your
praise shall sanc - ti - fy our rest.

We thank you that your Church, unsleeping
While earth rolls onward into light,
Through all the world its watch is keeping,
And rests not now by day or night.

Across each continent and island
As dawn leads on another day,
The voice of prayer is never silent,
Nor dies the strain of praise away.

The sun that bids us rest is waking
Your friends beneath the western sky,
And hour by hour fresh lips are making
Your wondrous doings heard on high.

So be it, Lord; your throne shall never,
Like earth's proud empires, pass away:
Your kingdom stands, and grows for ever,
Till all your creatures own your sway.

349   God, Who Made the Earth and Heaven
AR HYD Y NOS 8.4.8.4.8.8.8.4

St. 1, Reginald Heber (1827)
St. 2, 4, William Mercer (1864)
St. 3, Richard Whately (1838), alt.   Traditional Welsh melody (c. 1784)

God, who made the earth and heav-en, Dark - ness and light:

You the day for work have giv - en, For rest the night.

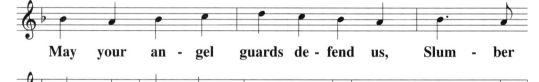

May your an - gel guards de - fend us, Slum - ber

sweet your mer - cy send us, Ho - ly dreams and

hopes at - tend us All through the night.

And when morn again shall call us
To run life's way,
May we still, whate'er befall us,
Your will obey.
From the pow'r of evil hide us,
In the narrow pathway guide us,
Never be your smile denied us
All through the day.

Guard us waking, guard us sleeping,
And, when we die,
May we in your mighty keeping
All peaceful lie.
When the last dread call shall wake us,
Then, O Lord, do not forsake us,
But to reign in glory take us
With you on high.

Holy Father, throned in heaven,
All-holy Son,
Holy Spirit, freely given,
Blest Three-in-One:
Grant us grace, we now implore you,
Till we lay our crowns before you,
And in worthier strains adore you
While ages run.

All Praise to Thee, My God, This Night   350
TALLIS' CANON LM

Thomas Ken (c. 1674)   Thomas Tallis (c. 1567)

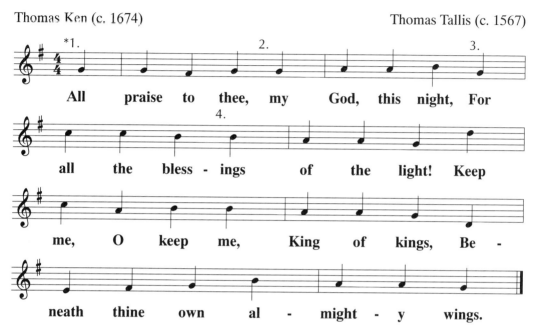

All praise to thee, my God, this night, For

all the bless - ings of the light! Keep

me, O keep me, King of kings, Be -

neath thine own al - might - y wings.

May be sung in canon.

Forgive me, Lord, for thy dear Son,
The ill that I this day have done,
That with the world, myself, and thee,
I, ere I sleep, at peace may be.

Teach me to live, that I may dread
The grave as little as my bed.
Teach me to die, that so I may
Rise glorious at the judgment day.

O may my soul on thee repose,
And with sweet sleep mine eyelids close,
Sleep that may me more vig'rous make
To serve my God when I awake.

Praise God, from whom all blessings flow;
Praise him, all creatures here below;
Praise him above, ye heav'nly host;
Praise Father, Son, and Holy Ghost.

351 Sun of My Soul, Thou Savior Dear

HURSLEY LM

John Keble (1820)   *Katholisches Gesangbuch* (1774)

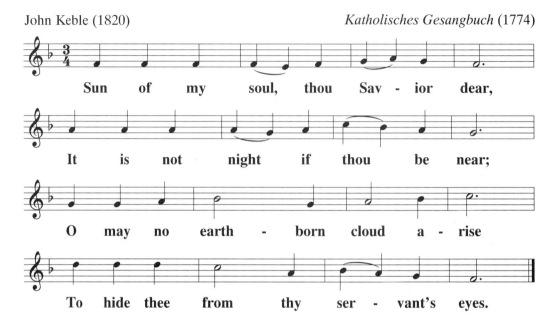

Sun of my soul, thou Sav - ior dear,

It is not night if thou be near;

O may no earth - born cloud a - rise

To hide thee from thy ser - vant's eyes.

When the soft dews of kindly sleep
My wearied eyelids gently steep,
Be my last thought, how sweet to rest
For ever on my Savior's breast.

Abide with me from morn till eve,
For without thee I cannot live;
Abide with me when night is nigh,
For without thee I dare not die.

Watch by the sick; enrich the poor
With blessings from thy boundless store;
Be ev'ry mourner's sleep tonight,
Like infants' slumbers, pure and light.

Come near and bless us when we wake,
Ere through the world our way we take,
Till in the ocean of thy love
We lose ourselves in heav'n above.

God of All Ages, Whose Almighty Hand   352
NATIONAL HYMN 10.10.10.10

Daniel C. Roberts (1876), alt   George W. Warren (1892)

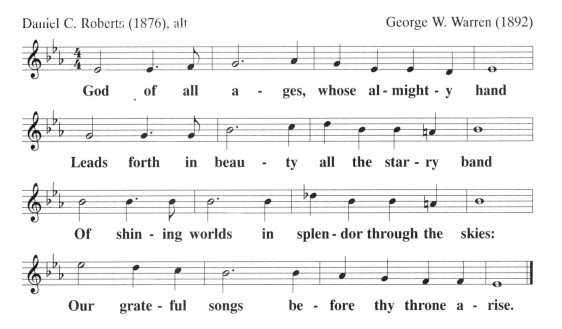

God of all a - ges, whose al - might - y hand

Leads forth in beau - ty all the star - ry band

Of shin - ing worlds in splen - dor through the skies:

Our grate - ful songs be - fore thy throne a - rise.

Thy love divine hath led us in the past;
In this free land by thee our lot is cast;
Be thou our ruler, guardian, guide, and stay;
Thy Word our law, thy paths our chosen way.

From war's alarms, from deadly pestilence,
Be thy strong arm our ever sure defense;
May true religion in our hearts increase,
Thy bounteous goodness nourish us in peace.

Refresh thy people on their toilsome way,
Lead us from night to never-ending day;
Fill all our lives with love and grace divine;
All glory, laud, and praise be ever thine.

353 Star-Spangled Banner

NATIONAL ANTHEM Irregular

Francis Scott Key

John S. Smith

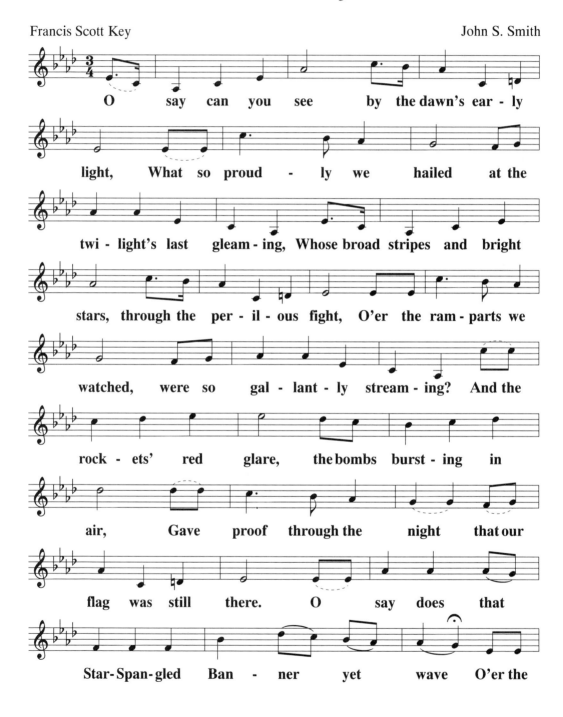

O say can you see by the dawn's ear - ly

light, What so proud - ly we hailed at the

twi - light's last gleam - ing, Whose broad stripes and bright

stars, through the per - il - ous fight, O'er the ram - parts we

watched, were so gal - lant - ly stream - ing? And the

rock - ets' red glare, the bombs burst - ing in

air, Gave proof through the night that our

flag was still there. O say does that

Star - Span - gled Ban - ner yet wave O'er the

land   of the   free   and the   home   of   the   brave?

On the shore dimly seen thro' the mists of the deep,
Where the foe's haughty host in dead silence reposes,
What is that which the breeze, o'er the towering steep,
As it fitfully blows half conceals, half discloses?
Now it catches the gleam of the morning's first beam,
In full glory reflected now shined on the stream,
'Tis the Star Spangled Banner O long may it wave
O'er the land of the free and the home of the brave!

O thus be it ever when free men shall stand
Between their loved homes and the war's desolation!
Blest with vict'ry and peace, may the heav'n-rescued land
Praise the Pow'r that hath made and preserved us a nation!
Then conquer we must, when our cause it is just,
And this be our motto, "In God is our trust."
And the Star-Spangled Banner in triumph shall wave
O'er the land of the free and the home of the brave!

354 My Country, 'Tis of Thee

AMERICA 6.6.4.6.6.6.4

Samuel F. Smith (1832)   *Thesaurus Musicus* (1744)

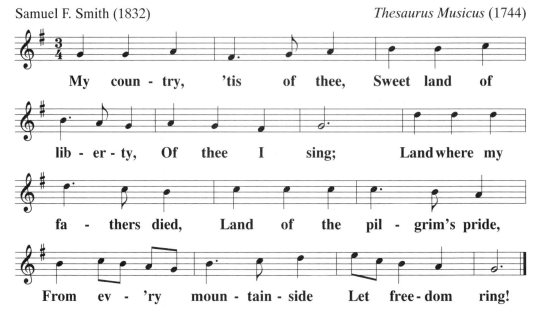

My coun - try, 'tis of thee, Sweet land of
lib - er - ty, Of thee I sing; Land where my
fa - thers died, Land of the pil - grim's pride,
From ev - 'ry moun - tain - side Let free - dom ring!

My native country, thee,
Land of the noble, free;
Thy name I love;
I love thy rocks and rills,
Thy woods and templed hills;
My heart with rapture thrills,
Like that above.

Let music swell the breeze,
And ring from all the trees
Sweet freedom's song;
Let mortal tongues awake;
Let all that breathe partake;
Let rocks their silence break,
The sound prolong.

Our fathers' God, to thee,
Author of liberty,
To thee we sing;
Long may our land be bright
With freedom's holy light;
Protect us by thy might,
Great God, our King.

Come, Ye Thankful People, Come   355
ST. GEORGE'S WINDSOR 7.7.7.7 D

Henry Alford (1844), alt.   George Elvey (1858)

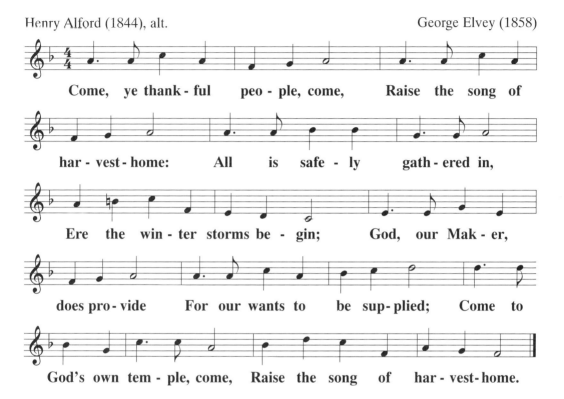

Come, ye thank-ful peo-ple, come, Raise the song of
har-vest-home: All is safe-ly gath-ered in,
Ere the win-ter storms be-gin; God, our Mak-er,
does pro-vide For our wants to be sup-plied; Come to
God's own tem-ple, come, Raise the song of har-vest-home.

All the world is God's own field,	For the Lord our God shall come,
Fruit unto God's praise to yield;	And shall take the harvest home;
Wheat and tares together sown,	From the field shall in that day
Unto joy or sorrow grown;	All offenses purge away;
First the blade, and then the ear,	Giving angels charge at last
Then the full corn shall appear:	In the fire the tares to cast,
Lord of harvest, grant that we	But the fruitful ears to store
Wholesome grain and pure may be.	In God's garner evermore.

Even so, Lord, quickly come
To your final harvest-home;
Gather all your people in,
Free from sorrow, free from sin;
There, for ever purified,
In your presence to abide:
Come, with all your angels, come,
Raise the glorious harvest-home.

356   America the Beautiful

MATERNA CMD

Katherine L. Bates (1893)   Samuel A. Ward (1882)

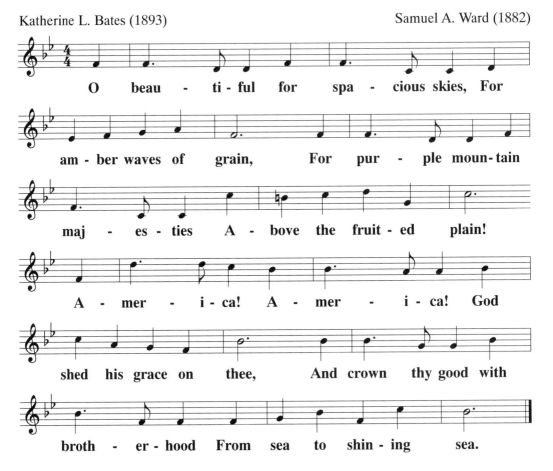

O beau - ti - ful for spa - cious skies, For am - ber waves of grain, For pur - ple moun-tain maj - es - ties A - bove the fruit - ed plain! A - mer - i - ca! A - mer - i - ca! God shed his grace on thee, And crown thy good with broth - er - hood From sea to shin - ing sea.

O beautiful for pilgrim feet,
Whose stern, impassioned stress
A thoroughfare for freedom beat
Across the wilderness!
America! America!
God mend thine ev'ry flaw,
Confirm thy soul in self-control,
Thy liberty in law.

O beautiful for heroes proved
In liberating strife,
Who more than self their country loved,
And mercy more than life!
America! America!
May God thy gold refine,
Till all success be nobleness,
And ev'ry gain divine.

O beautiful for patriot dream
That sees beyond the years
Thine alabaster cities gleam,
Undimmed by human tears!
America! America!
God shed his grace on thee,
And crown thy good with brotherhood
From sea to shining sea.

357   Battle Hymn of the Republic
BATTLE HYMN OF THE REPUBLIC 15.15.15.6 with refrain

Julia W. Howe (1861)   Attr. to William Steffe

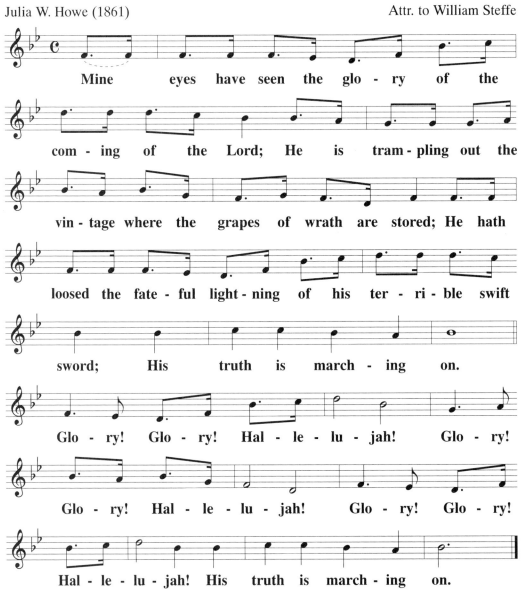

Mine eyes have seen the glo - ry of the com - ing of the Lord; He is tram - pling out the vin - tage where the grapes of wrath are stored; He hath loosed the fate - ful light - ning of his ter - ri - ble swift sword; His truth is march - ing on.

Glo - ry! Glo - ry! Hal - le - lu - jah! Glo - ry! Glo - ry! Hal - le - lu - jah! Glo - ry! Glo - ry! Hal - le - lu - jah! His truth is march - ing on.

I have seen him in the watchfires of a hundred circling camps;
They have builded him an altar in the evening dews and damps;
I can read the righteous sentence by the dim and flaring lamps;
His day is marching on.
    Glory...

He has sounded forth the trumpet that shall never call retreat;
He is sifting out all human hearts before his judgment seat;
O be swift, my soul, to answer him; be jubilant, my feet!
Our God is marching on.
   Glory...

In the beauty of the lilies Christ was born across the sea,
With a glory in his bosom that transfigures you and me;
As he died to make us holy, let us die that all be free!
While God is marching on.
   Glory...

358   Now Thank We All Our God

NUN DANKET ALLE GOTT 6.7.6.7.6.6.6.6

Martin Rinkart (1663)
Trans. by Catherine Winkworth (1858)

Johann Crüger (1647)
Harm. by Felix Mendelssohn (1840)

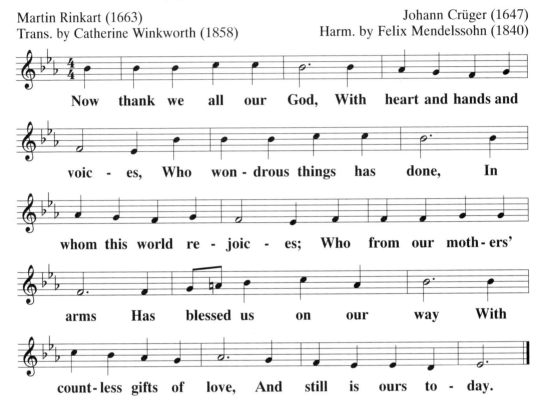

Now thank we all our God, With heart and hands and voic - es, Who won - drous things has done, In whom this world re - joic - es; Who from our moth - ers' arms Has blessed us on our way With count - less gifts of love, And still is ours to - day.

O may this bounteous God
Through all our life be near us,
With ever joyful hearts
And blessèd peace to cheer us;
And keep us still in grace,
And guide us when perplexed;
And free us from all ills,
In this world and the next.

All praise and thanks to God
The Father now be given;
The Son, and him who reigns
With them in highest heaven;
The one eternal God,
Whom earth and heav'n adore;
For thus it was, is now,
And shall be evermore.

Sing of Mary, Meek and Lowly   359
PLEADING SAVIOR 8.7.8.7 D

Christian Lyre (1830)
Harm. by Richard Proulx (1986)

Roland Ford Palmer (1838)

Sing of Mar-y meek and low-ly, Vir-gin-moth-er pure and mild, Sing of God's own Son most ho-ly, Who be-came her lit-tle child. Fair-est child of fair-est moth-er, God the Lord who came to earth, Word made flesh, our ver-y broth-er, Takes our na-ture by his birth.

Sing of Jesus, son of Mary,
In the home at Nazareth.
Toil and labor cannot weary
Love enduring unto death.
Constant was the love he gave her,
Though he went forth from her side,
Forth to preach, and heal, and suffer,
Till on Calvary he died.

Glory be to God the Father;
Glory be to God the Son;
Glory be to God the Spirit;
Glory to the Three-in-One.
From the heart of blessèd Mary,
From all saints the song ascends,
And the church the strain reechoes
Unto earth's remotest ends.

360 Sing We of the Blessed Mother

OMNE DIE 8.7.8.7 D

George B. Timms (1975)   *Trier Gesängebuch* (1695)

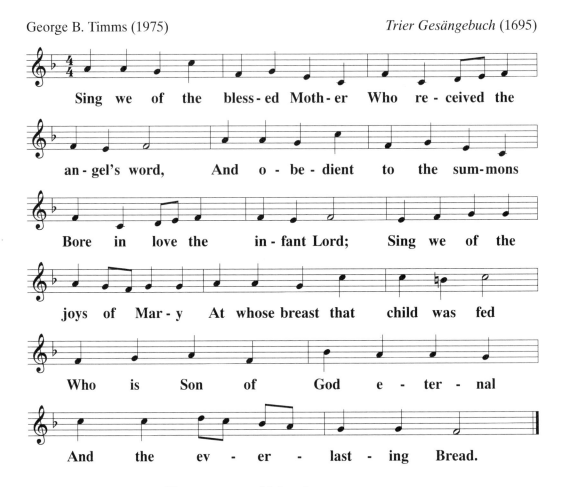

Sing we of the bless-ed Moth-er Who re-ceived the

an-gel's word, And o-be-dient to the sum-mons

Bore in love the in-fant Lord; Sing we of the

joys of Mar-y At whose breast that child was fed

Who is Son of God e-ter-nal

And the ev-er-last-ing Bread.

Sing we, too, of Mary's sorrows,
Of the sword that pierced her through,
When beneath the cross of Jesus
She his weight of suff'ring knew,
Looked upon her Son and Savior
Reigning from the awful tree,
Saw the price of our redemption
Paid to set the sinner free.

Sing again the joys of Mary
When she saw the risen Lord,
And in prayer with Christ's apostles,
Waited on his promised word:
From on high the blazing glory
Of the Spirit's presence came,
Heav'nly breath of God's own being,
Tokened in the wind and flame.

Sing the greatest joy of Mary
When on earth her work was done,
And the Lord of all creation
Brought her to his heav'nly home:
Virgin Mother, Mary blesséd,
Raised on high and crowned with grace,
May your Son, the world's redeemer,
Grant us all to see his face.

361   Immaculate Mary

LOURDES HYMN 11.11 with refrain

St. 1, Jeremiah Cummings, alt.
St. 2-7, Brian Foley (1971)

Traditional Pyrenean melody
Grenoble (1882)

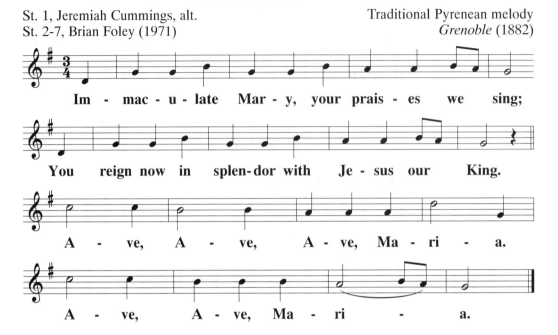

Im - mac - u - late Mar - y, your prais - es we sing;

You reign now in splen-dor with Je - sus our King.

A - ve, A - ve, A - ve, Ma - ri - a.

A - ve, A - ve, Ma - ri - a.

Predestined for Christ by eternal decree,
God willed you both virgin and mother to be. *Ave...*

To you by an angel, the Lord God made known
The grace of the Spirit, the gift of the Son. *Ave...*

Most blest of all women, you heard and believed,
Most blest in the fruit of your womb then conceived. *Ave...*

The angels rejoiced when you brought forth God's Son;
Your joy is the joy of all ages to come. *Ave...*

Your child is the Savior, all hope lies in him:
He gives us new life and redeems us from sin. *Ave...*

In glory for ever now close to your Son.
All ages will praise you for all God has done. *Ave...*

For All the Saints

362

SINE NOMINE 10.10.10 with alleluias

Hebrews 12:1
William W. How (1864)   Ralph Vaughan Williams (1906)

1. For all the saints, who from their la - bors rest,
2. Thou wast their rock, their for - tress, and their might;
3. O may thy sol - diers, faith - ful, true, and bold,
4. O blest com - mun - ion, fel - low - ship di - vine!
5. And when the strife is fierce, the war - fare long,
6. From earth's wide bounds, from o - cean's far - thest coast,

Who thee by faith be - fore the world con - fessed,
Thou, Lord, their cap - tain in the well - fought fight;
Fight as the saints who no - bly fought of old,
We fee - bly strug - gle, they in glo - ry shine;
Steals on the ear the dis - tant tri - umph song,
Through gates of pearl streams in the count - less host,

Thy name, O Je - sus, be for ev - er blest.
Thou, in the dark - ness drear, their one true light.
And win with them the vic - tor's crown of gold.
Yet all are one in thee, for all are thine.
And hearts are brave a - gain, and arms are strong.
Sing - ing to Fa - ther, Son, and Ho - ly Ghost:

Al - le - lu - ia! Al - le - lu - ia!

363   Faith of Our Fathers

ST. CATHERINE LM with refrain

Henry F. Hemy (1864)
Frederick W. Faber (1849)   Adapt. by James G. Walton (1874)

Faith of our fa - thers! liv - ing still

In spite of dun - geon, fire and sword:

O how our hearts beat high with joy,

When - e'er we hear that glo - rious word:

Faith of our fa - thers, ho - ly faith!

We will be true to thee till death.

Our fathers, chained in prisons dark,
Were still in heart and conscience free:
And truly blest would be our fate,
If we, like them, should die for thee. *Faith...*

Faith of our fathers! faith and prayer
Shall win all nations unto thee;
And through the truth that comes from God,
We shall all then indeed be free. *Faith...*

Faith of our fathers! we will love
Both friend and foe in all our strife:
And preach thee, too, as love knows how,
By kindly deeds and virtuous life. *Faith...*

I Sing a Song of the Saints of God   364
GRAND ISLE Irregular

Lesbia Scott (1929), alt.   John Henry Hopkins (1940)

1. I sing a song of the saints of God,
2. They loved their Lord so dear, so dear, And
3. They lived not on-ly in a - ges past, There are

Pa - tient and brave and true, Who toiled and fought and
his love made them strong; And they fol - lowed the right, for
hun-dreds of thou-sands still, The world is bright with the

lived and died For the Lord they loved and knew. And
Je - sus' sake, The whole of their good lives long. And
joy - ous saints Who love to do Je - sus' will. You can

one was a doc - tor, and one was a queen, And one was a
one was a sol - dier, and one was a priest, And one was
meet them in school, or in lanes, or at sea, In church, or in

shep-herd-ess on the green: They were all of them saints of
slain by a fierce wild beast: And there's not an - y rea - son
trains, or in shops, or at tea, For the saints of God are just

God— and I mean, God help - ing, to be one too.
no, not the least, Why I should-n't be one too.
folk like me, And I mean to be one too.

365   O Holy City, Seen of John

MORNING SONG 8.6.8.6.8.6

Revelation 21
Walter Russell Bowie (1909)

Wyeth's *Repository of Sacred Music* (1813)
Harm. by Charles Winfred Douglas (1940)

O Ho - ly Cit - y, seen of John, Where
Christ, the Lamb, does reign, With - in those four - square
walls shall come No night, nor need, nor pain, And
where the tears are wiped from eyes That shall not weep a - gain.

O shame to us who rest content
While lust and greed for gain
In street and shop and tenement
Wring gold from human pain,
And bitter lips in blind despair
Cry, "Christ has died in vain."

Give us, O God, the strength to build
The City that has stood
Too long a dream, whose laws are love,
Whose ways, the common good,
And where the shining sun becomes
God's grace for human good.

Already in the mind of God
That City rises fair:
Lo, how its splendor challenges
The souls that greatly dare:
Yea, bids us seize the whole of life
And build its glory there.

Jerusalem the Golden   **366**

EWING 7.6.7.6 D

Bernard of Cluny (12th C.)
Trans. by John Mason Neale, alt.
St. 4, *Hymns Ancient and Modern* (1861)

Alexander Ewing

Je - ru - sa - lem the gold - en, With milk and hon - ey
blest, Be - neath thy con - tem - pla - tion Sink heart and voice op -
pressed: I know not, oh, I know not, What joys a - wait us
there; What ra - dian - cy of glo - ry, What bliss be - yond com - pare!

They stand, those halls of Zion,	There is the throne of David;
All jubilant with song,	And there, from care released,
And bright with many an angel,	The shout of them that triumph,
And all the martyr throng:	The song of them that feast;
The Prince is ever in them,	And they who with their Leader
The daylight is serene;	Have conquered in the fight,
The pastures of the bless̀ed	For ever and for ever
Are decked in glorious sheen.	Are clad in robes of white.

Oh, sweet and bless̀ed country,
The home of God's elect!
Oh, sweet and bless̀ed country
That eager hearts expect!
Jesus, in mercy bring us
To that dear land of rest,
Who art, with God the Father,
And Spirit, ever blest.

367   Glorious Things of Thee Are Spoken

AUSTRIAN HYMN 8.7.8.7 D

Psalm 87:3, Isaiah 33:20, Exodus 13:22   Croation folk song
John Newton (1779)   Arr. by Franz Joseph Haydn (1797)

Glo - rious things of thee are spo-ken, Zi - on, cit - y

of   our God;   God,   whose word can - not be bro - ken,

Formed thee for his   own a - bode.   On the Rock of

A - ges found-ed, What can shake thy sure re-pose?

With   sal - va - tion's walls   sur - round-ed,

Thou   mayst smile   at   all   thy   foes.

See, the streams of living waters,
Springing from eternal love,
Well supply thy sons and daughters,
And all fear of want remove.
Who can faint while such a river
Ever will their thirst assuage?
Grace which like the Lord, the giver,
Never fails from age to age.

Round each habitation hov'ring,
See the cloud and fire appear
For a glory and a cov'ring,
Showing that the Lord is near!
Thus deriving from our banner
Light by night and shade by day,
Safe we feed upon the manna
Which God gives us when we pray.

Blest inhabitants of Zion,
Washed in our Redeemer's blood;
Jesus, whom our souls rely on,
Makes us monarchs, priests to God.
Us, by his great love, he raises,
Rulers over self to reign,
And as priests his solemn praises
We for thankful off'ring bring.

Acknowledgments/*continued*

297 Text: © 1958, renewal 1986, Hymn Society of America. All rights reserved. Used by permission of Hope Publishing Co., Carol Stream, IL 60188. Tune: Harm. © 1906, *The English Hymnal,* Oxford University Press

299 Text: © 1954, renewal 1982, Hymn Society of America. All rights reserved. Used by permission of Hope Publishing Co., Carol Stream, IL 60188.

300 Text: © 1989, Hope Publishing Co., Carol Stream, IL 60188. All rights reserved. Used by permission.

301 Text: © 1955, 1983, Jan-Lee Music Tune: © 1955, 1983, Jan-Lee Music; acc. © 1993, GIA Publications, Inc.

302 © 1982, Hope Publishing Co., Carol Stream, IL 60188. All rights reserved. Used by permission.

304 Text: © 1966, 1979, Willard F. Jabusch. Tune: © 1966, 1979, Willard F. Jabusch; harm. © 1975, GIA Publications, Inc.

308 Text: © 1961, *Seven New Social Welfare Hymns,* Oxford University Press

310 Text: © 1906, *The English Hymnal,* Oxford University Press Tune: Harm. © 1906, *The English Hymnal,* Oxford University Press

312 © 1971, Daniel L. Schutte, administered by New Dawn Music

313 Text: © 1982, Hope Publishing Co., Carol Stream, IL 60188. All rights reserved. Used by permission. Tune: Arr. © 1977, Robertson Publications. Used by permission of Theodore Presser Co. 1 Presser Place. Brn Mawr, PA 19010-3490

315 Text: © 1985, 1994, GIA Publications, Inc. Tune: Harm. © 1985, GIA Publications, Inc.

317 Tune: Harm. © 1989, United Methodist Publishing House

318 Text: St. 2-3 © The Church Pension Fund

320 Tune: © 1931, *Enlarged Songs of Praise,* Oxford University Press

322 © 1981, Les Presses de Taizé, GIA Publications, Inc., agent

324 Tune: Harm. © 1933, 1961, Presbyterian Board of Christian Education Westminster. John Knox Press, Louisville, Kentucky

327 Tune: Harm. © 1906, *The English Hymnal,* Oxford University Press

329 Tune: © 1906,*The English Hymnal,* Oxford University Press

331 Text: © 1979, Hope Publishing Co., Tune: © 1942, renewal1970, Hope Publishing Co., Carol Stream, IL 60188. All rights reserved. Used by permission.

336 Tune: © 1906, *The English Hymnal,* Oxford University Press

339 Text: Trans. © 1906, *The English Hymnal,* Oxford University Press

343 Text: © David Higham Assoc., Ltd. Tune: Acc. © 1927, *The Church Hymnary,* Oxford University Press

359 Tune: Harm. © 1986, GIA Publications, Inc.

360 Text: © 1975, *The English Hymnal,* Oxford University Press

361 Text: © 1971, Faber Music, Ltd., London. Reprinted from NEW CATHOLIC HYMNAL

362 Tune: © 1906, *The English Hymnal,* Oxford University Press

364 Text: © 1929, Lesbia Scott, used by permission of Morehouse Publishing Co., Inc.

365 Text: © 1909, Harper and Row

Index of Composers, Authors, and Sources/ *continued*

Index of Composers, Authors, and Sources/ *continued*

Index of Composers, Authors, and Sources/ *continued*

Topical Index/ *continued*

Topical Index/ *continued*

Topical Index/ *continued*

Topical Index/ *continued*

Topical Index/ *continued*

Topical Index/ *continued*

Topical Index/ *continued*

306 Where Cross the Crowded Ways of Life

REPENTANCE
165 Ah, Holy Jesus
87 All Glory Be to God on High
350 All Praise to Thee, My God, This Night
261 Amazing Grace
160 Beneath the Cross of Jesus
235 Bread of the World, in Mercy Broken
158 By the Babylonian Rivers
292 Christ for the World We Sing
341 Christ Whose Glory Fills the Skies
272 Come, Thou Fount of Every Blessing
125 Comfort, Comfort O My People
265 Dear Lord and Father of Mankind
159 Forty Days and Forty Nights
109 Glory and Praise to Our God
274 God Be in My Head
90 God of the Sparrow, God of the Whale
104 God Moves in a Mysterious Way
222 God of Grace and God of Glory
298 God the Omnipotent
349 God, Who Made the Earth and Heaven
113 Great Is Thy Faithfulness
181 Hail, Thou Once Despised Jesus
299 Hope of the World
276 How Firm a Foundation
212 How Sweet the Name of Jesus
247 I Need Thee Every Hour
249 I Sought the Lord
203 Jesus, the Very Thought of Thee
239 Jesus, Thou Joy of Loving Hearts
248 Just As I Am
238 Let Us Break Bread Together
307 Lord Christ, When First You Came to Earth
161 Lord Jesus, Think on Me
271 Love Divine, All Loves Excelling
296 Make Me a Channel of Your Peace
154 My Faith Looks Up to Thee
284 My Shepherd Will Supply My Need
264 Nobody Knows the Trouble I See
347 Now the Day Is Over
204 O Christ, the Healer
259 O Happy Day, That Fixed My Choice
152 Out of the Depths I Cry
48 Psalm 22:1-18, 25-31: My God, My God, Why Have You Forsaken Me?
53 Psalm 51:1-17: Have Mercy on Me, O God
55 Psalm 90: Lord, You Have Been Our Dwelling Place
58 Psalm 103:1-18: Bless the Lord, O My Soul
60 Psalm 116: I Love the Lord
63 Psalm 130: Out of the Depths I Cry to You, O Lord
64 Psalm 139: O Lord, You Have Searched Me
319 Rock of Ages
283 Seek the Lord
98 Seek Ye First the Kingdom of God
91 Sing a New Song
107 The King of Love My Shepherd Is
103 The Lord's My Shepherd
250 There Is a Balm in Gilead
166 There Is a Green Hill Far Away
112 There's a Wideness in God's Mercy
273 'Tis the Gift to Be Simple
163 What Wondrous Love Is This
170 When I Survey the Wondrous Cross
153 Wilt Thou Forgive that Sin
230 Wonderful Words of Life

REST
217 Come, Gracious Spirit
255 Come to the Water
344 Day Is Dying in the West
362 For All the Saints
349 God, Who Made the Earth and Heaven
212 How Sweet the Name of Jesus
327 I Heard the Voice of Jesus Say

366 Jerusalem the Golden
279 Jesus, Priceless Treasure
203 Jesus, the Very Thought of Thee
239 Jesus, Thou Joy of Loving Hearts
286 Near to the Heart of God
333 O Day of Rest and Gladness
46 Psalm 16:5-11: The Lord Is My Chosen Portion
49 Psalm 23: The Lord Is My Shepherd
54 Psalm 62:5-12: For God Alone My Soul Waits in Silence
60 Psalm 116: I Love the Lord
348 The Day You Gave Us, Lord, Is Ended

SAINTS
201 All Hail the Power of Jesus' Name
363 Faith of Our Fathers
362 For All the Saints
95 For the Beauty of the Church
332 God Himself Is with Us
66 Holy God, We Praise Thy Name
70 Holy, Holy, Holy! Lord God Almighty
302 How Clear Is Our Vocation, Lord
364 I Sing a Song of the Saints of God
366 Jerusalem the Golden
305 O God of Love, O King of Peace
50 Psalm 24: The Earth Is the Lord's
96 The God of Abraham Praise
83 Ye Watchers and Ye Holy Ones

SALVATION
87 All Glory Be to God on High
164 All Glory, Laud, and Honor
213 All Praise to Thee, for Thou, O King Divine
261 Amazing Grace
179 At the Lamb's High Feast We Sing
202 At the Name of Jesus
258 Blessed Assurance, Jesus Is Mine
37 Canticle of Praise to God
42 Canticle of Simeon
43 Canticle of Zechariah
183 Christ Jesus Lay in Death's Strong Bands
185 Christ the Lord Is Risen Today
194 Fairest Lord Jesus
339 Father, We Praise You
85 From All That Dwell Below the Skies
367 Glorious Things of Thee Are Spoken
181 Hail, Thou Once Despised Jesus
200 I Love to Tell the Story
247 I Need Thee Every Hour
157 Jesus, Keep Me Near the Cross
239 Jesus, Thou Joy of Loving Hearts
248 Just As I Am
127 Let All Mortal Flesh Keep Silence
307 Lord Christ, When First You Came to Earth
156 Lord, Who throughout These Forty Days
259 O Happy Day, That Fixed My Choice
275 O Savior, in This Quiet Place
228 O Zion, Haste
50 Psalm 24: The Earth Is the Lord's
51 Psalm 27: The Lord Is My Light and My Salvation
53 Psalm 51:1-17: Have Mercy on Me, O God
54 Psalm 62:5-12: For God Alone My Soul Waits in Silence
56 Psalm 96: O Sing to the Lord
60 Psalm 116: I Love the Lord
61 Psalm 118:14-29: The Lord Is My Strength and My Power
319 Rock of Ages
256 Savior, Like a Shepherd Lead Us
118 Savior of the Nations, Come
214 Sing, My Soul, His Wondrous Love
110 Sing Praise to God Who Reigns Above
233 Thanks to God Whose Word Was Spoken
210 The King of Glory
112 There's a Wideness in God's Mercy
199 To Jesus Christ, Our Sovereign King
67 We Believe in One True God
163 What Wondrous Love Is This

SALVATION HISTORY
205 O Love, How Deep
233 Thanks to God Whose Word Was Spoken

SEASONS
77 All Beautiful the March of Days
95 For the Beauty of the Church
113 Great Is Thy Faithfulness
65 Lord of Our Growing Years
73 Now Praise the Hidden God of Love
82 Praise to God, Immortal Praise
182 Welcome, Happy Morning

SECOND COMING
202 At the Name of Jesus
357 Battle Hymn of the Republic
229 Come, Labor On
355 Come, Ye Thankful People, Come
187 Crown Him with Many Crowns
362 For All the Saints
320 God Is Working His Purpose Out
149 How Brightly Beams the Morning Star
269 I Want to Walk as a Child of the Light
252 It Is Well with My Soul
366 Jerusalem the Golden
123 Lift Up Your Heads
271 Love Divine, All Loves Excelling
328 My Hope Is Built
295 O Day of God, Draw Nigh
365 O Holy City, Seen of John
206 Of the Father's Love Begotten
135 Once in Royal David's City
188 Rejoice, the Lord Is King
91 Sing a New Song
210 The King of Glory
124 Wake, O Wake, and Sleep No Longer
253 We Remember
163 What Wondrous Love Is This

SECURITY
318 Almighty Father, Strong to Save
262 Be Thou My Vision
101 Children of the Heavenly Father
295 O Day of God, Draw Nigh
46 Psalm 16:5-11: The Lord Is My Chosen Portion
63 Psalm 130: Out of the Depths I Cry to You, O Lord
312 Yahweh, I Know You are Near

SEEKING
232 Break Thou the Bread of Life
249 I Sought the Lord
152 Out of the Depths I Cry
50 Psalm 24: The Earth Is the Lord's
63 Psalm 130: Out of the Depths I Cry to You, O Lord
283 Seek the Lord
98 Seek Ye First the Kingdom of God
189 Spirit of God, Who Dwells within my Heart
325 Sweet Hour of Prayer

SERVICE
84 All People that on Earth Do Dwell
229 Come, Labor On
265 Dear Lord and Father of Mankind
242 Gift of Finest Wheat
274 God Be in My Head
76 God, Who Stretched the Spangled Heavens
257 I Am Thine
224 In Christ There Is No East or West
288 Jesu, Jesu
308 Lord, Whose Love in Humble Service
290 Lord, You Give the Great Commission
289 O Jesus Christ, May Grateful Hymns Be Rising
281 O Master, Let Me Walk with Thee
197 There's a Spirit in the Air

SHEPHERD
165 Ah, Holy Jesus

Topical Index/ *continued*

Topical Index/ *continued*

Topical Index/ *continued*

Scripture Passages Related to Hymns /*continued*

MATTHEW

2:1-2	O Little Town of Bethlehem 132
2:1-11	We Three Kings of Orient Are 148
2:1-11	Good Christian Friends, Rejoice 142
2:1-12	Angels, from the Realms of Glory 134
2:1-12	As with Gladness Men of Old 147
2:1-12	The First Nowell 128
2:1-12	We Three Kings of Orient Are 148
2:10-11	O Come, All Ye Faithful 133
2:11	What Child Is This 136
4:1-2	Forty Days and Forty Nights 159
4:1-11	Lord, Who throughout These Forty Days 156
4:16	Comfort, Comfort, O My People 125
4:24	The King of Glory 210
4:24	Your Hands, O Lord, in Days of Old 150
5:13	Gather Us In 240
6:25-34	Lord of All Hopefulness 287
6:33	Seek Ye First the Kingdom of God 98
7:7	Seek Ye First the Kingdom of God 98
10:42	There's a Spirit in the Air 197
11:25-30	I Heard the Voice of Jesus Say 327
11:28-30	Come to the Water 255
12:21	Hope of the World 299
13:21-43	Come, Ye Thankful People, Come 355
14:14	Love Divine, All Loves Excelling 271
14:22-33	How Firm a Foundation 276
14:22-33	I Sought the Lord 249
16:13-15	Tell Me the Stories of Jesus 277
18:10-14	My Shepherd Will Supply My Need 284
18:10-14	The King of Love My Shepherd Is 107
20:1-16	For the Fruits of This Creation 93
21:1-17	All Glory, Laud, and Honor 164
21:8-9	Tell Me the Stories of Jesus 277
21:33-43	Christ Is Made the Sure Foundation 223
23:37	O Jesus Christ, May Grateful Hymns Be Rising 289
25:1-13	How Brightly Beams the Morning Star 149
25:31-46	There's a Spirit in the Air 197
25:37-45	For the Fruits of This Creation 93
26:30	When, in Our Music, God Is Glorified 81
27:27-31	O Sacred Head, Now Wounded 168
28:6-9	Christ the Lord Is Risen Today 185
28:18	Alleluia! Sing to Jesus 186
28:18	Lord, You Give the Great Commission 290

MARK

1:1-8	Comfort, Comfort, O My People 125
1:12-15	Lord, Who throughout These Forty Days 156
1:29-39	Your Hands, O Lord, in Days of Old 150
1:30-34	O Christ, the Healer 204
1:40-45	Your Hands, O Lord, in Days of Old 150
4:26-29	For the Fruits of This Creation 93
4:35-41	How Firm a Foundation 276
5:15	O Christ, the Healer 204
5:21-43	O Jesus Christ, May Grateful Hymns Be Rising 289
6:30-34	I Heard the Voice of Jesus Say 327
6:30-34	There's a Wideness in God's Mercy 112
10:13-16	Tell Me the Stories of Jesus 277
11:1-11	All Glory, Laud, and Honor 164
11:8-10	Tell Me the Stories of Jesus 277
12:28-34	God Be in My Head 274
13:2	Lord Christ, When First You Came to Earth 307
14:26	When, in Our Music, God Is Glorified 81
15:16-20	O Sacred Head, Now Wounded 168

LUKE

1:26-38	Immaculate Mary 361
1:26-38	Sing We of the Blessed Mother 360
1:26-45	Savior of the Nations, Come 118
1:46b-55	Tell Out, My Soul, the Greatness of the Lord 120
1:46b-55	Canticle of Mary 41
1:68-79	Canticle of Zechariah 43
1:78-79	O Come, O Come, Emmanuel 121
2:1-10	The First Nowell 128
2:1-18	From Heaven Above 144
2:6-7	Savior of the Nations, Come 118
2:6-14	Silent Night, Holy Night 146
2:6-18	Angels, from the Realms of Glory 134
2:6-18	God Rest You Merry, Gentlemen 138
2:6-18	Go Tell It on the Mountain 140
2:6-18	What Child Is This 136
2:6-20	Infant Holy, Infant Lowly 126

2:7	Away in a Manger 130 131
2:7	Good Christian Friends, Rejoice 142
2:7	Lo, How a Rose E'er Blooming 119
2:7	Once in Royal David's City 135
2:7	Sing of Mary, Meek and Lowly 359
2:8-14	It Came Upon the Midnight Clear 141
2:8-14	While Shepherds Watched Their Flocks 137
2:10-11	God Rest You Merry, Gentlemen 138
2:10-11	Good Christian Friends, Rejoice 142
2:10-11	Go Tell It on the Mountain 140
2:10-11	It Came Upon the Midnight Clear 141
2:10-11	O Come, All Ye Faithful 133
2:10-11,14	From Heaven Above 144
2:10-14	Immaculate Mary 361
2:13-14	All Glory Be to God on High 87
2:13-15	O Come, All Ye Faithful 133
2:13-18	Angels We Have Heard on High 139
2:14	Canticle of God's Glory 38
2:14	From Heaven Above 144
2:15	O Come, All Ye Faithful 133
2:29-32	Canticle of Simeon 42
2:40	Sing of Mary, Meek and Lowly 359
3:4,6	On Jordan's Bank 116
4:1-2	Lord, Who throughout These Forty Days 156
4:1-13	Forty Days and Forty Nights 159
6:20ff	Be Not Afraid 266
7:11-17	Your Hands, O Lord, in Days of Old 150
8:22-25	How Firm a Foundation 276
9:57	O Jesus, I Have Promised 309
11:1-13	Seek Ye First the Kingdom of God 98
13:29	In Christ There Is No East or West 224
15:3-7	The King of Love My Shepherd Is 107
15:31-32	For the Fruits of This Creation 93
18:9-14	Gather Us In 240
19:37-38	All Glory, Laud, and Honor 164
23:33,44,50-53	Were You There 169
23:42	Jesus, Remember Me 322
24:1-2	Were You There 169
24:1-12	O Sons and Daughters, Let Us Sing! 180
24:34	Christ the Lord Is Risen Today 185
24:50-53	Alleluia! Sing to Jesus 186
24:51-53	Love Divine, All Loves Excelling 271

JOHN

1:1	At the Name of Jesus 202
1:1-5	O Come, All Ye Faithful 133
1:1-18	Christ Is the World's Light 196
1:9	I Heard the Voice of Jesus Say 327
1:9	O Gladsome Light 346
1:14	O Come, All Ye Faithful 133
1:14	Of the Father's Love Begotten 206
1:15-28	On Jordan's Bank 116
1:29	Canticle of God's Glory 38
3:5	Hark! The Herald Angels Sing 143
3:16	Christ Is Made the Sure Foundation 223
3:16	What Wondrous Love Is This 163
4:5-42	I Heard the Voice of Jesus Say 327
4:14	I Heard the Voice of Jesus Say 327
4:20	Christ Is the World's Light 196
6:	Eat This Bread 244
6:	I Am the Bread of Life 207
6:34	Gift of Finest Wheat 242
6:35-58	Deck Thyself, My Soul, with Gladness 241
6:35,51	Let All Mortal Flesh Keep Silence 127
6:41-59	Alleluia! Sing to Jesus 186
6:48	Hope of the World 299
8:12	Christ Is the World's Light 196
8:12	I Heard the Voice of Jesus Say 327
8:31	Faith of Our Fathers 363
9:1-41	Amazing Grace 261
10:	My Shepherd Will Supply My Need 284
10:	The King of Love My Shepherd Is 107
10:1-29	Savior, Like a Shepherd Lead Us 256
10:1-5	Gift of Finest Wheat 242
11:25-27	I Am the Bread of Life 207
12:12-16	All Glory, Laud, and Honor 164
12:13	Tell Me the Stories of Jesus 277
12:20-33	O God beyond All Praising 78
12:46	I Want to Walk as a Child of the Light 269
13:3-5	Jesu, Jesu, Fill Us with Your Love 288

Scripture Passages Related to Hymns /*continued*

Metrical Index of Tunes /*continued*

Metrical Index of Tunes /*continued*

Index of Tunes/ *continued*

Index of First Lines and Common Titles/ *continued*

Index of First Lines and Common Titles/ *continued*

Index of First Lines and Common Titles/ *continued*